To Mars ♡ W9-BNS-206

With deep thanks for
your friendship and help
at the Peace Corps!
Best wishes,
Chuck Hobbie 9-1-11

Buffalo Wings

Charles A. Hobbie

iUniverse, Inc.
New York   Bloomington

Buffalo Wings

Copyright © 2009 Charles A. Hobbie

iUniverse books may be ordered through booksellers or by contacting:

iUniverse
1663 Liberty Drive
Bloomington, IN 47403
www.iuniverse.com
1-800-Authors (1-800-288-4677)

ISBN: 978-1-4401-5198-9 (pbk)
ISBN: 978-1-4401-5200-9 (cloth)
ISBN: 978-1-4401-5199-6 (ebk)

Printed in the United States of America

iUniverse rev. date: 9/8/2009

Dedicated to my wife, children, brother, sister, other family, classmates, teachers, and friends, and to the citizens of Buffalo, New York, 1945-1963

* * *

And in grateful memory of Alix and John Hobbie

Charles A. Hobbie

This is written for my wife and children, with an apology, if what I write about is more than they ever wanted to know about me. My father left me his diaries after his death, covering the years 1914 to 1934. In the past several years I finally read them. As devoid as they were of really personal information, I came away very happy to have had even a limited, additional insight into his life from age ten to age thirty. I wish, however, that I had been able to read his diaries while he was alive, and had been able to ask him to elaborate on his cryptic notes.

My mother also left several small, diary-like books with notes of births, deaths, expenses, trips, and special events in her life, which I have read with great pleasure. They are crammed with memories. She also saved every letter I ever wrote home. I have recently revisited and enjoyed again the "Memories of Eighty Years" written by my great, great grandfather, Isaac Smith Hobbie (1820–1909) in 1906. It seems appropriate that a century later one of his descendants would write a similar summary. I hope that these six chapters, while probably not cryptic enough, may give some pleasure and insight to my family and others while I am still alive.

Since my parents died—first Dad in 1992 and then Mom in 1996—I have thought a lot about my upbringing and past life in general, wondering how events and people shaped me. I think it was Benjamin Franklin who said, "If you cannot relive your past, why not write about it?" I have never wanted to relive the past, except for a very few moments. I do feel an urge to remember and to pass on remembrances, in case they will be of some value to someone, and to my children in particular when they reach that time of life, which we all reach if we live that long, of starting to look back at their ancestors and to wonder what the "dash" (and it is both a figurative and literal dash) between the year of birth and the year of death really represents.

Time and imagination inevitably have clouded some of my memories. I have always loved to tell stories, and it is the storyteller's prerogative to exaggerate, but I have tried to resist embellishment and to provide a faithful account. Let me begin by quoting one of my favorite poets, Richard Hovey, Dartmouth College class of 1885, long forgotten as a poet by Americans who did not attend Dartmouth. Hovey opened a poem with the following words, which I think are fitting to open these memoirs:

The body is no prison where we lie,
Shut out from our true heritage of sun,
It is the wings wherewith the soul may fly....

Written in 1894 for the dedication of the bust of
Shakespeare in Lincoln Park, Chicago.

Chapter One—
Childhood Winters 1945–59

West Delavan Avenue from our porch

Buffalo is the city of big snows. Winds sweep from the west in winter across the more westerly Great Lakes and across Lake Erie, pick up moisture, and dump it as snow at the eastern end of Lake Erie on Buffalo. Or perversely, the occasional, northeastern blow from Lake Ontario has the same "lake" effect. Five miles from downtown Buffalo, the sun will be shining under blue skies, while the city is reeling in a blizzard of snow. The snow swirls and drifts around the buildings and trees, catching on the rough edges of siding, stone, and bark, so that even vertical surfaces are pocketed with white. Buffalo is a city of white in winter. In the late 1960s, teaching as a Peace Corps volunteer in the Far East, when I said I was born in Buffalo, Koreans would nod knowingly and ask how I had managed to survive in the Buffalo snows.

I remember snow. How it inevitably first arrived on Halloween evening, complicating whatever costume I was wearing in my trick or treating rounds up and down Bedford Avenue with my brother John Eyres Hobbie (b. 1935) and sister Cecilia Katherine Elizabeth Hobbie (b. 1938). My sister and brother had grown up mostly on Bedford, and for many years after the move to 453 West Delavan Avenue in 1945, we continued to go trick or treating on Bedford. Later, I went trick or treating without them on West Delavan, Ardmore, Baynes, Dorchester, Lafayette, and Richmond Avenues, and the blocks around Colonial Circle, where I grew up, with my gang of Public School No. 56 friends. I was partial to cowboy costumes with white, cowboy hats, especially the Lone Ranger or Hoppalong Cassidy outfits with twin guns and holsters. By the end of several hours of trick or treating, my cowboy hat and holsters would be well dusted with snow. Wherever we stopped, it seemed as though the people in the house knew us and would greet us like long lost friends, especially at the homes on Bedford Avenue, where my brother and sister knew everyone. It was very pleasant to be admired, fawned over, and given candy.

The Halloween snow never affected my enthusiasm for that night, which was one of my favorite events, despite the dire warnings of my parents about doctored candy and predatory adults, lurking behind the welcoming doors. I never encountered the old man in our neighborhood, who was rumored to heat a large kettle of shiny, copper pennies every Halloween and to cackle with joy when, at his invitation, overly greedy kids would grab a handful of pennies from the kettle, blistering their hands.

The snow would begin to accumulate in mid November. Other houses in our neighborhood were oriented so that the roofs sloped to the sides of the lot. Ours was the only house on our block that was a single family home, turned sideways. The steep roof of our house on West Delavan, where I lived my entire Buffalo life, would hold about eighteen inches of snow, before suddenly discharging an avalanche towards the street side and backside of the house. Visitors and our dogs, until they learned, would usually hear the rumble of the sliding snow, look up, and be momentarily buried, before they could duck under the over-hanging roof. I still remember the unmistakable look of chagrin on Tuffy's face (my second dog), when our family howled with laughter at his first avalanche encounter.

There was always a very satisfying mountain of snow under the roofline all winter long, until mid March. In the front of the house, snow shoveled from the side driveway and from the walks was piled onto the mountain, which could stand ten or twelve feet tall by February. My brother and sister, whom we called Ceci, introduced me to the joys of tunneling at an early age. I spent many hours building forts and tunnels in those snow mountains. In some years the vestiges of the snow piles lingered into May. After March, they were no longer satisfying or welcome.

Snowstorms often arrived in April. There was a healthy snowstorm in early April, 1945, on the day President Roosevelt died—the day before my birth on Friday the 13th. The snow made it hard for my parents to get to Children's Hospital in time for my arrival. I don't remember the storm, but until I was about ten, I thought I remembered being born. My memory of a bright, white light and a nurse, whose hair net I managed to grab, turned out to be from my tonsillectomy at the same hospital on Bryant Street in 1948, when I was three years old.

I lived on the longest avenue in Buffalo, stretching from the city's western end at the Niagara River to beyond the eastern city line. As such, Delavan was a heavily used route. Trucks and buses were part of the steady stream of traffic, passing our house at all hours of the night and day. In the bedroom in the northeast corner of the house, I remember lying in my crib at night and watching the lights from the passing cars, trucks, and buses play across the walls and ceiling. It took me quite a while to connect the lights with the traffic sounds in the street below.

Our house, which was a small, English style, stucco house with two floors, a basement, and an attic, was covered in ivy, in which dozens of English sparrows made their nests. During the daylight hours, their chirping and quarreling were constantly audible, even in winter with the windows and storm windows tightly closed. The sparrows' stirrings helped to drown out the street sounds just thirty feet from our front door. As a snowstorm approached, the sparrows would grow noticeably quieter. Lying in bed at night in a snow storm, you could tell the progress of the steadily mounting snow by the sounds of the passing traffic, with its chinc-chinc-chinc of chained tires, clinking with each revolution of the tire, and increasingly muffled noises. If in the morning there were almost no street sounds or sparrow sounds, chances were good that the snow was still coming and had been substantial enough to close schools, at least for a few hours.

Every morning we listened to WBEN radio at breakfast around 8 o'clock. Patti Page and the Andrews sisters were often featured. I particularly liked the "Tennessee Waltz" and "Mocking Bird Hill." Clint Buelman reported the news and weather and, most importantly, the school closings. I used to love the little ditty he sang on snowy days: "Leave for work a little early 'cause you'll find the streets are slick, and even if your brakes are good, you'll find you can't stop quick…." Clint referred to "Arthur Mometer" (our thermometer) to update the temperature. I thought Arthur was his partner and was pleased that we shared a name (Arthur being my middle name).

We ate in the kitchen at a round, oak table, looking out into the backyard. There were usually birds at our bird feeder. I remember squeezing oranges on the orange juice squeezing machine and toasting bread in the polished chrome toaster. The curved side of the toaster made your face look distorted as you peered at your reflection. For years, the toaster's reflection was the one mirror in our house I could easily peer into, so I thought I had an even more enormous nose than I actually have.

I think we were a generally happy family, with the usual amount of family fighting. My brother went to several elementary schools, ending up at Public School No. 56, from 1946 until 1949, then to Nichols High School until 1953. I followed him in both schools, ten years later. Teachers inevitably called me "John" most of the time. In winter my brother would leave for high school between 7:30 and 8:00 AM. My father (John Hayes Hobbie, 1904–92) would leave for work by 8:15. My mother (Maggie Alix Bray Hobbie, 1909–96) and I would drop off my sister at the Campus School, which she attended until 1952 and which she strongly disliked, about 8:30. My sister would often be very upset about leaving for school. Then I was left with my mother.

When I was young, my mother was the disciplinarian. She would occasionally yell at my sister. I don't remember either my brother or my sister being smacked by my mother, but it probably happened a lot before I was born—seven years after my sister and ten years after my brother. Sometimes I was spanked, but not often. In those days Mom had a temper. She got quite upset when one of us tracked snow or mud across the kitchen floor or forgot to carry upstairs the folded clothes, books, or other items, destined for the second floor, that were stacked on the bottom two stairs to be carried up.

My mother was truly a beautiful woman, extremely kind to people she knew and to animals, and very careful with money. She loved to play jokes on members of the family. Her favorite joke, when I was very young, involved an orange-colored can with a screw-on lid. A label on the outside said, "Delicious, roasted peanuts." If you shook the can, it rattled as though

4

there were peanuts inside. When you unscrewed the lid, out popped a spring, covered in green cloth to look like a snake, which had been tightly compressed inside. Somehow, I always forgot about the "snake" inside the can in my haste to get some peanuts.

Maggie Alix Bray Hobbie, October 14, 1933

Mom also loved to give us little presents, such as wind-up toys. These worked best on the smooth linoleum of the kitchen floor. Fake spiders or mice would scoot across the floor, changing direction as they encountered a chair leg, with our dog in hot pursuit. Mom and the rest of us would laugh until we cried.

She was always slim and nicely dressed. Her facial features were elegant, especially her perfect nose. People often told me how lovely Mom was. There was a picture of Mom in her wedding dress, hanging in my parents' bedroom.

I think because of the toaster's reflection of my nose, I was very aware of people's noses. Mom used to tell me to pinch my nostrils, so that my nose wouldn't spread. She also often cautioned me about making funny faces, because my face might permanently freeze in the objectionable, funny face. I guess my early delight in extending my tongue into one of my nostrils prompted these warnings, but the thought of going through life with my tongue frozen in place by an act of God, poking into one of my nostrils forever, never deterred me. Usually, her anger was directed at my father and either involved a money matter or revolved around something that affected her mother—my grandmother Schultz (Margaret Elizabeth Eyres Schultz, 1880–1954), who lived nearby, and, I think, incited my mother to complaints.

In the winter, when we were confined to the house more than in the other seasons and visited my grandmother daily, my mother was more edgy than in other seasons. I remember her saying often that I had ruined her day by something I had done, indirectly raising the horrible specter of coal in my stocking if Santa Claus found out. Her anger, however, was always short-lived. If she had really gotten angry with me during the day and was feeling guilty, we would walk over to the Parkside Drug Store, on the corner of Potomac and Elmwood, for a sundae. My favorite was a Royal Sundae—chocolate sauce and marshmallow sauce over vanilla ice cream, with peanuts, whipped cream, and a cherry.

Twice each month, my mother picked up a wonderful, German woman, who came to our house to clean, but was more like a beloved aunt than an employee. Emily Specht was a short, white-haired woman, about twenty years older than my mother. I used to help her polish silverware in our dining room, and I liked to vacuum the downstairs rugs under her direction. She had lost a finger on one of her hands. A kind, robust, and practical woman with a great sense of humor and a way of always looking at the funny side of a problem, she could get us all laughing at what my mother had started to address as a crisis. Emily was someone that a child could go to with a problem and be assured of a sympathetic ear. Our dogs would talk to Emily with a gentle and rambling yowl, whenever they saw her, as if describing all the happenings in our household since she was last there. Emily was our beloved "nanny." I saw the television broadcast of Queen Elizabeth II's coronation in 1953 at Emily's house. We didn't have a television.

In contrast to my mother, my father was hardly ever mad, was full of humorous stories, and had an endearing quality of breaking into laughter, as he neared the end of telling a joke, in anticipation of the punch line. My father never met a stranger he didn't immediately engage in conversation and like, it seemed. He was almost too gregarious. He loved sports, history, geography, music, and nature. He had an incredibly wide range of knowledge and an ability to remember and quote literature of all kinds that always amazed me. An excellent singer, he also played the piano beautifully, well into his eighties. He was handsome in an ordinary sort of way, wore glasses, and was balding. He had a big nose, but not too big. He could wiggle his ears better than anyone I ever knew. He could also curl his tongue lengthwise. My mother couldn't do either. The only two things I didn't like about my father were his habit of retelling the same jokes and his short fuse when he was driving. He never used obscenities but would get extremely angry about other drivers' bad driving. Dad felt that in the car was one place where he could release his frustrations.

Dad worked hard at two jobs. Until the 1950s, he was the head, manufacturing pharmacist in my Grandfather Hobbie's pharmaceutical company—P. Harold Hayes & Company—and worked evenings at local drug stores. He worked for many years, additionally, at Volk's Drugstore on Delaware Avenue near Gates Circle. I remember watching out the front windows of the house for him to come home from work, walking down the street in the dark from the corner bus stop. When he opened the front door, I would fly into his arms.

John Hayes Hobbie, 1925

After dinner was a fine time. There was nothing like sprawling in the living room on the floor, in front of the fireplace and radio, on a winter's evening and listening to "The Lone Ranger," sponsored by General Mills (Cheerios and Wheaties), at 7:30 on Mondays, Wednesdays, and Fridays, and to "Sergeant Preston of the Yukon" at the same time on Tuesdays and Thursdays. I will always feel indebted to Buffalonian Fran Striker, from my old neighborhood, who created the "masked man, Tonto, Silver, and Scout." Big debt also to Rossini for the *William Tell Overture*, which added so much to the excitement, and which I still love.

I shoveled a lot of snow in Buffalo. I got my first shovel when I was four years old, for Christmas, I recall, and put it to good use. Once, when a babysitter named Pat McKinnon, Ceci, and her friend Gretchen Halbin were home, probably teasing me, I was outside the house on a dark evening, dressed in the snow pants and coat I hated when I was young, which were so bulky I could hardly walk. For some reason, Pat, Gretchen, and Ceci had locked the back door and would not let me into the house, when I tried to come in. I remember their laughing faces, looking out at me through the small glass windows in the back door on the side of the house, and my howls of frustration. I was tantrum mad. Finally, I remembered my new shovel, then stored in the shed in the backyard. With some difficulty I got through the snow in my snow outfit and retrieved the shovel. I then brought it around to the side door and bashed in two of the small windows with it. That shut up

Pat quickly, and the girls let me in. My parents were not pleased, when they came home. Pat never babysat for me again. I always liked her anyway.

When I was about eight years old, I started shoveling in earnest. After I had completed our front sidewalks and side driveway, I would clear a path around the backyard for our dog and cat. Elderly neighbors on both sides usually were willing to pay good money to have their walks and driveways cleaned. I could earn a dollar for each job. My grandparents on my mother's side, Margaret and Charles Henry Frederick Schultz (1878–1963)—whom I always considered my real maternal grandfather, although he was actually a "step" grandfather—who lived about two blocks away at 715 Richmond Avenue, had a long driveway, which went all the way to a four car garage in the backyard. Shoveling their walks and driveway was an all-day commitment. Miss Gertrude Angell, the Headmistress for almost five decades at the Buffalo Seminary (the girls' high school, where my mother, two aunts, and sister Ceci all went to school), lived on Dorchester Road, around the corner from my grandparents' house. My grandmother, mother, and I used to have afternoon tea on occasion with her when I was very little, and my grandfather and I would often shovel her walk together.

My grandfather and I also shoveled the driveway and sidewalk of other old friends on Dorchester Road: Hazel and Judson Rumsey. Mrs. Rumsey, who was one of the best snow shovelers I ever saw, even when she was seventy years old, called my mother "Ottie," because their daughter, Dallas, used to call my mother that when she had baby-sat Dallas decades before. Judson Rumsey was an especially nice and kind man, with thick, owlish-looking glasses, who always wore a bow tie. His wife, who was very outspoken and critical of "newcomers" to the neighborhood, sometimes scared me with the fast way she spoke, like a machine gun. Both were dear friends of our family.

I enjoyed shoveling. I had a feeling of accomplishment, when I finished a shoveling job, and never minded that, within a day, either new snow or drifted snow required starting again. After I began elementary school at P.S. No. 56, I rarely shoveled alone. Usually, one of my neighborhood buddies—Mike Weinberg, Bruce Bleichfield, Nicky Losicero, Enn Teivas, John Mooney, or Richard Bassett—would share the work and reward. We would break up the monotony of particularly big jobs by throwing snowballs at passing cars. At my Grandfather Schultz' house one snowy afternoon, an especially lucky throw by Mike Weinberg went through a car's open side window, hitting the driver in the face. Mike and I hid in my grandpa's cellar, after sprinting up the driveway, around the back, and into the back door, with a cursing driver hot on our heels.

Dad in front of 453 West Delavan Avenue, 1954

Before I was allowed to go outside in winter by myself, I often played indoors with two childhood friends—April Lee Haydon, who lived around the corner on Richmond Avenue with her mother and grandmother and went to kindergarten and pre-primer with me at P.S. No. 56, and Mary Jo Collins. Mary Jo lived a few doors west from us on Delavan Avenue, in the flat below Mrs. Davidson, who used to be my mother's piano teacher. Both April Lee and Mary Jo were my first good friends outside of the family.

April Lee's mother and grandmother were very protective of her and guarded us, as we played or walked to school together, as though we were in imminent danger of being kidnapped at any moment. While it is true that one of the heads of the Buffalo mafia and other reputed mafia members lived in our neighborhood, because of them our neighborhood had a reputation of being very safe, so I never understood their concern. April Lee and I registered for kindergarten together in the summer of 1949 and met Miss Mulligan and Miss Kick, who taught us in the kindergarten classes at P.S. No. 56 in 1949–50.

Mary Jo, in contrast to April Lee, was a maverick, with an older brother, Tim, and a younger brother, Mike (who was called "Worm" by his mother). We spent a lot of time hiding from her parents, while they called her by name throughout the neighborhood. Her mother had a piercing voice. Mary Jo went to a Catholic elementary school, had cute freckles and red hair, and seduced me when I was five.

The three of us often played together during the winter in our attic, where there was a small, gas stove to keep the attic warm. The attic was a glorious place, with dark, enclosed eaves in which to hide and make forts, a pool table, and lots of space in which to play—even to play doctor and nurse. As I recall, it was Mary Jo who suggested that game, in which we took off our clothes, inspected each other, and took each other's temperature by a rectal pencil. I learned a lot. April Lee wouldn't play, and my mother put a stop to it when she found out somehow (April Lee ratted us out).

Until I was seven or so, I was not allowed to go out in a snowstorm. The Buffalo *Courier Express* (the morning paper) and the Buffalo *Evening News* (the evening paper) both had articles about adults and children becoming lost and freezing to death in snowstorms, which my parents assiduously brought to our attention. I would watch the snow fall silently and heavily for hours, and sometimes days, from the bay windows in the front of our house, and delight in the way the bushes that lined our backyard would catch the snow, bend under the weight, and create dozens of secret, hiding places, under snow-laden branches. When I was old enough to be allowed out in a storm, I liked nothing better than to walk around the neighborhood in a heavy snowstorm—so heavy that the houses and trees were obliterated by the driving snow, traffic was stopped, and the only sound was the wind. As soon as the snow stopped, we went outside to build snow forts, incite snowball fights, and etch snow angels in the new snow.

In the 1940s and 1950s, huge, mature, elm trees lined all of the streets on Buffalo's west side, typically one or two in front of each house. Their branches formed a canopy over the streets. Their three or four-foot wide trunks marched down the streets and parkways like guardians, reassuring in the heaviest of snows, for even when the streets and houses were invisible in the snow, I could always go from tree to tree in the whiteness and know when I reached the tree in front of our house. After a storm, the trees supported snow-filled arches overhead, forming bowers of silver and sparkle above each street. The best physical part about our neighborhood was the nearby forest of American elms, planted in five rows, which stretched about one mile, from Colonial Circle to Soldiers Place, on Bidwell Parkway. It was magnificent in every season.

I remember being really cold only once in Buffalo's snows—in fact, "colder than a witch's tit," as a friend, Bill Morgan, used to say. (I thought that was a cold bird for many years.) Delaware Park was about one mile from 453 and accessible by walking east on West Delavan Avenue to Bidwell Parkway, north up the parkway to Soldiers Place, and then up Lincoln Parkway to the park. Both parkways had hundred-foot wide medians, filled with giant elms, and presented inviting routes to Delaware Park for kids with sleds. At the park, several long hills sloped down the sides of ravines, leading to the park lake. As soon as a storm was over, sled trails would appear on the hills. I spent many happy afternoons on those hills, with a long sled and with an old toboggan that held about six kids. We competed, of course, to see who could make the longest run.

Once, in early December when I was about ten, before the park lake had completely frozen over, I had a spectacular run on my sled, which dropped me onto the lake's ice and then into the water beyond the rim ice. It was no problem to get out of the lake shallows, but I remember running the mile or so home, covered with water and ice, with friends dragging the sled and toboggan, and wondering if I would make it home. I was no worse for wear.

We also skated on the Delaware Park Lake and on rinks around Buffalo, although I preferred sledding, until I was old enough to go skiing at Holiday Valley or Kissing Bridge, which were the nearest ski resorts. Ceci and her friends first took me skating on the park lake. We rented skates. My sister's friends laughed and laughed at my falls. I was pretty mad at them at first but gradually began to enjoy the speed of skating, and the cups of hot chocolate that we bought at the old concession stand next to the lake.

I deeply regretted not becoming a good enough skater to play high school hockey, although I spent many afternoons, flooding makeshift rinks in my backyard and in friends' backyards with water from garden hoses, and playing in pickup hockey games on those rinks, until I went to high school. The best backyard rink we ever made was in Mike Weinberg's backyard, where one winter we nurtured the ice for several months, with the help of Mike's dad. Great hockey games there were made more challenging by the Weinberg's single tree and large brick barbecue, which intruded on the rink. Nothing was as satisfying as checking someone hard into that tree or the barbecue. Some of my favorite Christmas presents were hockey pucks or sticks.

In my earliest years, Buffalonians burned coal to keep warm in the winter. A big, coal truck would back into my grandparents' driveway, or into our driveway on West Delavan. You would hear the rumbling growl of that big, dump truck engine and know what it was. A chute would be attached from a small opening at the rear of the truck to, and through, a small window in the basement. Then the driver would climb into the cab and slowly raise the front of the truck's bed, until the coal started to slide down the bed and into the chute with a happy rattle. When the truck was empty, the bed was lowered, the chute disassembled, and the truck pulled away. A huge pile of coal invited inspection in the basement.

Dad and Grandpa Schultz asked me to help them shovel coal into the furnace every day in winter. Just inside the furnace door was a pan of water to create humidity. It was my job to fill that pan up with water by using an old kettle. At Grandpa Schultz' house my grandparents also used coal in the kitchen stove, so another job assigned to me was lugging the coal scuttle up from the basement, filled to the brim with coal. It sat next to the stove and was filled at least once a day. In the early 1950s the coal furnaces, and my grandparents' kitchen stove, were replaced by oil heat and a gas stove, respectively. One day they were gone, and I never saw the coal truck again, although the coal dust lingered in the corners of the basement for a long time afterwards, and for years we saved a small pile of coal to fill the bucket each Christmas in which the Christmas tree was anchored.

Our backyard in early winter, 1956

Lake Erie often froze solid. By January it was safe to go out on the lake. My family rented a small cabin each summer in Canada, about fifteen miles west of Buffalo, on a wild sweep of shoreline called Holloway Bay, just to the west of Point Abino on Lake Erie's north shore. To get there we crossed the Erie Canal and the Niagara River on the Peace Bridge, acknowledging with appropriate whoops, as we passed by, the flags in the middle of the bridge: American, United Nations, and Canadian. I liked the United Nations flag, with its round map of the world on a sky blue field, and felt that it belonged on the *Peace* Bridge. I have always shared my father's deep love of maps and have had a world map on the wall of my office. That was my first knowledge of the United Nations. It was comforting to know that its flag flew stolidly next to the Canadian and American ones on the bridge. I also was very happy with the new Canadian Maple Leaf flag.

If my grandfather Schultz was with us, as he often was, our entry to Canada (and our re-entry to the U.S.) was considerably faster than usual. Grandpa Schultz had worked his way up in the U.S. Customs Service to chief inspector, before retiring. As a result, with him in the front seat and a special sticker on the windshield in the shape of a badge, the immigration and customs inspectors on both sides of the bridge would snap to attention, greet, and salute him, waving us through without inspection. I missed this pomp, when he was not with us, and it would sometimes take ten minutes to get through the inspection line. "Where were you born? What is your citizenship? What do you have to declare?" My father always responded to the first question by stating "Tonawanda" as his birthplace, after everyone else in the car had answered "Buffalo" in rapid succession. He was always pleased, I think, to be able to answer with a different place of birth. Once the immigration officer startled him by asking, "Why were you born *there*?" Without blinking an eye my father replied that his mother was there in Tonawanda, and he wanted to be near her.

After crossing the Peace Bridge, we drove west, past summer, lakeside communities on Bertie Bay, Thunder Bay, and Abino Bay, to Holloway Bay, where many of our Buffalo neighbors had summer homes. The more lavish summer homes were on these bays. As you got farther from the city, the size and impressiveness of the homes decreased, I always thought. After Labor Day these summer communities tended to be mostly deserted. In winter they were like ghost towns with an occasional, lighted store or school and a scattered house, decorated with Christmas lights, which we knew to be occupied by a Canadian, year-round resident. The roads were empty of vehicles, the fields stretched endlessly on either side, and the lines of trees, separating field from field, traced silhouettes against the winter sky. We often saw herds of deer, struggling through the windswept and snow-drifted fields.

The last two miles to the community of rented cabins and small houses known as "the Kennels" were south on the Holloway Bay Road, a one-lane, gravel road, leading from the Port Colburne highway through open fields of snow. The fields gradually gave way to the woods of maples, oaks, and evergreens surrounding the thirty or so small, summer houses and cabins I called "the beach," nestled just north of the sand dunes lining Holloway Bay. Others called the community "the Kennels," I guess, because the cabins were very small, like kennels. The cabins *were* small and lacking in audio privacy, but woods and thick brush screened each place from the others. So although you could hear parents yelling at their kids, or at each other, in the summer, you couldn't see them. In the winter the cabins seemed smaller and closer together. Our rented cabin was among the smallest. Although we rented several different cabins in the almost fifty or so years at the beach, they were almost all two rooms with a large screened-in porch. The outhouse, with its summer spiders, mosquitoes, and the occasional skunk, was located about thirty feet behind the cabin. After the first twenty years, we got indoors plumbing.

We went to the beach several times each winter. Snow-clogged roads often made us park our old Chevrolet on the edge of Holloway Bay Road and walk a mile or so in to the beach, through the snow. If the road was passable, but with a covering of snow, we would tie a sled behind the car with a long rope and ride it behind the car, three or four kids jammed on the sled.

Sometimes, my father would drive pretty fast. We had to be careful to avoid slamming into the car, if he had to brake fast. We would drive like this as far as possible along the deserted road, until we could go no farther, then park in the snow on the side of the road and walk in. Where the sun had melted bare patches on the gravel, the sled's steel runners gave off satisfying sparks on these sled tows.

I loved the solitude of winter at the beach. There was usually no one else there in December or January. Summer sounds of waves, banging screen doors, and radios were totally absent, but jays and chickadees were still noisy in the fragrant trees. The woods of spruce, hardwoods, and pine were deep in snow, as were the sand dunes and beach. In the woods the smell of the pine and spruce was clean and unencumbered by the sultry, summer smells of grass, lake, and wildflowers. From the cabin to the beach was about four hundred yards, with a ridge of sand dunes between the cabin area and the beach. We climbed up and over the sand dunes and were rewarded at the top with a view of the bay, stretching from Port Colborne to the west to Point Abino in the east. The frozen lake was before us, as far as the eye could see. The American shore could not be seen from our beach, so Lake Erie seemed like an ocean of ice.

The beach was indistinguishable under the snow from the ice. We carefully walked onto the beach and ice, and, if the ice was thick enough, ventured out as far as a mile or more. People sometimes drove vehicles onto the ice. Usually, in early January the ice would be relatively flat and have wind-blown surfaces that were smooth and skateable. By February there would be mountains of ice and snow, forty or fifty feet high, pushed up by the wind's action on the ice. With the wind whistling across the frozen lake's surface, and the spectacular, ice mountains, I liked to imagine that I was in the arctic. After hours on the ice, where mountain climbing, skating, and snowball fights exhausted us, we would retreat to the cabin. A small, wood stove and hot chocolate with marshmallows would welcome us.

On these winter trips my father would never let deep snow hinder his gathering of downed branches from the woods or of driftwood, poking through the beach snow. The smaller pieces would be stacked next to the cabin for the wood stove. The larger limbs would be sawed into four-foot lengths, stacked in the trunk of the car, and smuggled into Buffalo for our living room fireplace. My dad spent hours collecting wood there and sawing it, winter or summer. I have the same gene. Nothing gives me more pleasure than sawing, splitting, and stacking wood. The beach was a northern escape in both winter and summer. You could always count on it being soothing and friendly.

Dad sawing wood at Holloway Bay with Port Colborne in background

On several occasions, our family took winter afternoon trips to Chestnut Ridge State Park, just outside of Buffalo, where the major attractions in winter were the toboggan slides. As I recall, there were three or four of the slide platforms at the top of a quarter-mile long hill. You climbed up about thirty steps to the top of the platform with your toboggan. From the edge, a steep wooden slide, about two feet wide and fifty feet long, dropped to the hill, like a small ski jump. We got five or six people on a toboggan, inched towards the edge of the platform, and then careened down the slide and hill with screams. My father injured his back once, I remember, when we were struck broadside by an errant toboggan and crew that had strayed out of its path and was traveling much faster than we were. On another occasion, when I was riding in the first position, all of the others on the toboggan fell off, permitting me a glorious ride all the way to the end of the hill—the only time I was able to go so far.

My parents were very good about allowing our friends to go with us on our outings. John had good friends from Boy Scouts—Fred Turner and Billy Cook—and later some Nichols High School friends—John Talbott and Jim Herlan—who sometimes came with us. Patsy Runk, Pat Zimdahl, or Gretchen Halbin or another girlfriend frequently accompanied Ceci, and one or more of the usual culprits in my close circle of early elementary school friends—Enn Teivas, Richard Mann, Mike Weinberg, Richard Bassett, John Mooney, Bruce Bleichfield, Joel Lippes, Danny Fraustino, and Chuck Turco—joined me.

My school group reflected the neighborhood's diversity of origin and religion: Estonian, German, Italian, Sicilian, Irish, and English; Jewish, Catholic, and Protestant. Our immediate neighbors were mostly Sicilian:

Grisanti, Shillaci, Gregorio, and Leone to name just a few of dozens. They were good neighbors and passionate people. Some of their customs were different from my family's way of doing things, and they often intrigued me. I watched in awe, once, when Sonny Leone's mother brought home a live chicken from the Black Rock Market, wrung its neck in their kitchen, plucked off all the feathers, and cut it up for dinner. The Cox family and the Collins family were other nearby neighbors. They were Irish Catholics. The Siegels—German and Jewish—lived across the street. Their son Ernie, who was my sister's age, played a mean trumpet.

Our neighborhood was not very diverse racially, which I greatly regret now. I remember one lovely, African-American girl—Melodye Darnell—and one Mohawk Indian girl, with beautiful, braided hair—Kathy Henry—in our eighth grade class of about ninety kids. I considered both of them friends. Kathy also was in Sunday school at St. John's Episcopal Church. William Lovelace, a kindly, African-American man in his mid fifties, was the sexton at our church for a long time. Mr. Lovelace knew how to solve any problem at St. John's. I never saw an Asian or Hispanic face in my childhood in Buffalo that I can remember, except for the Chinese bishop who confirmed me. Although it was wonderful in so many ways, our west side neighborhood did not provide the rich diversity of races and cultures that I have loved, and been enriched by, in later life.

My early, winter life also included many trips to Lewiston, where my father's parents lived on what was then called the River Road. Lewiston is a small town on the Niagara River, about twenty-six miles north of Buffalo and five miles below or north of Niagara Falls. To get there from Buffalo, we drove out Niagara Street from West Delavan, past the automobile assembly plants, power station, and Hooker Chemical Company lining the river, to the south Grand Island Bridge, which we would cross onto the island—a shortcut down the river. My father never lost an opportunity to give us a history lesson on these trips.

Just before the bridge at the northwest end of Grand Island, we passed what was called "Burnt Ship Bay," which was an inlet on the Niagara River above Niagara Falls to the north of Grand Island. The French had anchored several ships in this small bay during the French and Indian War in 1759, on the way from Venango on Lake Erie to relieve the French garrison at Fort Niagara. Upon learning that the fort had already fallen to the British under Sir William Johnson, the French burned the ships before retreating to Detroit. According to my father, the bay had been haunted ever since. We eyed it apprehensively ever time we passed it, fully expecting ghost ships to rise from the reeds and challenge our passage.

After crossing the bridge, we drove around the City of Niagara Falls, past the Bell plant, to the Niagara Escarpment, which is an imposing ridge, stretching from east of Rochester, New York, a thousand miles or more to Wisconsin. My father called it a "cuesta" from the Silurian Age, and I would always think of the vast inland sea it once bordered, as we dropped over the edge on the River Road and down the steep incline, under the railroad bridge, to the cozy town of Lewiston. (The escarpment is most famous, of course, for the cliff over which the Niagara River forms the famous Niagara Falls, for which it is named.) There was always a competition among the kids in the car, as we approached the escarpment, to see who could first spot Brock's Monument on the Canadian side of the river and on top of the escarpment. The monument is an imposing tower, topped by a statue of General Brock, commemorating both the Battle of Queenston Heights, in which the British repulsed the Americans during the War of 1812, and the death in that battle of Major General Sir Isaac Brock, the British commander of troops defending against the American invasion.

As we drove through Lewiston on its sole commercial street, we passed the Perrigo house on Main Street, where my grandparents once tried in vain to get me to take voice lessons from Bessie Perrigo, an elderly friend of theirs, whose voice could break glass. Bessie had given my father singing lessons when he was young. I was told that the skeleton of a Civil War soldier had been found plastered up in the living room wall in that old Victorian house—originally Kelsey's Tavern—built in 1820. I agreed to one lesson, so as to be able to inspect that wall, but then I was out of there! Another landmark was the old hotel on Main Street, called the Frontier House, where General Lafayette and other famous people (James Fenimore Cooper, Jenny Lind, President McKinley, and Charles Dickens) had stayed. The last time I was there it was a McDonald's.

Leaving the town of Lewiston, we drove north down the river past a nineteenth century house on the riverbank, where a former tailor of nineteenth century Lewiston, Josiah Tryon, was rumored to have sheltered many slaves in an underground railroad terminus called "Tryon's Folly." The house, owned by the Harper family when I was young, is built atop the Niagara Gorge, with four descending cellars leading toward the Niagara River, which provided an excellent hiding place and escape route for the former slaves' late-night crossing into Canada. From there to my grandparents' house at 4667 Lower River Road was about one quarter mile north, past the Morgan Farm's apple, peach, pear, cherry, and plum orchards, its red barn, chicken coops, and other outbuildings, its bee hives and barnyard, and its fields of corn, barley, wheat, oats, and hay.

These landmarks along the way to my grandparents' house in Lewiston marked a palpable, growing excitement in the car, as we got closer to it.

We never failed to point out to any guests in the car their significance, and spotting each was a cherished ritual.

My paternal grandparents—Dr. John Albert Hobbie (1874–1962) and Mary Belle Charlton Hobbie (1876–1963)—had their home on the River Road, initially as their summer residence and then as their year-round home, for over eighty years, until the estate was sold in 1982. The large, Queen Anne style house, with a comfortable, wraparound front porch, sat back two hundred feet from the Niagara River gorge on about four acres, amidst spacious lawns, a tennis court, a half-acre garden, and towering oak, elm, and black walnut trees. There was a horse block in front of the house on the curving driveway, comprised of several large stones with a flat stone top, from which in the past you stepped into carriages or onto horses. For me the horse block was one of several forts on the grounds to be defended against marauding French soldiers or Iroquois.

Grandpa Hobbie was a calming presence. He was a physician, specializing in asthma and related conditions. I liked the way he whistled softly to himself, under his breath, as he worked around the house or on the grounds of the Hobbie estate. He told me many stories about his adventures with his cousin "Mile Zero" when he was young. I thought that name was the best I had ever heard. It was years later that I figured out the cousin was Miles Ayrault (Ayrault was the maiden name of my great grandmother, who was married to Issac Hobbie, mentioned above). My grandfather commuted from Lewiston to his office on Delaware Avenue in Buffalo, across the street from the old Temple Beth Zion, virtually every day, through snow and rain, until he had a stroke at the age of about eighty-four. I often drove to and from Lewiston with him. He had a "rhythmic foot" on the car's accelerator, which created a lulling alternation of speed and coasting.

Grandpa Hobbie, 1958

When I was about ten, Grandpa Hobbie and I drove from Buffalo, through dense fog, down the river towards Niagara Falls, crawling at about ten miles per hour and following the red tail lights of a dump truck ahead of us for what seemed like an eternity. Finally, the truck stopped, and the driver got out and walked back to us, asking if we were lost. We were in the middle of a vast expanse of dirt and rocks, which turned out to be the still-dry bottom of the Niagara Power Commission's newly-created reservoir, which would soon be flooded, as part of the largest power plant of its kind in the world. In the fog, we could have driven into Lake Ontario and not known it. The kind driver led us out to the road to Lewiston. My grandfather seized the occasion to tell me that the land we had been lost on had belonged to the Tuscarora Indian nation, but had been taken by the government for the reservoir. A split Supreme Court decision had permitted the New York Power Authority to take the land from the Indians, despite the treaty giving them the land long ago. One dissenting Justice, the great Hugo Black, wrote, "I regret that this Court…breaks faith with this dependent people. Great nations, like great men, should keep their word." Grandpa Hobbie agreed with Justice Black.

My grandparents' imposing house had five bedrooms and two baths upstairs, and a large living room, dining room, kitchen, library, and half bath on the first floor. French doors opened on to the front porch from the dining room and the living room. There was a huge fireplace in the living room and one in the front bedroom upstairs, overlooking the river. Above the living room fireplace was a scary portrait of ancestor Enoch Hall (1792—1850), which always set our dogs into fits of barking. His eyes followed you wherever you moved in the room. Both Pepper (dog number three) and Tuffy (number two) avoided the living room like the plague. Enoch's father, General Amos Hall, was the commander who surrendered Buffalo to the British in the War of 1812.

Behind the house to the northeast was a magnificent, black walnut tree, with a forty-foot long swing, hung from one of its largest limbs. Between the house and the extensive garden was an old apple tree, in which my grandfather had built a triangular, tree platform, with rails and wire mesh on each side. A metal ladder led up twenty feet to this platform, which was another stronghold against the various dangerous animals and enemies, lurking everywhere at Lewiston in my childhood.

My grandparents' property extended about one half mile east from the river to the abandoned fields of a neighbor's farm and into the river on the west, encompassing a small, stony beach at river's edge and a treacherous path through poison ivy down the one-hundred-foot shale bank. To the south lay the Morgan farm, belonging to the family of my Aunt Betty (Elizabeth Morgan Hobbie, 1909–2002), who was the wife of Uncle Tom, my father's twin brother (Thomas Charlton Hobbie, 1904–86). To the north lay several imposing estates, including several owned in the past by ancestors. The two-lane River Road snaked along the top of the gorge between the house and the steep riverbank. The village of Lewiston was two miles south of the Hobbie place and historic Fort Niagara about five miles north.

In the winter, we often spent Thanksgiving and part of Christmas day, or the day after Christmas, at Lewiston. My family would be joined there by my mother's parents (she was an only child) and by the families of Uncle Tom and Aunt Betty Hobbie (six girls) and of Aunt Betty Craig (my father's sister, Mary Elizabeth Hobbie Craig, 1909–79) and her husband, Bob Craig (Robert S. Craig, 1905–76). Aunt Betty Craig and Uncle Bob had twin daughters, named Molly and Kitty. The older of my father's sisters, Aunt Kate (Katherine Emily Hobbie, 1906–2004), who was a college professor in Oneonta, New York, also would usually attend, as would several elderly family friends with no close relatives with whom to share the holidays. So for the holiday meal at Lewiston, we typically had a crowd of about two dozen people.

We entered my grandparents' house past the outside dinner bell, which hung next to the backdoor, through the back door, and up the back stairs, which brought us right into the kitchen through an entryway. The smell of roasting turkey and baking pies permeated that kitchen, even when nothing was cooking. My grandfather Hobbie had mounted a long, bird-feeding shelf just outside the double kitchen windows, facing the gardens, and a suet feeder on a pole just beyond. Whenever you entered the kitchen, you checked the bird feeders first for the cardinals, jays, chickadees, finches, titmice, and nuthatches gathering there. There was usually a woodpecker on the suet feeder.

The second kitchen stop was the cookie jar on the counter, next to the dining room door, to check for gingersnaps or Christmas cookies. The third stop was the closet, off the entryway from the back stairs, to be sure my grandfather's BB gun and the horn were in their proper places. The horn was an old, dented coach horn, with a two-foot long neck, which we used to blow from the riverbank in salute to the *Cayuga* on its daily trip down the Niagara River, from Queenston and across Lake Ontario to Toronto and back.

My grandmother Hobbie sometimes had an older woman who helped in the kitchen—Mrs. Murphy—but I remember that meal preparations on these occasions were everyone's business. The kitchen was packed with people! We always had turkey with two types of cranberry sauces, stuffing, mashed potatoes, candied squash, a big bowl of fruit, and green beans. Apple pie or pumpkin pie with ice cream often followed. The ice cream was invariably peach flavor, which was Grandpa Hobbie's favorite. My Aunt Kate usually organized the cleanup afterwards, helped by all the cousins. To this day, when

I wash dishes, I think fondly of her. My parents were the most influential adults during my childhood. Aunt Kate was a close second.

Aunt Kate was a special person. She never married, but I was visiting her one winter in Oneonta, New York, in the 1950s, when she confided to me that earlier that day the university president had proposed to her. I bet that she had a lot of marriage proposals in her life. I wouldn't call her beautiful, but she was pretty. Her spirit and sense of right were her beautiful qualities. She told me that her career as a teacher and an administrator began in Damascas, Syria, at the American School, where she was one of only five Americans in that city in 1930. Later, in 1942 she was so incensed at the internment of the Japanese-Americans that she resigned her teaching position in New York and headed for the camps. She lived there in U.S. Army tarpaper-covered shacks, behind ten-foot-high, barbed-wire fences, at Tule Lake, California, from 1942 until 1945, teaching internees in a desolate, so-called relocation center, where the temperature ranged from twenty degrees below zero in winter to over one hundred degrees in the summer.

When I visited Aunt Kate that winter, she was teaching at the New York State Teachers College at Oneonta and was about to become the Dean of Professional Studies. It was fun to walk around the campus with her and to have virtually all the students and faculty greet her respectfully as Dr. Hobbie.

When I was about five years old, she showed me a cardinal for the first time in the bushes next to the kitchen window at the Lewiston family home, and later that year showed me a Baltimore oriole in the walnut tree next to the tennis court there. She taught me both birds' songs. These were the first two of hundreds. I once complained to her that my kindergarten teacher would not let me practice in school my imitation of a cardinal. I always think of her when I see or hear a cardinal.

At Christmas at Lewiston, seated at the piano in the living room, she led us all in Christmas carols. On many occasions I heard her on visits in Oneonta or Lewiston, playing the piano and singing by herself, or joining with my father in a duet. Besides being a fine musician, she was an incomparable reader! She could really make a story come alive and delighted in doing so. When I was very young, she made the *Freddy the Pig* series of children's books and the Thornton W. Burgess books (*The Burgess Bird Book for Children*, *The Burgess Animal Book for Children*, and *Mother West Wind Stories*) an important part of my life. When I read *Charlotte's Web* to my own children, I recalled Aunt Kate's consternation at the bawling of my cousins, Molly and Kitty, and me the first time she read it to us at Lewiston. Later, she gave me such books as Sir James Frazer's *The Golden Bough*, ensuring that as an adult I had the understanding necessary to enjoy literature to the fullest. I still read them and dozens of other books that are inscribed to me from Aunt Kate as birthday or Christmas gifts.

Aunt Kate was a trusted sounding board, a kind of compass by which many of us steered our lives. If she approved, you felt comfortable going ahead. She strongly opposed the Vietnam War and refused to pay the percentage of her federal taxes that funded it. It was Aunt Kate who most encouraged me to go to Korea as a Peace Corps volunteer. She told me of her love of the Far East and accurately predicted that my life would be changed completely and positively, if I went. Later, she was a strong voice of support, as I struggled to resolve what to do when I received my draft notice for the Vietnam-era army. Still later, as a strong supporter of labor unions, she encouraged me to begin a career in union-side labor law. At the age of eighty-eight, with her elderly friends, she reportedly helped to organize the workers' union at the mushroom farms near Kennett Square, Pennsylvania, where she lived in a retirement community. She lived to be ninety-eight years old and was as sharp as a tack to the very end.

At my grandparents' house we ate meals at a long, oak table in the dining room. There was a set of chimes, hanging on the dining room wall, next to the door leading to the front hall. You played these chimes with a mallet. Of course, every child had to have a turn at banging out the dinner call on the chimes. We were discouraged from creating such a racket at any other time, but before dinner it was required. Also on the wall was a painting of eight piglets, each of which was named for a grandchild.

After the holiday meal, very often virtually all of the adults found chairs or sofas in which to snooze and snore in front of the living room fireplace or in the library. I once counted six sleeping adults in the living room after a Thanksgiving dinner. Each had a distinct snore or whistle, but Grandpa Hobbie had the most interesting: a combination rumble and sharply rising and then descending whistle. Grandpa Schultz was a close second, and Grandma Hobbie usually held her own. She was a tall, big-boned woman, much taller than my grandfather, and a former member of the Wellesley basketball team and of the class of 1898. Her snore always suggested to me that she must have been ferocious on the basketball court, although she was very kind to her grandchildren.

Grandma Hobbie was a comfortable woman. She was at ease with people, belonged to many church organizations and the Lewiston Garden Club, and relished having garden parties for her family, friends, and neighbors. I rarely saw her angry at anyone. She taught German in high school for many years. When German prisoners-of-war were housed near Lewiston at Fort Niagara during World War II, and worked at the fruit farms along the river and Lake Ontario, she invited them for meals. She received a fine education at Wellesley and had an air of self-confidence about her that commanded respect. She called my grandfather "Bert" or "Father." He called her "Mother." Most significantly, she could turn her eyelids inside out, which gave her eyes a horrible, bloody red, supernatural appearance and delighted her eleven grandchildren. She raised four remarkable children.

Grandma Hobbie, Christmas 1959

Most of the snoozing adults in the living room at Lewiston would snort in their sleep, when the grandfather clock in the hall tolled the hours and the Westminster clock, on the shelf next to the fireplace, chimed the quarter hours. While my grandparents and other adults dozed after the meals, the kids escaped upstairs to the second floor and attic, where we could play "Spike and Louie" or Hide-and-Seek, slide down the banister, or search for the silver teapot set, which my grandmother had hidden, and then forgotten its hiding place, when she had traveled to Europe decades before. The reward was twenty-five dollars. Supposedly, it was hidden on the second floor or in the attic. My grandfather also claimed to have hidden money—not more than a couple of five-dollar bills—in several books in his extensive library between the living room and the dining room. We would diligently search the library books for those five-dollar bills, never realizing that we were indirectly dusting those old books in the process. (My cousin Kitty finally found the silver service in the attic rafters after decades of searching. No five-dollar bills were ever found, to my recollection.) We also played Bagatelle on a fine old board, which had been handmade by my grandfather, or Pick-Up-Sticks. Or we would dress in our jackets and wool hats and head for the riverbank or the Morgan farm, known formally as Red Bank Farm (in honor of the reddish, shale riverbank at which the land ended), next door.

The riverbank was usually off limits officially. In the winter the wind howled up the river like a banshee and set the leaves of the oaks at the top of the bank to rattling ominously. I had a special tree on the riverside, to which my brother and sister had introduced me: a gnarled cedar, which leaned precariously out from the bank about thirty feet down. The tree had partially fallen, but its main twelve-inch trunk stuck out at a right angle to the steep bank for about ten feet, then curled upwards for a few feet to where its branches began. My perch was another ten feet or so up the trunk. As there were no branches to hold on to for the first ten feet, it was tricky to get to the branches leading upwards to the perch. Cedar bark is smooth and slippery, especially with ice on the trunk. The drop from the trunk to the bank below was at least twenty feet at first and then sharply increased as you inched further out on the trunk. But the view in both directions was magnificent, especially in the leafless winter. You looked up the river to the south towards Lewiston Heights and Brock's Monument, where you could imagine the fighting, one hundred fifty years before, and down the river to the north towards Fort Niagara. Unknown to my grandparents, I made it a point to always climb to my perch in the cedar, to check out the river and Canada on the far side, shortly after arriving at Lewiston each visit. That perch was the best perch and world perspective I ever had.

Scovell's steps were easier to navigate. To the north of the cedar, a neighbor had built a staircase of ninety-two steps from the top of the bank down to a small platform, about sixty feet above the beach. In the winter these steps were always hopelessly covered with ice and snow, but if you really wanted to get to the platform, you could back down the icy steps, like a ladder, avoiding the occasional rotten step. Below the staircase, the awesome Niagara swirled and eddied with ice flows and whirling seagulls. On several occasions, we got the grandfathers, uncles, and my father to bring out my grandfather's .22 caliber rifle. From the platform, we shot at the icebergs, rushing past.

More often, however, instead of visiting the riverbank, the kids were tempted to trek south across the peach orchard, through the drifted snow, to the Morgan farm. There was a well-worn path, even in winter, between the Hobbie property and the farm, which was a year-round Eden of sorts. The path crossed row upon row of barren peach trees, which served in snowstorms as guideposts across the orchard. With the farm's extensive fields and orchards stilled under deep snow, our winter visits were limited to the pigpen, chicken coops, horse stables, milking room, and the second floor of the barn.

The pigs were often named after the Hobbie and Morgan grandchildren, so it was obligatory to greet them. The several chicken coops were not pleasant places, as they reeked of chicken excrement, but the nesting boxes usually hid freshly laid eggs, which we felt obliged to gather for the Morgans. The trick was to slide your hand under a nesting hen, without disturbing her, and find an egg, removing it carefully, without getting chicken poop on your hand. In the milking room the six cows were sometimes named for cousins, too, but I remember three of them—Mrs. Wogus, Mrs. Wurtzburger, and Mrs. Wiggins—being named after the cows in the classic *Freddy the Pig* books by Walter R. Brooks, which I have already mentioned.

The barn was designed so that the ground level housed the horses to the left and the cows to the right. You climbed a small incline to enter the barn's main door in front on the main floor, from which you had to go down steps inside to reach the milking room. Dutch doors in back connected both the stables and the milking room to the barnyard. A tall silo joined the milking room on the right side, usually filled to the brim with silage. Above the main floor of the barn, with its stored farm machinery and grain bins on each side, were the haymows, accessible by ladders.

The haymows were another area officially off limits to kids, but irresistibly tempting, with their mountains of loose hay to slide down or jump onto, and stacks of hay bales, conveniently tied with twine and just about the right size to be blocked into tunnels, forts, and castles. You needed a flashlight to see in the dim light and down in the tunnels of hay bales. Many flashlight batteries wore out there, during our hours and hours of cavorting in the hay. Of course, matches were strictly forbidden anywhere in the barn. On the wall of the left haymow a thirty-foot ladder crept up to a small window with a magnificent northern view of the farm buildings, the peach orchard, and the Hobbie place about a quarter of a mile away. Jumping from this ladder into the hay below was just one ingenious way of risking life and limb in the barn.

In winter the unheated barn was chilly, although the heat from the animals in the stables and milking room below kept the temperature tolerable. The smell of hay, silage, and manure lingered pungently throughout the barn, like the scent of incense in a cathedral. I learned to love these smells. To this day they evoke the joy of swinging on a rope, stretching from one of the barn's overhead beams, and the comfortable rustling of horses and cows in the straw in their stalls.

A trip to Lewiston always exhilarated me. Returning to a comparatively drab Buffalo was a letdown. But winter could be fun at home. Many happy, winter days were spent at Public School No. 56, or at home in the attic with my friends, playing with toy soldiers, my brother's model railroad, or other toys, such as Lincoln logs or the wooden blocks my grandfather Schultz had made for us. Hundreds of castles and forts were built in my early years, and hundreds of miniature battles were staged on the floor, amidst the folds of rugs. My sister and brother were adept constructors of tents, made out of sheets draped over tables and chairs, and passed along their trade to me. They were also fine teachers of such skills as the best places to hide, when we played

Hide and Seek, or when we turned off the lights at night and played Flashlight Tag, throughout the house.

During the days of winter, my mother taught me a lot of card games. We often played Fish, Double Solitaire, Canasta, Hearts, and Cribbage, among many other games, when it was too cold to go outside and my brother and sister were at school. I would usually resist her order to take a nap after lunch, but recall hearing her playing the piano in the music room downstairs, as soon as she thought that I was asleep. She was a magnificent pianist and taught piano at our home in my early years. Canasta was Grandpa Schultz's favorite card game. Until he died in 1963, my mother and I played Canasta with him virtually every Sunday night, and often during the weekday evenings.

At our house on West Delavan Avenue, you entered the front door by climbing four steps onto a porch and then accessing the front door through a glass-enclosed vestibule. It was murder to clean all those little glass panes. From the front door, you entered our living room directly. To the right was a cozy area in front of the fireplace, with its carved, mahogany mantelpiece. A couch, covered with a yellow, floral print, faced the living room's windows from the south wall. Above it was my favorite painting in our house—a very large print by Karl Biese of winter in the German Alps, depicting a snow-covered lodge in the foreground and snow-covered, dawn-tinged mountains in the background.

Our house in a storm, January 1953

To the left as you entered was a kind of arch into another room with a large, bay window. I guess I thought of this as the music room, because there was a baby grand piano in one corner and later an upright piano in another corner. It was probably my most beloved room at 453, for it had four windows, letting in light, and our Christmas tree was usually placed in the bay window.

In this room a small circle of English immigrants, who lived on Buffalo's west side, held their monthly "culture club" meetings in the first decades of the twentieth century, my grandmother told me. When I was five and my brother was fifteen, we sang together in this room for one of my mother's many, club gatherings. John played the guitar, while we sang "Streets of Laredo" together. I remember happily playing with my Lincoln logs under the piano with my cousin, Kathy Dudden, for several afternoons, when her family visited us, just after my eighth birthday. Her father, Arthur Dudden, was my mother's first cousin. He was a professor at Bryn Mawr College. Kathy was my age and very pretty.

Through another arch, you came to the dining room. The music room could be shut off from the dining room and from the living room by pulling out sliding, wooden doors from the sides of the arches. When I heard the faint rumble of the doors being pulled shut, I knew that my mother either was teaching with a student or was going to practice by herself. Even at an early age, I sensed both exuberance and sadness in her playing, and it was evident that she was an exceptional pianist. My favorite composers have always been Chopin and Schumann, since those winter afternoons, which rang with Mom's glorious music. To this day, a Chopin etude or waltz evokes overwhelming and fond memories of her and her piano music.

Gypsy, Tuffy, or Pepper—our successive dogs over a period of twenty-five years—used to come to the piano and lie under it, whenever Mom played. You could tell that they loved to hear her music. Whenever I practiced violin, each dog would disappear to the basement to get as far away from the sound as possible. Gypsy used to howl piteously, when I practiced.

In the center of the dining room hung an old globe chandelier, which I never liked much. On the west side of the room was a large china cabinet. The space between the china cabinet and the wall was one of my favorite hiding places, when I was small. A portrait of George Washington hung on the south wall, next to the twelve-glass-pane door, leading out to the garden.

Between the living room and the kitchen, in the center of the house, was the upstairs staircase. The first three of the sixteen steps were usually laden with folded laundry, magazines, and books to be carried upstairs. There was a bedroom in each corner of the house. When I was very young, I slept in my parents' bedroom in the northeast corner of the house. My mother had a small, framed print of Maxfield Parrish's "The Dinkey Bird." I was sure that the naked lady, swinging in a swing before the distant castle, was my mother, since the picture was on her dresser. Later, my room moved to the northwest corner. I remember there was a copy of one of Edward Hicks' "Peaceable Kingdom" paintings, with the lion, wolf, and bear, peacefully mixing with a lamb, ox, and other animals. I liked that painting a lot

After naptime, we would visit my maternal grandmother and mother's friends, weather permitting. My mother seemed to know every elderly person within blocks of our home, and felt compelled to check on them daily, especially in winter. We trundled over to their houses for a cup of tea and cookies on most afternoons in the years before I started school. I would be dressed up. One pinkish outfit with black buttons (probably inherited from my sister) I particularly detested and would fight like crazy to avoid wearing. I also disliked wearing the bulky, snow pants, winter coat, and rubber, snow boots into which I was stuffed on these expeditions. The winter clothes had cumbersome zippers, which froze, and the boots had tricky metal buckles, which soon became encased in ice and impossible to open when you needed to take off the boots.

A very enjoyable part of these winter visits to housebound, elderly friends was food. Cookies and cake have always helped to make a boring situation bearable. My mother taught me to make and to frost cakes at an early age. I loved to beat the batter and to pour it into greased pans, standing on a stool in our kitchen, next to the refrigerator, and then to frost the finished product. I remember when we got our first electric beaters, which made cake-making much more exciting. We would take the cakes, or parts of them, with us on our visits.

The old houses on Buffalo's west side, set in virtually identical rows on each block, always smelled a little funny—like a combination of talcum powder, dust, and old wood. On the outside, each house looked very similar to all the others. A driveway, about twelve feet wide, separated one house from another. They were mostly duplexes, with one family living on top of the other. Often, a family's elderly members would live on the first floor, with the children and their children living upstairs. Very roomy and well laid out, the duplexes usually had beautiful, dark woodwork inside and interior doors with stained glass.

The ancient, Burton sisters on West Delavan Avenue, who lived a half block west of our house and across the street, old Ms. Martha Meissner on Baynes Avenue, and Hazel and Judson Rumsey often invited us to visit on winter afternoons. The sisters Burton attended my grandmother when she gave birth to my father and Uncle Tom in 1904. Ms. Meissner was a seamstress, who had been a dear friend of my grandmother Schultz. My mother's former piano teacher, Mrs. Frank Davidson, who lived several doors away, as well as Gertrude Angell, my mother's former high school headmistress, as I have previously mentioned, also often called our telephone number—ELmwood 2979—with invitations for us to visit.

The front of our house, December 1958

We were also frequent visitors to my grandparents' house at 715 Richmond, about one and one half blocks from our house and around the corner. I don't remember very much about my maternal grandmother, except that she was English, spoke with a very slight, British accent, sometimes mispronounced words like "aluminum," was pretty strict with children, and constantly complained to my mother about grandpa's manners and attitude. She could be very loving sometimes, too. She also seemed to be overly anxious about how she was regarded by other people.

I remember Grandma Schultz had a tea table with wheels, almost like a little cart, which I was allowed to push into the dining room at her house. The tea service would be elaborately displayed on this tea table, after I had unfolded the table's leaves. Before she became ill in the late 1940s, my grandmother Schultz often hosted little tea parties in her dining room, to which she welcomed several, elderly, neighborhood friends, including the Rumseys, Stitchells, and my mother's former headmistress at the Buffalo Seminary, Gertrude Angell, all of whom lived around the corner on Dorchester Road, as I have previously mentioned. Sometimes, those tea parties seemed to last forever.

One of my mother's favorite stories from my childhood was the time she left me in the care of my brother John one wintry day, while she went to visit my grandmother. In the middle of her visit, my mother looked outside, and there I was, three and a half years old and alone in the driveway in my snowsuit, having navigated by myself the one and a half blocks to my grandparents' house, and having crossed two busy streets. I have no memory of that but don't doubt this early and compelling testimony to my courageousness…or stupidity. Upon returning home with me, my mother confronted my brother, who had not missed me.

After Grandma Schultz' heart attack, she was mostly confined to her bed at home, until she died in 1953. I heard Dr. Schnatz, her physician, often urge her to get up and exercise, but she seldom left her bed. Her death, when I was eight years old, is the first death of a loved person that I can remember. I was mad at my brother, because he wasn't crying as I was.

By Christmas, there was usually a fine accumulation of snow—one or two feet most years. The downtown stores would begin decorating around December 1st. Decorations at St. John's Episcopal Church, in the form of several dozen wreaths of evergreen boughs and evergreen roping along the walls and aisles, would be hung around the second week in December. We always shopped for a Christmas tree as a family, usually at one of the Christmas tree lots on Niagara Street. This was a favorite outing for me, until my brother and sister left for college in the 1950s. With them gone, shopping for a tree each year seemed kind of lonely or forlorn. We would examine dozens of trees, it seemed, until we found the perfect one, no more than seven feet high nor less than six. The tree was tied to the top of our old Chevy, taken home, and allowed to stand in the backyard, until its branches fluffed out. Then, we would saw off the bottom three inches of the trunk, bring the tree indoors, anchor it in a bucket filled with coal and sugar water, place it by the front windows (often in the bay windows in the music room), and decorate it together. It was one of my favorite events of the year. We also decorated the mantle piece with an old, Christmas village, consisting of several houses and a church, with a Christmas light inside each, surrounded by mounds of cotton snow and pine branches. It was pure magic to turn off the lights in the living room and music room and see the village and our Christmas tree all lit up!

In the weeks before Christmas we would make several shopping trips downtown to buy gifts. The Christmas displays in the Kleinhan's, Berger's, AM&A's and Hengerer's department stores' windows were always spectacular. One year, I recall that one of the stores featured an igloo in one of its windows, with Eskimos sitting around a fire. You could meet the Eskimos inside and take a short sled ride (on wheels), behind a team of dogs, and we did. My father spoke to one of them and verified that he was indeed an Eskimo from northern Canada. That was almost as good as meeting Santa Claus himself, which I did religiously at Hengerer's Department Store for many years.

At least one day before Christmas was devoted to Christmas cookies. My mother would make the dough the previous day and shape it into four-inch balls, which sat in the refrigerator overnight. On Christmas cookie day, these were rolled into flats of dough, one quarter inch thick, by John, using our old rolling pin, which used to hang in the closet, next to the clothes chute in the kitchen. Then, Ceci and I, and any friends who were participating (there were always some) used cookie cutters to cut out the shapes and place them on baking pans. My favorite cookie cutter was the reindeer, but you had to be careful in handling the cut dough lest the horns fall off. After baking the cookies, the real fun began, as we all spread frosting of many different colors on the baked cookies and heaped small candies, nonpareils, colored crystals, and chocolate jimmies on the frosted cookies. The finished cookies were divided up: some for friends to take home, some for teachers, at least six for Art (the mailman), some for my parents' friends and relatives, and several dozen for us.

Another Christmas ritual began several weeks before the big day: a nightly reading of my favorite childhood poem, "Twas the Night before Christmas," by Clement Clarke Moore. This was the first poem I ever memorized by choice, just because I liked it. We sang a musical adaptation of Moore's poem at school every year for the Christmas program in elementary school.

On most Christmas Eves, we went to church for the candlelight, midnight service, which actually started at 11 o'clock and ended at midnight. St. John's Episcopal had magnificent, stained glass windows and a thunderous organ. It was a beautiful church. Our minister, Dr. Walter Russell Lord, to whom we addressed every prayer ("Dear Lord"), baptized me there on August 19, 1945. Before I became an acolyte, I sang in the youth choir, from the age of about seven until ten, joining my father, who was a tenor in the choir for over fifty-six years. In the twelve years during which I actively participated as either a choirboy or as an acolyte, the Christmas Eve service topped all other services, with its beloved nativity story and Christmas music.

On Christmas morning I would usually be up at the crack of dawn, so excited that I could hardly stand it. I was never disappointed, as it seemed that Santa always got the letter I wrote him in November and posted at the mailbox on the corner of Delavan and Richmond, or at the post office on Elmwood Avenue. The rule was that I could ask for one small thing from him, since the sleigh had limited space. I trusted in Santa Claus, long after most of my friends had stopped. After all, the cookies and hay left by the fireplace on Christmas Eve had always been eaten, and thank you notes had been left in a large and exotic handwriting, probably reflecting his advanced age and Dutch background.

The first person up had to wait for the entire family to put on bathrobes before we all trooped down the stairs, turned on the Christmas lights, and admired the scene, including the presents stuffed in the stockings on the mantle piece and piled under the Christmas tree. We were allowed to take down the stockings before breakfast. Each was filled with apples, oranges, walnuts, and Hershey kisses, as well as one or two small presents. Socks and mittens were candidates for stocking gifts. After breakfast in the kitchen, we would put some Christmas music on our old record player and open the presents. Over the years, my preferred presents evolved from dolls (or accessories for Peggy—a large, old doll, inherited from my sister) and stuffed animals to toy guns, toy soldiers, hats, sports equipment, records, and books. I always enjoyed buying gifts for others, but I frankly enjoyed getting gifts more!

We often had Christmas dinner at noon, at home, with my Buffalo grandparents and several elderly, family friends, who were without nearby family. Turkey, ham, or lamb, with French style green beans, a fruit salad, and mashed potatoes, with blueberry pie (a favorite of my mother's) for dessert, could always be relied on as fare. Sometimes, my mother made a delicious, English, fruit trifle with a touch of rum. But the locale alternated from year to year among the Richmond Avenue house, our house, and the Lewiston house.

Wherever we were, we sang Christmas carols, accompanied by my mother, father, sister, or Aunt Kate, who were all excellent pianists. My sister studied piano, my brother studied cello, and I studied violin, so for a number of years we played carols together as a trio, as everyone sang. If my Hobbie and Craig cousins were joining us for Christmas, as they sometimes did, other instruments were added to the mix. In later years many neighbors would remark to me that they had enjoyed watching the family, through our bay window, making music on these occasions.

The Hobbie Trio: John, me, and Ceci in the music room, Christmas 1957

There was a letdown after Christmas. My friend Mike Weinberg could always be counted on to have a fine party on his birthday, December 31st. Several years he had his party at Skateland on Main Street, where I learned to stumble around a roller skating rink. We rarely did anything exciting for New Year's Eve, except listen to Guy Lombardo's New Year's Eve program on the radio. After the holidays, it was a long time to my birthday in April, not to mention spring. There was Valentine's Day, which provided some excitement.

Mom in the kitchen after a New Year's party, 1956

It was a big deal in our home to make valentines out of colored paper for all of the family, relatives, and close, family friends. One of these was my godmother, Ruth Culliton. I made special valentines for her. Ruth was a lovely lady, who taught English at Kensington High School. When she was young, she probably had red hair, but in my childhood I remember her white hair, very blue eyes, and porcelain-like skin. When she walked down the wintry sidewalks of the west side, she seemed to balance deliberately from one step to the next, like a graceful flamingo. I could recognize her blocks away, just from the way she walked. (When I was young, I never liked to wear glasses, with the result that, until I got contact lenses at the age of fifteen, I learned to recognize distant people by the clothes they wore or the way they walked.) She was a close friend and classmate of my mother's, from Mom's year at Lafayette High School. Ruth lived with her father and sister, Florence, on Auburn Avenue, several doors from the bank on the corner of Auburn and Elmwood. Her father was very sick, confined to a bed on the first floor, and died in the late 1940s. Her sister collected cats. I remember that there were dozens of cats in their house. The house, and Ruth, smelled of cats.

After their father's death, the two sisters and the cats moved to Potomac Avenue, again several doors from a bank, this one on the corner of Potomac and Elmwood. I think of Ruth when I meet cats and enter banks. I loved Ruth dearly. She was extremely kind and gentle. I imagined that she must have had a hard time, teaching English to high schoolers and keeping order in her classroom, because she was so soft spoken and gentle. But she never talked about that. Kensington High School had a well-known girls' synchronized swimming team in those days, which we went to watch with Ruth on several occasions. She was one of the several, very influential teachers in my early life, who discussed books and music with me at an adult level. I still use the dictionary that she gave me when I was fourteen.

Another special valentine was made for Aunt Edna Hopkins, who was an old friend of my grandmother Schultz, living in North Buffalo. As with many of my mother's friends, I called her "aunt," although she was not a true relative. Aunt Edna was a sweet lady, with white hair cut in a pageboy style. She baked brownies, when we visited her apartment, and had several flavors of ice cream in her icebox. The smell of baking chocolate permeated her apartment and masked the other smells I associated with older people when I was young. Her birthday was the day before mine: April 12th. Aunt Edna was a Christian Scientist, and died in 1964, after she broke her hip in 1963 and refused medical treatment.

My father's birthday provided more excitement on February 25th. His twin brother Tom, who was a small town doctor in Sodus, New York (about a three hour drive away), would often join us with his family to celebrate, either at Lewiston or in Buffalo. The Tom Hobbie girls ranged in age from ten years older than me to seven years younger. When our families got together, my sister suddenly had six allies—Mary, Beth, Sukie, Kate, Margaret, and Ellen—in teasing me and my brother—seven, if you count Aunt Betty Hobbie, who was a wonderful tease. Aunt Betty and I exchanged Valentine's Day cards for over fifty years. My other cousins—Molly and Kitty Craig—also identical twins, lived in New York City in my early years, but sometimes joined in the birthday celebration, as their birthday was February 24th. In the late 1950s, they moved to the small, white house that used to belong to Aunt Mabel and Uncle George, next to my grandparents' house on River Road. Woe was me, especially when my brother John was absent, in the face of the overwhelming gender odds against me.

If the birthday celebration was at Lewiston, the birthday cake board was brought out. This was a round, wooden board, about sixteen inches in diameter and one inch thick, with seventy-six, one-quarter inch holes drilled around the perimeter. It was always used for birthdays. The board had been in the Hobbie family for over four generations. With the birthday cake in the middle and candles lit around it, two children could barely carry the board.

My father and his twin brother were similar enough in appearance to sometimes cause confusion among their friends, or even among the Hobbie grandchildren. On one occasion, my cousin Kate, who was then about six years old, waltzed into the living room at the Lewiston house and plopped down on my father's lap with a hug, turning beet red as she realized slowly that this was not her father. When my father was in Sodus, visiting his brother, confused citizens called him "Doc Hobbie." Likewise, my uncle was called "John," whenever he visited Buffalo and met friends of our family. A sweet, tenor voice, a deep love of music, an engaging laugh and handshake, and a passion for stories and jokes were characteristics shared by my father and uncle. I always tremendously enjoyed those occasions with my cousins.

Looking east towards Richmond Avenue from our front porch, 1958

A couple of times each winter my father, brother, and I would go to the Buffalo Auditorium, or the "Aud," where the Buffalo Bisons played in the American Hockey League. I loved the excitement of those games, the smoke curling up towards the ceiling, the smells of beer and hot dogs, the scrape of the skate blades, the bang of the puck against the boards, and the fast action on the ice. We usually sat up pretty high, some would say in the cheap seats. But I preferred being able to see the whole rink. I especially loved the Hershey Bears in their dark brown uniforms and the crowd's inevitable, mocking song: "N-E-S-T-L-E-S, Nestles makes the very best...chocolate." There is nothing like a herd of Buffalo hockey fans, and nothing as noisy as a game at the "Aud," with the organ's throbbing pulse, sirens, and the screams for Larry Wilson or Art Stratton to score.

Once every winter in January, the Episcopal Dioceses of Western New York sponsored a "hockey night" for the boys who served as acolytes. The acolytes from my church, St. John's Episcopal, would go as a group with our fathers and the minister. We attended a late afternoon service at St. Paul's Cathedral downtown, had dinner together at the Loeb's cafeteria, and then attended a hockey game. When I first heard about this event from my brother, who had attended for several years, I decided to become an acolyte at our church. God works in strange ways. This was a high point of winters in Buffalo for me for over ten years.

More often, we would go to hockey games at Nichols High School, which had the first, indoor, ice rink in Buffalo. My brother graduated from P.S. No. 56 in 1949, when I was four. He went to Nichols during the years 1949–53, and I remember that he seemed to disappear from my early life, upon entering high school. He was always at school, either studying or involved in athletics. But my parents, Ceci, he, and I often went to high school hockey games at Nichols, which were terribly exciting. Although my brother's winter sport was squash, his friends were hockey team stars. My love of hockey grew from those high school games.

Winter was not my favorite season in Buffalo. It lasted too long. After months of snow, the novelty of snowplows and trucks, carting snow to the parks, wore off. About the second week in February, after valentines had been cut and pasted and given to classmates, family, and friends, I began to wish that the snow I had wished for all autumn and early winter, which now lay in two and three-foot drifts wherever the wind could pile it up, would quickly melt. But we often had spring snowstorms in March and April, and at least twice it snowed on my birthday, April 13th. By March, the snow had become black with soot from the Lackawanna steel mills and from the coal furnaces, and as it slowly melted, the accumulated winter's trash became visible everywhere.

April was not much better, except that, by my birthday, it was usually warm enough to have a party outside, during the mud season, between the snow piles still in the parks, if there were fields dry enough to play on. By my sister's birthday on the 26th, about two weeks after mine, the daffodils and forsythia would be out, and sometimes even the japonica in the northeast corner of our backyard, with its fragile, pink blossoms.

So winter usually lasted five months in Buffalo. I survived eighteen winters there, then four in New Hampshire, one in Wisconsin, and three in Korea, before living in Virginia. Buffalo had the most snow. The snow touched everyone and everything. The sound of the spinning wheels of a car was a call to action in Buffalo for all within earshot. Every neighbor, who was able to shovel, attacked a snow-covered sidewalk. My west side neighbors, some of whom spoke only Italian or Sicilian, and my family and friends lived the Italian maxim (loosely translated), credited to Luciano de Crescenzo: "We are, each of us angels with only one wing; and we can only fly by embracing one another."

I never fully understood that winter could be different, or actually sometimes snowless and warm, until I came to Virginia in 1972. Our winters in the South give the term "winter" a bad name. I have always missed those satisfying, childhood snows and embracing wings on the Niagara Frontier.

Chapter Two—
Childhood Springs 1945–1959

Mirror Lake in Forest Lawn Cemetery, April 1958

Only someone who has squinted over snow since Halloween can fully appreciate spring in Buffalo! In March, while the ice on Lake Erie shuddered and crackled from the early, spring gales, whistling in from the west, the constant breeze off the lake ice kept the air wintry in Buffalo's west side. In downtown Buffalo the ropes, strung up along the sidewalks in winter, for people to grab for support against the wind, were still taut and singing, like violin strings played by a wintry bow. The long, slow transition, from dark to light, from cold to warm, and from bleak to brilliance, whipped my anticipation of spring into a frenzy.

I was a spring baby, together with my Grandpa Hobbie (April 3, 1874), Aunt Edna Hopkins (April 12, 1886), sister Ceci (April 26, 1938), mother (May 17, 1909), brother John (June 5, 1935), my brother's friend, Fred Turner (June 6, 1937), and Grandma Hobbie (June 22, 1876), to name only a few. I was born at 10:41 AM and weighed 7 lbs. 6 oz. I had a lot of dark brown hair and blue eyes. I still have blue eyes.

Because I was the only one in our family with blue eyes, it dawned on me, when I was four, that I must have been adopted. I wondered about that for years, especially when a waitress in Vermont, when I was five, confirmed my doubt. She said something to me like, "Oh, what beautiful blue eyes you have. Whom did you get those from?" And then, after looking at the other four members of my family, with their beautiful, brown eyes, retreated in confusion, saying, "I'm so sorry." That was food for thought.

My mother told me my birthday was a very "auspicious" date, for on April 13, 1907, her father, Arthur Lewis Bray, had left England from Liverpool for the United States on the *Etruria*. (My grandmother, Margaret Elizabeth Eyres, sailed from England on August 8, 1908, on the *Corsican*, and they married in Toronto, Canada, on August 16, 1908. I think they knew each other before her departure. My mother was born, almost exactly nine months later, on May 17, 1909.) I later found out that her grandfather—my great grandfather John Arthur Bray—had died on April 13, 1931, so "auspicious" was both good and bad. Friday the 13th has always been a lucky day for me. Dad often reminded me that Thomas Jefferson and John Hanson shared my birth date, along with Lord Frederick North and Samuel Beckett. I disagree with T.S. Elliott. April is not "the cruelest month."

I was named after my step grandfather, Charles Schultz, and after my mother's natural father, Arthur Bray, and her favorite cousin, Arthur Dudden.

Right after the twin, presidential holidays on February 12th and February 22nd (also Richard Bassett's birthday), and my father's birthday on February 25th, I began to look forward to a new season of holidays, birthday parties, outdoors play, baseball games, and natural splendor.

Along the shores of the lake and the Niagara River, the cherry, apple, pear, peach, and plum trees seemed ready to burst into their spring color at any minute, as mid March and the vernal equinox approached. I would wait and wait and wait for the blossoms, which were often a month away. Chunks of ice streamed down the river towards Niagara Falls. The rushing, white ice made the water seem bluer and faster, every time I gazed at it. The ever-present, circling gulls urged the water on with their cries. Some caught rides on the mini icebergs, which swirled around the ferry and other boats that my mother and I watched from Broderick Park at the foot of West Ferry Street. Over two miles wide as it emptied from Lake Erie, the Niagara was fierce in its rush to the escarpment. I have never seen a more glorious or intimidating river.

Finally, one day the ice would disappear magically from Lake Erie and from the river. When I was young, my mother and I spent a lot of time on the waterfront, watching the lake and river, especially in the spring, when the urge to get outside and to exult in the beauty of the water overwhelmed all other feelings. There were a police barracks and stables with horses in those days, at the foot of Porter Avenue in Front Park, not far from the water treatment station closer to the water's edge. We took apples and fed the horses. I remember how the horses frisked in the spring air and how every mother in Buffalo seemed to be out with a baby carriage, strolling along the waterfront in nearby LaSalle Park. There was also a wonderful concession stand, which opened every April, where you could buy great ice cream cones! I especially liked the contrast on the waterfront between the sting of the wind off the cold water and the warmth of the sun on my face. Just by turning your face into, or away from, the wind, you could feel wintry or springy.

Buffalo and the Niagara River in spring from the Canadian shore

The front of our house on West Delavan Avenue faced north. The huge piles of snow on that side of the house, accumulated over the past five months from the snow slides off the roof and from snow shoveled from our driveway and front walks, often hid any signs of spring, until mid April. But in the backyard, on the south side of the house, the snow piles from the roof avalanches were usually almost gone by the end of March.

By April Fool's Day, crocuses, daffodils, and tulips would begin to poke up in the flowerbeds, and the backyard grass started to green. A gentle infusion of tiny leaves would creep over the house, as the ropes of ivy, covering our house, came to life. With the warmth came renewed energy for the birds and a frenzy of nest building and quarreling among the English sparrows in the ivy. I once counted a dozen nests on the backside of our house, and the daily commotion of chirps and complaints, from dawn until sunset, suggested there might have been three times as many birds. I thought that the ivy probably held our stucco house together, so as long as the birds were there, I knew the ivy and the house were secure.

**Me, on the steps of my grandparents' house,
715 Richmond Avenue, spring 1947**

April Fool's Day was a good day. I would sneak downstairs very early in the morning to prepare the morning's tricks, which were the same every year, but never failed to surprise and amaze my parents. I switched the salt and sugar first, so that my parents' coffee and cereal would taste very salty. One of them would get the false spoon, which had a round hole in the center, so that cereal would dribble through the spoon, when used. The other would get the fake knife, which bent when you tried to cut something. Or Ceci or John would get the plastic ice cube in their glass of orange juice. The cube had a dead fly in the middle, which resulted in a happy reaction, when spied by the drinker.

We also had Whoopee Cushions, which were strategically slid under a cushion in a chair or on the couch in the living room and made an embarrassing noise, when you sat down on them and squeezed the air through the neck of the cushion. This trick particularly delighted me, when I was young. Grandpa Schultz never seemed to notice the slight bulge in the cushion, before he sat down and "farted."

At Lewiston on one April Fool's Day, my other grandfather was equally accommodating. My mother had brought home a trick device, consisting of two, rubber, hollow bulbs, connected by a tube, one sort of flat and the other squeezable. When the flat bulb was placed under a plate on the table, under the tablecloth, and the connecting tube was also carefully hidden under the tablecloth, the trap was set. When I squeezed the large bulb (hidden in my lap), forcing air through the tube into the flat bulb under the plate, the bulb expanded rapidly, making the plate jump. I did this several times, before Grandpa Hobbie noticed the jumping plate, suddenly grabbed it with both hands, and made a great show of being totally befuddled. My mother had collected these prizes over the years and kept them in the same drawer as our regular knives, forks, and spoons. She loved playing tricks on family and friends. I inherited that gene.

One year, on the evening before April Fool's Day, I heard that my sister would be out late on a date, returning after midnight. I think I was about nine years old, so Ceci must have been in high school. After my parents went to bed and our dog Tuffy had retired for the night, I came downstairs, bent on mischief. First, I got a broom and wedged it into one of the kitchen chairs, upside down, so that the head was up. A clothes hanger was then balanced on the head of the broom, and my father's overcoat draped over the broom and clothes hanger, creating a sinister looking figure, near the kitchen table, facing the back hallway, where my sister would enter the house. This was topped off by placing my father's hat on the broom's head. With the lights off, in the dark my creation was quite lifelike! I then unscrewed the light bulbs in the back hallway, on the cellar stairs, and in the kitchen, so that my sister would have no access to any light in the house when she entered.

The anticipation of the event was almost as delicious as the actual anxiety I watched my sister experience, when she arrived home, as she gasped upon entering the back hallway, froze in the dark, fumbled for light switches, which did not work, and finally heard my stifled laughter. I never played a better trick on her.

The robins arrived from the south shortly after April 1st, most years. It was important news in our family, when someone reported seeing the first robin or the first crocus or daffodil in bloom. My grandparents' house on Richmond Avenue had several huge forsythia bushes in both the front and back yards, as well as a lovely japonica in the back. We had several forsythia bushes, too, along the Grisantis' fence on the west side of our back yard. Our japonica was along the fence between our yard and the Ralphs' driveway on the east side of the backyard. The Stitchell's yard, which backed onto my grandparents' backyard from the north, had an old cherry tree that leaned over my grandparents' garage. The blooming of the yellow forsythia, crimson japonica, and the pink cherry tree, each in its turn, was cause for wonder and celebration every spring.

You could never tell about Easter and flowers. Crocuses and daffodils sometimes would be in full bloom on Easter, and the air would be so warm that no winter coat was needed for the trip to church and back on Easter morning. Other years, we would have snow on Easter. I remember walking with my brother and sister, one Easter afternoon, out to the creek at the east end of my Grandpa Hobbie's estate at Lewiston, to look for pussy willows. There was a thin film of ice on the creek, underneath the large bushes of pussy willow next to the creek. We cut dozens of pussy willow branches for the Easter table, because there were no flowers out yet. With their silver buds, those branches made a fine centerpiece. On other occasions in the spring, my Aunt Kate led the pussy willow expeditions.

John, Mom, Dad, and me in front of our house, Easter 1953

When I was seven, Easter fell on my birthday—April 13, 1952. On that happy, double holiday my parents took several friends and me to the South Park Conservatory for my birthday party. The conservatory was a huge, glass-enclosed series of gardens with magnificent flowering bulbs, all out at once, at Easter time. It was breathtaking! The sweet smell of the hundreds of Easter lilies was almost too much to bear for nostrils hungry for a sniff of spring. My pals and I reeled from the delicious fragrance. To top off this feast of vision and fragrance, the Easter Bunny itself was there and handed out chocolate, foil-wrapped eggs and chocolate bunnies. This was the only time I ever met the Easter Bunny. It didn't say anything, but gave me an extra chocolate bunny, when told that it was my birthday. I trace my life long addiction to chocolate to that day. when the Easter Bunny itself started me on the habit.

Actually, it probably is not fair to say that my chocolate addiction started in 1952. It would be more honest to admit that, from the moment I gulped my first breath of air and squealed at Children's Hospital, I was hooked on chocolate. The best chocolate candy in the world was sold in Buffalo at the Quaker Bonnet, a restaurant owned by my father's cousin, Harold Hayes, located on the corner of Bryant Street and Elmwood Avenue, about two blocks from the hospital. We went there often for lunch or dinner and never failed to have a piece of chocolate. Cousin Harold would wave his hand near my ear and give me the quarters he found hidden there. It took me several years to realize that the tantalizing smell of chocolate from the Quaker Bonnet easily reached Children's Hospital and was undoubtedly among the first smells I experienced in April, 1945.

A few days before Easter, my mother would buy several dozen eggs and a package of Easter egg dyes and decorations. The dyes came in little round tablets of all the colors of the rainbow. My favorites were blue and green. We placed a tablespoon of vinegar in the bottom of a glass for each color, and then plopped a dye tablet into the vinegar. After hard-boiling the eggs, we mixed the vinegar and dye in each glass with enough water to cover an egg. The dye package came with little, wire egg holders, wax crayons, and small stencils of pictures and symbols. Each egg was carefully lowered with its wire holder into the dye in the glass. The longer the egg was in the dye, the brighter or deeper the color of the egg became. You could make eggs with several colors on each egg, if you were careful. The wax crayons were used to add writing or other designs on the eggs, since the dye would not color the egg where the wax had been applied. You applied a stencil to an egg, after the egg was dyed, by moistening the stencil, placing it upside down on the egg, and then rubbing the stencil onto the egg. We created some fantastic Easter eggs over the years. Some came out gray or black, when we tried to use too many colors on one egg. The eggs were then distributed to family and friends on Easter morning, with at least two saved for each of our family's Easter baskets.

We left a little saucer of milk out for the Easter Bunny on the evening before Easter. The milk was gone on Easter morning. Either our black cat Jinx, or our black spaniel Gypsy, or the Easter Bunny had to have lapped it up, and since Jinx was always exiled to the basement for that one night of the year, and Gypsy was upstairs on my bed, there was only one explanation. In the morning at the crack of dawn, I would be up, waiting for the rest of the family to slowly straggle downstairs. I had to wait for everyone at the foot of the staircase that rose through the center of our house, with the doors to the living room and to the kitchen, from the base of the stairs, closed.

With all assembled downstairs, the hunt for the Easter baskets could begin. Each basket was hidden somewhere on the first floor. Each had a name on it. If you found someone else's basket, you had to ignore it and not give away the hiding place. I soon learned that in the pianos, behind the curtains in the dining room or living room, in the fireplace, in the china cabinet in the dining room, in the oven, under the kitchen sink, or in one of the kitchen cupboards was fertile ground for Easter baskets. Somehow, I usually found my basket first. If I was having a hard time finding my basket, my mother would say that the Easter Bunny had told her where it was hidden, and then would guide me by saying "warmer," as I got close to it, or "colder," as I moved away from it, until I found it. Those were excruciatingly happy hunts!

The baskets themselves were marvels. There were several dozen jelly beans of different colors and flavors, hidden in the green, paper "grass," which stuffed the basket, along with several, yellow, marshmallow chicks. Of course, the eggs we had made were also hidden in the grass. Somehow, the Easter Bunny unfailingly found the eggs in the refrigerator, where we had left them for it. Best of all were the chocolate eggs—foil wrapped, some large and some small, some with a rich filling and some solid chocolate—and chocolate animals—usually a large bunny and sometimes a rooster. This Easter tradition continued until I was about thirteen. I abandoned it with great regret.

We went to church on Easter. I loved our church building with its soaring arches, gorgeous, stained glass windows, century old bell, and history. It was reputed to be one of the finest examples of gothic architecture in the city. President Grover Cleveland's alleged mistress, Maria Halpin, went to St. John's, before he had her committed to the state insane asylum on Forest Avenue and Elmwood Avenue, about eight blocks from the church, after she supposedly bore him a son. Cleveland's opponents memorialized his indiscretion, which he admitted, in their political chant: "Ma, Ma, where's my pa? Gone to the White House, ha, ha, ha!" I thought it interesting that Ms. Halpin did not name her son "Grover" after his alleged father, but rather named him after Cleveland's law partner, with whom she had also been intimately acquainted, according to church lore. The law partner had died before the son was born, charging Cleveland with taking care of his widow and young daughter. The President married the daughter in the White House some years later.

When I was very young, the Sunday school children marched around the Sunday school building each Sunday morning, led by the older children, carrying a cross, an Episcopal Church flag, and an American flag. We would sing "Onward, Christian soldiers, marching as to war, with the cross of Jesus going on before. Christ, the royal Master, leads against the foe; forward into battle see His banners go! Onward, Christian soldiers, marching as to war, with the cross of Jesus going on before." I will never forget that hymn, which I liked, but thought a little out of place in church, even when I was young. I wondered who the unlucky "Dafoe" (the foe) was. The hymn was later banned from the hymnal.

St. John's Episcopal Church. June 1954

On Easter morning, we paraded around the sanctuary of the church with the acolytes, choirs, and Reverend Easter, who was almost as aptly named as my first minister—Dr. Lord. St. John's Episcopal was beautifully decorated with Easter lilies and other flowers for that day, and the church was so packed that there were even people in the balcony. There was a magnificent organ in St. John's. With all the stops out and the choir in full voice, the music of the service was overwhelmingly beautiful. Handel's *Messiah* was often on the program, or at least the "Hallelujah" chorus. There were some wonderful singers in the choir. Mr. and Mrs. Rosenberger, especially, had magnificent baritone and soprano voices, respectively, and often sang superb duets. My father had an excellent tenor voice. I often dreamed of singing in the choir with him.

In those early years I sat with the Sunday school children in the right front pews of the church for the first part of the service. Grandfather and Grandmother Schultz and my mother sat in the sixth pew from the front on the left side. My father was in the choir, trading whispered comments with his tenor buddy, John Putnam, in their seats behind the pulpit. I remember that my brother was an acolyte, and that my sister was in Sunday school with me for at least a couple of years. I also remember John's playing the organ on several occasions, when the church was empty. The children stayed in the service for the first half hour and then went to church school, which was deadly boring most of the time, except for the exquisite Judith Miller and Trudy Noehren, both of whom I had crushes on, when I was six or seven.

My favorite Sunday school teacher was a friend of my mother, Mrs. "Dee" Matzinger, who had twin girls my sister's age. She was a good teacher, and most of what I learned about the Bible in my early life I learned from her. Another favorite Sunday school teacher was Mrs. Dudden, whose daughter Ann was in my sister's high school class. Our family did not read from the Bible or talk much about religion, although we always prayed before meals. We usually went to church on Sundays, unless we were at my grandparents' Lewiston home or at the beach cabin. As soon as I could, I joined the youth choir, about the age of seven, to escape from as much of the time in the Sunday school class as I could, and to join in the making of that glorious music.

I spent several years in the choir and enjoyed it a lot. The adult choir members were very kind and anxious to teach the younger members. Richard Bassett and Janine Hannel—both P.S. No. 56 classmates—and I sang soprano. Many of the fundamentals of music, and the religious pieces we learned in those days, together provided the foundation for my four, happy years in Dartmouth's glee club, more than a decade later, singing bass.

What I really loved about services at St. John's—especially on Easter or Christmas—were the music, pageantry, and opportunity for quiet thought. I rarely listened to sermons, and the prayers did not seem to interest me, unless I had something urgent to pray about. On the other hand, the music often moved me to tears. I loved carrying flags and the cross, ringing the old bell, helping with the communion, or lighting and snuffing out the candles. I also liked the moments of silence, or when the sermon was droning on, the chance to think quietly about events and people. And I liked the people at church: caring adults in the choir, my parents' friends, and lay readers, such as Jimmy Guest, who always had a new joke to tell me, or our gang of acolytes. Hank Priebe, John Richmond, Enn Teivas, Richard Bassett, Neal Hodgson, and I served faithfully and happily together as acolytes for many years.

I remember four ministers particularly well: George Easter, Alec Pudwell, and Clare Backhurst, all from my childhood, and later Peter M. Bridgford, whom I knew through visits to Buffalo in the 1980s and 1990s. Reverend Easter had a somewhat wild son, who dated my sister. Reverend Pudwell, who was Canadian, had a fine, horse farm on the Canadian shore of the Niagara, south of Niagara Falls, which the choir often visited for picnics, since his sons sang in the choir. I loved those picnics. Reverend Backhurst was the St. John's minister I knew best, and I liked him a lot. His son, David, was a year behind me, also attended Nichols High School later, and was an acolyte, too.

Reverend Peter Bridgford and his wife were very kind to my parents in their older years. I liked them immensely and was glad that Peter presided at their funerals. I still remember Peter asking my father, on his deathbed in the hospital in 1992, what he was feeling and experiencing, as my father lapsed in and out of consciousness, but had several, very lucid moments. Peter was searching for insight into profound, near death experiences, I felt uneasily. My father in response, starting into lucidity, told us the story of the fireman he had once seen, riding on the end of the ladder on an old hook-and-ladder truck, many years before, when Dad was a fire warden, during the war. The end of the ladder, where there was a seat for a fireman, had become detached from the truck, and the ladder with the fireman seated on it was swinging wildly from side to side, as the truck careened down a Buffalo street. The seated fireman was holding on to the seat for dear life. The fire truck made a sharp turn at high speed, which resulted in the ladder swinging out over the sidewalk and flinging the fireman into the air. He ended up flying through the air and crashing unhurt, through a store window, none the worse for wear. What a ride, my father commented, laughingly! Then he drifted off again. I had never heard that story before, and I never heard another story from Dad. I wonder if Peter got the message.

On Easter afternoon, if the weather was good, my parents took flowers over to Forest Lawn Cemetery, which is about one and half miles east of our house on West Delavan Avenue. Forest Lawn is a beautiful cemetery, linked to Buffalo's large central park, Delaware Park. I passed it every day on my way to high school in later years. My family's ancestors, going back three or more generations, are all buried there. It is a huge expanse of rolling hills, old trees, and winding roads. Scajaquada Creek meanders through the hills, with their dusting of headstones. Our family shares a plot in section H with relatives of my father's family—the Hayes family. I liked that our plot is on one of the highest hills in the cemetery and that a large obelisk, which has "Hayes" on three sides and "Hobbie" on the fourth, marks it. My father's grandparents, uncles, and aunts are all there. One day, I noticed that our next-door neighbors to the east on West Delavan—Howard Ralph and his wife and daughter Dorothy—are also our neighbors at Forest Lawn, buried right next to our family's site. I thought it was neat that, out of the tens of thousands of gravesites in Forest Lawn, the Ralphs and Hobbies ended up neighbors in death, as in life. My grandmother Schultz and my grandfather Schultz are buried in Forest lawn also, as are my grandfather Bray and my great grandmother Bray, his mother. Grandpa Bray's grave and his mother's grave are not marked by any stone. I guess my grandmother was too poor to afford them in 1916. We went to the cemetery on Easter to put flowers on the graves and pay our respects.

In the middle of Forest Lawn is a lovely, small lake—Mirror Lake—fed by a spring, near West Delavan Avenue, called Jubilee Spring. In the spring, when the cherry trees surrounding the lake were in full bloom, we went there to feed the ducks and geese stale bread. I saw lots of pheasants there and an occasional deer. It was a splendid oasis in the middle of the west side. In the center of Mirror Lake, on an island, is a small, bronze statue of a little girl. I thought that she looked lonely all by herself, except in the spring, when there were lots of ducklings and goslings, playing in the waters around her. I have fond memories of that cemetery. And I have memories of being terrified there on occasion, when my mother was teaching my sister how to drive our old car on the cemetery's twisting roads. I sat in the back seat, cowering, as my mother punctuated the lessons with sudden screams of "Stop!" that were supposed to teach my sister to react quickly in an emergency, but had the effect of making both my sister and me neurotic at an early age.

Besides the graves of people who died learning to drive there, Forest Lawn Cemetery has hundreds of war memorials and graves of soldiers. I wondered why our country seemed to have so many wars and so many dead soldiers. In the tranquility of Forest Lawn it was difficult to imagine what war must be like. Although I had been born in the waning years of the Second World War, I remembered nothing about it, unlike my brother and sister and their friends, who had experienced rationing and the deaths of family members and neighbors' sons. As the vestiges of that war faded in the late 1940s, a new war in Korea began in 1950, so war became a reality, even for post-war kids like me.

One of my favorite, childhood stories was about war. Grandpa Hobbie, and later Dad, often recounted it as a bedtime story. Grandpa Hobbie began the story by telling me that he had been first told the story, when he was about six years old, by a man named Martin Woods, who was married to the step aunt of his mother, Susan Hobbie—my great grandmother:

> In the early part of the nineteenth century, the Woods family lived on the south shore of Tonawanda Creek, about a mile east of the Niagara River, not far from Buffalo. They lived in a log house made from trees cut down by Martin's father, when clearing the woods for a farm. The family consisted of Martin's father and mother, a baby sister, and Martin, who was then about seven years old.
>
> One night in late autumn, during the War of 1812, when Martin had been sleeping for a while, he was suddenly awakened by his father and told not to make any noise. He got dressed quickly and went out to where his mother, with Martin's baby sister in her arms, was seated on the family's only horse. There was a red glow, barely visible through the dark trees of the forest, surrounding their farm. A neighbor's house, several hundred

yards away, was on fire, and shadowy figures of men were dancing around the fire and whooping and yelling. Martin knew that they were Indians. His father put Martin up on the horse behind his mother and told him to hang on tightly to his mother. His father then led the horse and the family's cow through the pitch-black woods in the chilly darkness.

After traveling for what seemed like several hours, they reached a creek, which Martin's father knew was fordable. Martin was rather sleepy by this time, but he woke up, when the creek's cold water hit his feet. As the horse started up the creek's bank on the other side, Martin sleepily let go of his mother's waist and fell off the back of the horse into the cold water. Luckily, he was able to grab onto the horse's tail and got pulled up the creek bank to dry land. A short time later, they were challenged by soldiers with familiar accents and knew that they were safe in the American lines. They never returned to see what happened to their farm. Instead, they moved east to Batavia, New York. His father, and later Martin, farmed in that region.

I asked to hear that story so often that I knew it word for word, when I was young. Later, when I thought about it, I realized how scary it must have been for Martin and his family that autumn night in a war on the Niagara Frontier, so long ago.

I recall when I first became really aware of a modern war. My parents and I had walked over to Thompsons' Delicatessen, next to the candy shop, on the southeast corner of Elmwood Avenue and Bidwell Parkway. We sometimes went there for a light dinner. There were several, round tables with chairs around them at the back of the store. A television sat on a shelf. As we ate dinner, we watched movie footage of planes, dropping bombs, and of bombs, exploding on the ground. I guess these were scenes of either World War II or of the Korean War. I had nightmares about those bombs for weeks afterwards. About a year later, at school one day our teacher passed out comic books, depicting the Korean conflict. Again, there were scenes of bombs, dropping and exploding. I ripped up my comic book on the way home.

Our neighborhood had been built up in the first decade of the 20th century. Grandpa Schultz could remember when our house, which was one of the first built, had fields around it. Now there were only the two story duplexes and driveways. Most had small backyards, but some of these were completely filled by garages. All had porches on the street side, except Dr. Metson's house, which was the only house on the block with no porch. Some had porches on the backside, too. Grisantis' house had front porches on the top and bottom flats, but none on the back. Ralphs' house had porches on both levels on the front and back. Our house had a large, first floor, front porch on the street side, with a gently sloping roof, which ran from just below the second floor windows.

When the air warmed, our neighbors began to come out onto their porches. As the grass greened up and began to grow, everyone on the west side, it seemed, started to cut the grass and to clean up the winter debris that had collected next to the curbs and on the lawns. If I mailed a letter for my father at the corner mail box on Richmond Avenue five houses away (not counting the corner house), I would be greeted, as I walked, by someone from each house, either from the porches' rocking chairs or from behind a push mower. Old Howard Ralph next door and his upstairs tenants Matt and Nancy Mesci, Mrs. Leone on her porch next to the Ralphs' porch, calling for the Leone kids, Marie or Sonny, or Dr. Metson, the neighborhood dentist in the next house, always seemed to be outside. Mr. and Mrs. Grisanti, with their daughter Rose Marie, our neighbors to the west, and Mr. Grillo in the flat above them, were fixtures on their respective porches, once spring arrived. Nothing ever happened in our neighborhood without someone seeing it and commenting on it.

Windows opened in the spring, and the sounds of our neighbors' lives spilled out. A lot of yells, directed at our neighborhood's kids, echoed in the driveways from the houses up and down the block. Someone named Anthony played the saxophone about five doors west. Ernie Siegel's trumpet practiced from across the street. In the evenings you could tell who was listening to Jack Benny on the radio. More than a few were listening to classical music on the Canadian Broadcasting Corporation, which was my favorite radio station and the only classical music station available in Buffalo, after WBEN stopped playing good music. It was as though the entire neighborhood was awakening from a muted sleep that had been blanketed by snow.

When I was very young and still confined to the house, I welcomed the people who knocked on the back door several times a week to bring their business to our home. My mother reminded these men to clean the mud off their boots or shoes on the mud scraper, which was located just outside the backdoor. (I never saw another mud scraper anywhere. It was a little metal cross bar, between two metal arms, about six inches high.) I remember that the man from the bakery had a large, glass, carrying case, suspended from his neck in front, in which there were pies, small cakes, fresh baked bread, doughnuts, and cookies. I called him the "whistler," because he was always whistling, as he emerged from his little truck. Mom usually bought something small from him, like a pie or a chocolate éclair.

The front of our house

Then there was the milkman, who stopped by twice a week. When I was very young, the milkman arrived in a little milk wagon, pulled by a horse. His glass bottles jangled against the metal of his milk carrier, as he walked up the driveway. We had a standing order of three quarts of milk. Next to our back door was a small opening, built into the wall of the back hallway, with a door on the outside and a door on the inside: our milk box. A small hook locked the outside door. The milk box held six quarts. I could easily squeeze through the opening, until I was about five. If I was very good, my mother sometimes ordered a pint of chocolate milk for me, which was almost as good as Coca-Cola! We placed our empty milk bottles in the milk box for retrieval by the milkman.

Occasionally, other men came to the house to repair pots, or to sharpen scissors and knives, or to collect rags. The rag man, whose name was Freddy Gugenheimer, was quite bent over and pushed a cart filled with rags. I think he was German, because Grandpa Schultz frequently stopped to talk with him, if we saw him on the street. We always waved to him and greeted him, respectfully.

And of course, every day brought Art the Mailman to our house. He was a very special person—like a member of our family. Our wonderful mailman, Art Markwardt, delivered mail to 453 West Delavan Avenue for over thirty years. I can still hear his "Hi ya, Charlie," which was the prompt for me to ask if I could accompany him down the block, helping him carry the bundles of magazines and stuff mail through the slots in our neighbors' doors or into their mailboxes. I would often go with Art around the entire block. Art gave me lots of advice, usually about women, even when I was still in kindergarten. "You can't live with them; you can't live without 'em," he would say. He was always interested in the happenings of my life and in my girlfriends. Art had been a soldier in Korea, before he became our mailman. Years later, when I told him I had decided to go to Korea as a Peace Corps volunteer, he said that he thought the Peace Corps was a great thing, but that I should reconsider going to Korea. The war there had been terrible for him.

In the 1950s, all of these visitors, except Art, stopped coming to our neighborhood. I missed them tremendously. They had carried news of our neighbors: who was sick, who had died, who had had a baby, or who had left for college or the army. First, it was the baker, then the milkman, then the others—all of whom disappeared. They vanished as the elm trees began to die on our street. It was as though they had nourished the community with their visits and tied us together with our neighbors and the trees.

When I graduated from a baby carriage to my blue three-wheeler, my mobility increased, and I got to know our block and neighborhood. My big, blue tricycle had large diameter wheels with rubber tires, so it was virtually impossible to overturn. I used to pedal on the sidewalk in front of our house, which stretched from Richmond Avenue on the east to Baynes Street on the west. All the streets on the west side had sidewalks about five feet from the street curb. In the grassy strips, between the sidewalk and the curb, were magnificent American elms in the nineteen forties and fifties—usually one in front of every house. Our house had two. Each sidewalk slab was separated from the next by a crack, which you could feel through the tricycle's wheels. With your eyes closed, you could pedal as far as you wanted and know where you were by counting the cracks, as you crossed each, providing you kept the front wheel straight and accounted for the driveways. I was learning to count at that age. There were eight cracks in front of our house and fifty-two cracks and five driveways from the edge of our driveway to the corner mailbox. I often crashed into the elms, which seemed unperturbed.

On the West Delavan side of our block there were twenty-four houses, plus a big, empty lot on the corner of Baynes and West Delavan. Turning the corner and passing that lot, you came to three houses on Baynes, before you hit Ardmore Street. Turning left onto Ardmore, you passed twenty-four houses on Ardmore, including Patsy Runk's house, before you came to the corner of Richmond and Ardmore. Willa Buffum's family lived in the corner house. There were six houses on the Richmond Avenue side of our block. You turned left at the mailbox on the corner, and our house was in sight. Fifty-seven houses were on our block in the 1950s. It took about ten minutes to go around the block on my tricycle. Later, when I was six and on my blue Schwinn American Rider bicycle, my personal record was two minutes and thirty-six seconds.

The year that I learned to ride my bike was the spring that my tongue turned purple. I guess it would be more accurate to say that my pediatrician discovered that I had a condition called "geographic tongue" and treated it by painting my tongue with an antifungal agent—a medicine called "gentian violet." My tongue was bright purple. I cried and cried, and refused to let my mother paint my tongue each week, as prescribed by Dr. Brown, unless Ceci also had her tongue painted. So both of us had purple tongues for several months. (My sister was enormously grateful for this opportunity to have a purple tongue.) I later learned that "geographic tongue" (benign migratory glossitis) is a condition that occurs in up to 3% of the general population. Geographic tongues are ridged and furrowed and often have areas of strange and wonderful coloration. I kept the secret of this disfigurement from all my friends. The gentian violet had no effect, and my treatment soon stopped, to my sister's great relief. I still have a geographic tongue, which my dentist points out to every new dental assistant in his office, when I visit.

My mother usually shopped for groceries at Gwellis' corner market on Hoyt Street and West Delavan, about two blocks west of our house. There was also a butcher's shop on Bird Avenue, near Hoyt Street, and a dry goods store next door. Stewarts' Butcher Shop was also a favorite store, located next to the barber's shop, near the corner of West Delavan and Elmwood. (Mr. Stewart's daughter, Tana Lee, was a classmate and an object of my affection in sixth grade.) Near Stewart's shop, but on the corner, was the nearest drugstore to our house: Wards Pharmacy. It was a sad day when the soda fountain in Wards disappeared one day, when I was seven. Next to Wards was an Italian market, which later was Clayton's Toy Store for a few happy years. Clayton's moved to the corner of Bidwell Parkway and Elmwood Avenue, across the street from what used to be a seductive ice cream parlor and candy shop. Two of my favorite places were across the street from each other.

In those days of small, family-run grocery stores, usually there was just one person manning the store. Whoever was on duty used a long pole, with a grabber on the end, to reach the item you wanted to buy from the high shelves, loaded it into your basket, and then checked you out at the cash register. Later, my mother preferred the new supermarket, Loblaws, on Elmwood Avenue near Breckenridge Street. You did all your own shopping at Loblaws, depositing items into a shopping cart, with a child's seat in back, on which, of course, I rode up and down the shopping aisles, all around the store. Our small, neighborhood stores closed within a year after Loblaws opened.

The other important, neighborhood places in my youth were our church, on Colonial Circle about two blocks away; the two closest public libraries on Elmwood Avenue and Highland Avenue and on West Ferry Street near Grant Street; Police Station No. 5, about five blocks west of our house on West Delavan Avenue; and Public School No. 56, where my mother ('26), brother ('49), and I ('59) all attended. In March of 1954, another important place came to my attention: the home of the mother of Harry Taub, on Elmwood Avenue near Highland Avenue, where I started to study violin with Harry.

Harry Taub was my violin teacher from 1954 until about 1962. He was a young man of about thirty, when my mother arranged for me to have two, one-hour lessons each week. We paid him a reduced rate of $3.50 a lesson, which he never raised. I loved the violin, and he was a wonderful teacher and friend. From the first day he told me to call him "Harry." And he did have lots of hair. How he tolerated my limited practicing, all those years, I will never understand. I think he understood that baseball, friends, and other distractions, as I grew older, were powerful forces, competing with my desire to play the violin well. Harry Taub was a fabulous violinist (associate concertmaster of the Buffalo Philharmonic Orchestra for over fifty years), a professor of music at the State University, a gifted composer, and a sympathetic and patient teacher. He often played my favorite piece for me—the "Lone Ranger" part of Rossini's *William Tell Overture*. Later, he liked to play part of Lalo's *Symphonie Espanole*, which was another favorite of mine.

Some of my happiest moments were playing the violin with my mother, with Harry, with my brother and sister as a trio, in the student symphony at P.S. No. 56, or in the Buffalo Youth Symphony, where my friend Danny Fraustino was the concertmaster and I was the assistant concertmaster. (The famous conductor, Josef Krips, who conducted the Buffalo Philharmonic Orchestra, and one year conducted our youth orchestra, threw his baton at Danny and me, during a rehearsal, to stop us from talking.) One of the big regrets of my life is that I did not continue studying the violin. Harry Taub and my parents gave me a rich musical education that has given me pleasure every day of my life.

My musical education included Sunday concerts with the Philharmonic at Kleinhans Music Hall. I loved those concerts, as well as the Pop Concerts on Wednesday evenings. I first heard Tchaikovsky's *Violin Concerto in D, Opus 35*, on a Sunday afternoon in Buffalo, played by Nathan Milstein. It has been my favorite musical piece ever since. But what I liked best about those concerts at Kleinhans was watching Harry Taub, in the front row of the violins, with his formal black coat—the only one unbuttoned among the violins, so that his white shirt unmistakably marked him—and the effortless, but passionate, way he played. When I visited Harry backstage during the intermission, he would be wiping the sweat from his face with a big, white handkerchief, as he told me how glad he was to see me. He was one of the greatest older friends I ever had.

The back of our house, June 1955

My best neighborhood friends, Mike Weinberg and Bruce Bleichfield, lived at 68 Colonial Circle and 703 Richmond Avenue, respectively, each about one and a half blocks from our house. There was a well-worn rut in the sidewalk between the Hobbie house and the Weinberg and Bleichfield homes. My other closest friends, John Mooney and Enn Teivas, lived on Bird Avenue, over a mile away, and on Lafayette Avenue, about half a mile away, respectively.

Mike Weinberg's father owned and operated several dry cleaners, called "Campus Cleaners," because his first store was out on Main Street near the campus of the University of Buffalo. Mrs. Weinberg was a very attractive, blond woman with a deep, allover tan, who wore high heels. She sometimes walked around her bedroom in just her high heels, with the door open, and once asked me to bring her a glass of water, as she sat in front of her dresser, in her high heels. Lester and Esther. I loved their names! They were very kind to me over the years. Lester often chewed on a cigar, or smoked one, and his breath always smelled of tobacco. He used to play catch with us, and he was a good ball player. Esther used to make us delicious "beef on weck" sandwiches for lunch (roast beef on a kimmelweck roll, which is basically a Kaiser roll topped with lots of pretzel salt). Before "Buffalo wings," this was Buffalo's best-known food. Mike's family had a big, electric cooler on their back porch, filled with cold Cokes, to which Mike and I helped ourselves, even on the coldest, winter days. There is nothing like a "beef on weck" with a bottle of Coca-Cola.

The Weinbergs had a huge house (twice as big as ours) on Colonial Circle, which was a prestigious address. The mayor of Buffalo, Frank Sedita, later lived on Colonial Circle, too. Our church's rectory was across the circle from Mike's house. The Weinberg's house had a long, curving banister along the stairs, leading from the large, front hall room to the second floor—great for sliding down! On the first floor was a bathroom with all mirrored walls. The Weinbergs also had a new, Buick convertible in the early fifties and later a pink, Eldorado Cadillac. I was very jealous. Mike's grandmother, whom Mike called "Nana," was often at the Weinberg house and was always glad to see Mike's friends.

I spent many happy nights at Mike's house on sleepovers. We had a deal with Mike's parents. If Mike would finish his homework first, and if I would test his spelling (his major academic weakness was spelling), they would pretty much give us the run of the house. Mike had a lot of trouble once spelling "geography." Then our fourth grade teacher told us to remember it this way: "George Elliot's Old Grandmother Rode A Pig Home Yesterday."

In the den was a large, black and white television. We didn't have a TV in our house, until I was in high school. So when we were in elementary school, on Saturday mornings at Mike's house, we watched cartoons faithfully. On Sundays, we watched baseball games in the spring and pro football in the fall, all afternoon.

In those early years, my favorite baseball team was the Brooklyn Dodgers, and my favorite player was outfielder Duke Snider, the "Duke of Flatbush." Buffalo had no football team, until my beloved Bills arrived in 1960. So in the fifties, our favorite football team was the Cleveland Browns, and our hero was the Brown's huge, awesome fullback from Syracuse, Jim Brown, who ran through tacklers as if they were made of cardboard. I will never forget how powerful he was.

Mike had two attractive sisters. Randy, his older sister, often had her girlfriends or cousin Ronnie at the Weinberg house, and Mike and I would plot against them at every opportunity. Randy had a tendency to try to get us into trouble with her mother. Mike's younger sister by a few years, Candace, liked to play with us and pestered us to let her. Of course, she was too young for us to play with, especially since she was prone to run around the house in her underwear, or worse, and we considered her a pain in the neck, although she was otherwise a nice kid. I remember that she was pretty, petite, and into tap dancing, as were Mike and Randy.

Esther Weinberg liked to dance. One year, almost every time I visited Mike's house, I saw Mike's parents, dancing in the large, checkered-tile floor room at the foot of the stairs. They liked cha-cha, rumba, and samba, especially, and were quite expert. We often watched the dance instruction and the handsome dance teacher, who came to their house. Mike was sometimes cajoled into dancing with his sisters, but I refused. Dancing was not for me, until a few years later. But I admired Mrs. Weinberg's dancing.

One day Mike discovered his father's movies of nudes. These were not pornographic at all, but none of us had ever seen anything like them before. In our house the only even mildly provocative pictures were in the *National Geographic*. The movies caused great excitement among all Mike's friends, including me. Until Mike was old enough to operate his father's movie projector, we used to sit in Mike's closet, with the reels of film, and hold the film up to the light to view the frames. Sometimes, most of the film was off the reel and on the floor, as we excitedly peered at it. On one such occasion, Mike's father suddenly came into Mike's bedroom. Three of us in the closet—Bruce Bleichfield, Enn Teivas, and me—frantically tried to get the film wound back on the reel, as quickly and quietly as we could in the darkness. Of course, we were soon discovered. Mr. Weinberg was initially mad, but then laughed and laughed. After that he would wink at me, when he saw me, and ask if I had seen any good movies recently. He actually gave us permission to watch some of his movies, when we were older and had been taught at P.S. No. 56 how to load film into a projector and operate it.

Mike and Lester took me to my first Buffalo Bison baseball game, when I was about eight years old. The Bisons were in the International League— Triple A. They played at old Offerman Stadium, constructed around 1924, on the corner of East Ferry Street and Michigan Avenue. I loved that stadium. It was cozy and friendly, seating about 15,000. The center field scoreboard was forty feet high and was 420 feet from home plate. Only one player ever hit a home run over that scoreboard: Buffalo's big first baseman, Luke Easter. And Luscious Luke did it twice. When Luke came to bat (he always batted cleanup), we all yelled "Luuuuuuuke." Luke Easter was a legend. He could *crush* a baseball, and he was a very nice person, who signed several of his Cleveland Indian baseball cards for me. A cabby in Houston told me that a robber killed Luke Easter in 1979.

Mr. Weinberg drank a lot of beer and bought us a lot of popcorn, peanuts, and cracker jacks at the games that followed over the next seven years. He used to play right field for Canisius College and once hit a home run at Offerman, he told us. We went to several dozen games together, before Offerman Stadium closed in 1960. I also went to baseball games there, occasionally, with my father. At one game, against the Havana Cubans, Buffalo's stellar, center fielder, Bobby Del Greco (down from the Phillies), jumped at the base of the scoreboard to make a fantastic catch, then turned and threw a perfect strike to the catcher to nail the runner on third base, who had tagged-up and was trying to score. Four hundred and twenty feet in the air! Dad always said he was glad to have been a witness to that feat. It was the best play I ever saw.

When I was ten, my father and I drove to Rochester, New York, about a two-hour drive on the new Thruway, to watch a ballgame there, between the Bisons and the Redwings. We left after eight innings, with Rochester ahead by thirteen runs. As we arrived in Buffalo hours later, I turned on the car radio to WEBR, which used to broadcast the Bison games. The game was tied and in the fifteenth inning. Buffalo finally won. I learned an important lesson: never turn off the radio in the middle of a game, no matter how far behind your team may be.

After the Bisons moved to War Memorial Stadium, I never felt the same about baseball in Buffalo. Memorial Stadium was a *football* stadium and huge. The old intimacy was gone forever. The ghosts of shortstop Lou Ortiz, manager Phil Caveretta, Del Greco, and Easter didn't hang around this stadium.

As soon as I could throw a ball, baseball was kind of an obsession for me. My brother taught me to catch and throw, when I was about four. John and I would play catch in our backyard, which had enough room for a game, when I was very young, despite the raspberry patch in the southwest corner, the pergola in the middle of the back part of the yard, and Grandpa Schultz' tomato garden in the southeast corner. As I grew stronger, John and I would play catch over the house. He would stand on the street side, with a tennis ball, and loft it over the house. I would be waiting in the backyard, trying to pick up the flight of the ball, as it cleared the ridge of the roof and came down towards me. Sometimes, I would collide with the pergola or fall among the roses, as I concentrated on catching that ball. That game helped me a lot in later years. I could always track a baseball in flight pretty well, even when I picked up the ball's flight late, and I became a good outfielder. After John went to high school and college, my friends and I often played catch that way. Or I would lob a tennis ball onto the roof and catch it as it rolled off. Later, to my father's dismay, I would fire baseballs at the brick chimney and catch them as they rebounded.

In the spring, baseball was foremost on my mind. Mike Weinberg and I used to buy tons of bubble gum at a little store on Baynes Street, across the street from Public School No. 45, just to get the baseball cards. Or we would stop at Pringles on Elmwood Avenue on our way to school. Pringles was a candy store, but old Mrs. Pringle also sold Topps bubble gum, with baseball cards. Then we would trade the cards back and forth. I once had over five hundred cards, which I kept in old cigar boxes. One of my favorites was Glen Hobbie, who was a young pitcher with the Cubs and, according to Dad, a distant cousin. I thoroughly disliked Mickey Mantle, because he was a hated New York Yankee. I used to fasten his rookie cards (I had about a dozen) with a clothespin to the wheel frame of my bike, so that the cards made a whirring sound, like a small motor, when they snapped against the turning spokes of the wheel. All my baseball cards vanished mysteriously when I went to college—my life's fortune up in smoke.

We started out playing baseball in our backyard. A home run was anything hit beyond the pergola (about forty feet). By the time I was seven, a home run had to clear the back fence (about eighty feet). After we outgrew the confines of Hobbie Field, we moved our games to the open, grassy spaces around Colonial Circle or in the middle of Bidwell Parkway. The only problems with those playing fields were the ominous police signs on the trees that warned, "No ball playing. Violators will be prosecuted."

We played on Colonial Circle and Bidwell Parkway for many years. The magnificent elms substituted for bases and outfield fences. When the police came on their periodic raids, we would grab our equipment and run like hell, rendezvousing in Mike Weinberg's backyard, and being careful not to run directly there, but to use a circuitous route, through neighbors' backyards. Our backup plan, if the police seemed to be following us to Mike's backyard, was to cut through Nicky Locisero's backyard to our backyard fence, climb the six-foot fence at the telephone pole in the corner, and gain refuge at our house. Once, when I was executing the backup plan and tearing through Nicky's backyard, a clothesline, which his mother had unexpectedly strung across the yard, caught me at my neck and flipped me, completely knocking the wind out of me. I thought I was dead. Amazingly, no police arrived to lead me away in handcuffs to be "prosecuted," and my friends soon revived me.

On another occasion, my precious baseball mitt—inherited from John— was inadvertently left behind, as we fled the scene. My father went with me to the police station in our neighborhood to retrieve it. Except for that one time, we never really had problems with the police, who rarely left their car, after yelling at us. The only other time I ever was inside station No. 5, all those years in Buffalo, was to pay a speeding ticket—my first—in 1971, when I was twenty-six, on my first day back from Korea.

In fifth grade we started playing serious baseball at the asphalt-covered playground behind P.S. No. 56. For four years, we had glorious games there in the spring and summer, whenever we could get enough kids together to have two teams—no less than ten players: pitcher, first base, shortstop, and two outfielders at a minimum. One of the batting team usually played catcher temporarily for the team in the field, if we were short of players. Some of our most heated arguments involved plays at home plate, when that was the arrangement, because the catcher, from the opposing team, often did not take too seriously his sworn pledge to play honestly.

Home plate was at the far end of the playground. There was a short, left field fence about one hundred feet from home plate, but twenty feet tall. Anything hit over that fence was an automatic double. The school walls formed the other outfield boundaries, ranging from about two hundred feet in right field to about one hundred fifty feet in dead center from home plate. Anything that hit the school was a home run. If you broke a window, it was an automatic out, and the game ended quickly.

Mr. Schwartz, the school custodian, lived in a house behind the school, next to the playground. His house was the last school "cottage" in Buffalo, he proudly told me. Apparently, many of the public schools used to have cottages on the school grounds, where the school's custodian lived. He was a quiet, unassuming man and had at least one very nice daughter— Donna—at P.S. No. 56, when I was there. He approached me one day and said that, if I reported any broken windows to him immediately, he would not investigate further or blame anyone. He just wanted to know when and where he had to repair a broken pane. He was as good as his word and never reported any of us. Since I was the hitter who most often broke windows, I was happy with the arrangement and always considered him a friend.

My neighborhood pals were easy-going guys. We had our fights, but among our group these were short-lived. We had a great ball team: Danny Fraustino at pitcher; Ronnie Hoover at first base; Mike Weinberg at second base; Ronnie Carey at shortstop; Joel Lippes at third base; Enn Teivas, Richard Bassett, and John Mooney in the outfield, and Bruce Bleichfield at catcher. I was a sort of jack-of-all-trades and played any position. Because I was the biggest kid in our group (I was almost six feet tall in eighth grade), I had a strong arm and could hit the ball pretty well, not because I was better than anyone else, but just because I was bigger.

My other close, neighborhood friend was Bruce Bleichfield, who lived on Richmond and was a year younger than the rest of us, and a grade behind. Bruce's father, who was a lawyer, owned a burlap bag company. He was a very smart, kind, and friendly man, who lounged around the Bleichfield house in a white undershirt, a drink in one hand, and a cigar in the other. Mrs. Bleichfield was constantly saying to him, "Jack, take that cigar outside." She was a sweetheart, baked delicious brownies, and was always fussing after her daughters, Molly and Debbie. Both girls were very pretty in different ways. Molly had lovely, red hair and freckles, was two years older than me, and was always very friendly. I used to see her a lot at Volk's Drugstore, where she worked part-time for several years with my father. Debbie was my brother's age and a pretty brunette. She was also very kind, like her parents. I think she and John once dated.

Although Bruce was younger and smaller than the rest of the gang, he was smart, feisty, quick to stand up for his rights, and respected by all of us. His Aunt Ruth Rose lived on Ashland Avenue, around the block from my grandparents, and was a teacher, I recall. She knew my Aunt Kate, my godmother Ruth Culliton, and my next-door neighbor, Dorothy Ralph, who were teachers, too. All teachers in Buffalo knew each other. Bruce's aunt often visited the Bleichfields' home, when I was there, and spoke with us kids as though we were adults (as only a good teacher can). I thought she was a special person. I sometimes consulted with her about school projects.

Bruce's family had a large, summer home in Canada on Lake Erie, right on the beach at Waverly Beach. I often went there with Bruce. Besides the lovely beach and shallow bay, which were perfect for swimming when I was young, there was an old, abandoned, amusement park about one mile to the northeast, called old Erie Beach. It was aptly named "eerie," because it was overgrown with grass and bushes. But you could see where, forty or fifty years before, elegant buildings and amusements had stood: a dance hall, concession area, old tracks for some sort of railroad, and paved paths among the bushes and grass. It was a great place to ride bikes and to play cowboys and Indians or cops and robbers. Bruce and I spent many happy hours at old Erie Beach in the spring, before the summer heat and mosquitoes arrived. I often imagined how it must have looked in its heyday, splendid in its amusement park kind of glory, with the smells of hot dogs and popcorn and the ancient longings of young couples, hanging in the air, and the buildings of downtown Buffalo, looming on the horizon, just across the end of Lake Erie.

I preferred our beach on Holloway Bay at the Kennels to any of the other Canadian beaches nearer Buffalo. My family would "move" over to the beach and start to stay there on weekends in mid May. On the way to the beach from Buffalo, after crossing the Erie Canal and Niagara River on the Peace Bridge, with its snapping flags, we stopped at the ice rink in Fort Erie to pick up ice. In the trunk of our black, 1940 Chevy sedan we carried a metal tub and a pair of ice tongs. At the rink we pulled up to the back, where there was a loading dock. For twenty-five cents we ordered a fifty-pound block of ice, which my father picked up and carried from the dock with the tongs. Sometimes we forgot the tongs. Then we had to struggle to maneuver the slippery block into the tub with our bare hands and strain to get the tub and ice into the trunk.

Several years later, the ice rink's sale of ice became automated. We put a quarter into a slot and then listened intently, near an opening in the wall on the loading dock, which was the end of an inside chute for the ice blocks. After a few seconds, you heard a distant rumble from way inside the building somewhere, which got louder and louder, as the block banged down the chute, until the ice block popped out of the hole. The arrival of the ice was occasionally sooner than expected. Once or twice I fell off the dock, trying to get out of the way.

After picking up the ice, we drove west towards Port Colborne and through the town of Ridgeway, past the water tower at Crystal Beach, past the place we called "Skunk Hollow" nearby (because there was usually a dead skunk in the road at this sharp curve, through a small woods), and past the horses in the Bassett Farm's endless, white-fenced fields. We finally came to a favorite landmark: the Triangle Store. This little, country market was the closest food store and gas station to the Holloway Bay Road, which led to the Kennels. We stopped there to pick up last minute supplies and, most importantly, to get ice cream cones. The Triangle Store had heavenly ice cream, especially the chocolate. Canadian ice cream was much tastier than American ice cream. From there to the cabin was about three miles.

Those last three miles wound through fields of timothy grass, clover, and spring flowers, a grove of hardwood trees, and finally a forest of pine, spruce, and second growth trees that ended at the sand dunes on the lakeshore. I remember a family of groundhogs, whose burrow we usually stopped to inspect, where the road entered the woods. At the end of the road on the left, there was a chain-link fence and gate. After we passed through the gate, we came to a large parking area.

This parking area was known as the "parking lot," although it was more like a large field, crisscrossed with gravel roads. It was the center of group activities for the thirty or so families who rented cabins each spring and summer at the Kennels—our baseball field, fair ground, and point of departure for expeditions to the beach, to the drive-in movies near Sherkston Quarry, or to the closest town, Ridgeway, Ontario. On one side were two posts, supporting a wooden message board with news of upcoming events and reminders about trash pickup and other community housekeeping details. You had to cross this parking area to get to the sand dunes and the beach beyond. The gravel was murder on your bare feet.

From the parking lot, three, small, gravel and dirt roads fanned out into the woods. At the entrance to each was a wooden post, from which were suspended wooden plaques, with the names of the families who lived on that road. The names didn't change much for the almost fifty years we rented our cabin. As the parents grew old and died, their children took over the cabins. Generations of Guckers and Greevers, Harwoods, Hobbies, Henrys, and Halbins, as well as Benzows, Beyers, Bordens, Turners, Nitteraurers, Devonshires, Sloans, Sanders, and Shanks, to name only a few families, grew up in that community. Ours was the road on the left.

Our cabin in the 1940s was one of six in a row on that road, which was about ten feet wide and led about one quarter mile from the parking area to a dead end in the woods. The first cabin was the Greevers'—they owned a flower shop on Delaware Avenue for years and then one on the southwest corner of Elmwood Avenue and Bidwell Parkway, about six blocks from our Buffalo home. Gretchen Greever was in my sister's high school class.

The second cabin on the road belonged to the Gucker family. The Guckers' daughter, Gigi, used to babysit for me when I was very young. I remember her as being extremely lovely. I think she was a model; she certainly looked like one. I was distraught, when I heard that she was getting married, when I was about five. She married a handsome Egyptian by the name of Ken Malick.

One of their two daughters is a famous movie and television actress: Wendie Malick (*The American President, Dream On,* and *Just Shoot Me*).

The Sloans, who were former neighbors in Buffalo from Bedford Avenue, where my family lived before I was born, as I have mentioned, rented the next cabin. They had three sons: Buddy, Johnny, and Ricky. Next to us on the south side was a cabin alternately rented by the Turner family, whose children were Martha, Ann, and Fred (one of my brother's best friends), and by the Halbin family, whose kids were Peter and Gretchen, who was my sister's good friend. These were all Bedford Avenue neighbors, also. Mr. Turner was my godfather. The next to last cabin in the row was our small cabin in 1945–52, and finally the Bordens at the end of the road. In the mid 1960s another small cabin was built across the road and south of our cabin. Woody Smith and his family rented it for years. A family sometimes rented a cabin for only two months, and then another family would take over. From year to year, who rented what cabin changed a lot, but the same families came back year after year. I knew them all.

The first cabin rented by my family that I can remember was painted dark green. It consisted of two rooms and a large, screened-in front porch, where my brother, sister, and I slept in a bunk bed and on a cot. Glorious! My parents had the small bedroom inside, and the main room was where we ate. There was a small, pot-bellied stove in the main room, which quickly warmed up the cabin on brisk, spring mornings. The main room also had a sink—but you couldn't drink the water—and an old-fashioned icebox. On the porch inside the screens there were roll-down sunscreens made of bamboo, which were lowered to keep the sun or wind and rain out, when necessary. Hanging from the roof outside was a wren's house, invariably occupied in the spring and summer by the busiest and most vocal pair of wrens in existence.

When we arrived at the Kennels, we drove slowly down the dirt road to the cabin in our old car, calling out to friends in the neighboring cabins. The car was backed up to the cabin and unloaded. As soon as the block of ice was safely carried into the cabin and placed in the top of the icebox, my father would break out the bottles of Coca-Cola and chip pieces of ice off the block for our paper cups. I insisted on pouring my own Coke from the bottle, as soon as I could hold it. Nothing on earth compares to the sight, sound, smell, and taste of the foam on the top of Coke poured over ice. It only lasts a minute, but the sensation of the gas bubbles rising into your nose and mouth, as the essence of ice-cold Coke is ravished by your tongue, is one of the marvels of the twentieth century!

Dad would then walk around the back of the cabin, clearing away the cobwebs from the path that led about twenty feet, through the second growth, to the outhouse. Mom and Ceci wouldn't let him do anything at the beach until he had checked out the outhouse, flushed out the skunks in the vicinity, and cleaned out the spiders and snakes. I would usually follow right behind him to watch and make sure that he didn't miss any creatures. Dad never checked the areas *under* the double-holed seat in the outhouse, however. Sitting on the seat—although I used the outhouse as little as absolutely possible—I always wondered about two things: what spiders and snakes lurked beneath me, out of Dad's reach, waiting to take a bite out of my bottom, and why were there two holes in that seat? Who would ever share that creepy experience—the smell, darkness, and crawling things—with someone else on the second hole at the same time? Or was the second seat the backup seat to be used when the pile of deposits was too high under the first seat to be safely sat above?

We spent a lot of time on the porch of our cabin, playing games, reading, or just listening to the distant roll of the waves, the wind in the pines, the muffled sounds of our neighbors' lives, and the trilling of the wrens or the "meowing" of the catbirds. We drank in the sweet smells of the grass, bushes, pines, and beach. It was languidly peaceful at the cabin. In the spring, about dusk the spring peepers would tune up, punctuated by the bass fiddling of bullfrogs. The view on all sides was of bushes and low trees. As the leaves came out and filled in the branches, the winter bareness transformed into a lush, impenetrable wall of green. I imagined myself in a frontier cabin, two hundred years before. There was nothing better than lying in the bunk bed on the cabin porch in the early morning and losing yourself in the sounds and smells around you. Whenever I hear the "meowing" call of a catbird, I think of the cabin porch, where I spent many happy hours, daydreaming or reading.

Although my favorite book as a young child was "Make Way for Ducklings," by Robert McCloskey, later I especially liked books about the French and Indian War. I imagined how the early frontiersmen and Indians stole silently through the forests of New York State. I was also extremely fond of books about a farm near Centerboro, New York, some miles south of Rochester, where a pig, named Freddy, learned to read and talk. Freddy and his farm friends—Jinx (the black cat), Charles (the voluble, vain rooster), who my sister said reminded her of me, Mrs. Wiggins (the wise cow), and many others—had marvelous adventures on their farm, which was like the Morgan Farm at Lewiston in many ways. I read each of Walter R. Brooks' two dozen or so *Freddy* books at least fifty times, and the cabin was an especially great place to read. But it was the beach that drew us all.

On the northern shore of Lake Erie, our beach, which faced southwest, curved gracefully from Point Abino in the southeast to Pleasant Beach in the west. From the lighthouse on the tip of Point Abino to the high fence at Pleasant Beach was a forty-minute walk—about two and a half miles of soft sand and lapping waves, without a house in sight. You could pretend that you were on a deserted island, if you ignored the smokestack at Port Colborne—the highest in Canada—in the distant west. The wind and the waves were the only sounds besides the gulls. Except on Saturday and Sunday mornings in the summer, when the shore of the bay might have several dozen people sun bathing or swimming on our beach, it was empty and inviting most of the time. In March or April you seldom saw anyone.

To get to the beach from our cabin at the Kennels, you first walked down our little road to the left past four cabins, retracing the route in, back to the parking area. At the far end of the parking area, a path of boards led up and over the sand dunes to the beach. Dunes rose up on both sides of the path, creating a little pass in the sand, which stretched about one hundred yards from the parking area to the beach. We called such a pass through the dunes a "cut." Our cut was constantly changing shape from one spring to the next, as the winter winds picked up the sand and sculptured hills and dales in new places. Old wooden fences of slats on both sides, together with gnarled bushes and trees, unsuccessfully tried to keep the sand in place.

As you emerged from the cut onto the beach, the incomparable view hit you, with the sweep of water to the horizon. No land was visible across the water, even on the clearest of days. Lake Erie always looked a little different every time you saw it. The texture of the surface was sometimes like glass, or sometimes rippling with little waves, or sometimes tossing with huge mountains of water. Erie's color was blue-green under sunny skies, gray under a low cloud cover, or black, when a storm was brewing. The sky above the lake was sometimes a mirror of the water, or sometimes filled with puffy clouds of all shapes that cast dark, moving shadows on the water's surface, or sometimes pushing ominous rain clouds, rolling with thunder. The combination was always different, always changing, always lovely. Near the cut on the beach was an old, broken, concrete water intake, like a giant, concrete pipe about five feet high and twenty-five feet long, which stuck out into the water several feet. When I arrived at the beach, I went first to my perch on the end of the intake to take in the sky and water. It was also the best place to find frogs.

The beach had fine sand. In the spring the sand was never too hot for bare feet, and in the early morning or late evening felt cool on your toes. My family loved to walk on the beach, usually with our dog Tuffy, skipping in and out of the surf and barking at the sandpipers, plovers, and gulls. In the late 1940s and early 1950s you could find wooden floats washed up on the beach. These were six-inch long, three-inch diameter, wooden cylinders with a hole in the middle for a rope, used to float fishing nets, I was told. We collected all we could. They made great fuel for the cabin's stove. In later years the wood floats changed to plastic, but we still collected them and strung them up in the cabin. Of course, we also looked for shells, interesting driftwood, and items that had been lost overboard.

The best time of the year to find floats and other treasures was the early spring, before other beachcombers got to the winter's deposits of lake refuse.

Our beach walks often went as far as the lighthouse at Point Abino. In the two-mile stretch of beach to the lighthouse, there were not more than a dozen houses visible from the beach. The closest to our cut was the Malicks' house, about five minutes walk up the beach, built on the edge of the sand dunes in the 1950s. Gigi Gucker Malick, as I mentioned, had babysat for me, when her parents were in a neighboring cabin. The Guckers later built a large house about a quarter of a mile down the beach, which the Malicks took over. When I was a teenager, I sometimes watched Gigi and Ken's three kids for them—Darcie, Wendie, and Ken—and always enjoyed visiting their house, with its incredible view. We walked past the Malick house to either the first or second cut, about half a mile and one mile from our beach, respectively, and then climbed up through the cut, over the range of dunes, and dropped down into the deep woods on the leeward side of the dunes. Paths led from the cuts to an old, overgrown dirt road, which ran through the woods parallel to the line of dunes and beach edge. At one end, the road linked up with houses at Point Abino. In the other direction, it led back to our parking area at the Kennels.

The woods were carpeted with ferns, jack-in-the-pulpit, and white, pink, and purple trillium in the spring. The road was laced with spider webs, shimmering with dew. We broke off branches to sweep down the webs, as we walked. If we moved quietly, we could see foxes or deer. Before the mosquitoes came out in late spring, this woods was one of my favorite places to visit. The solitude, songs of the wood thrush and veery, and woodland flowers were missing from the rest of my life, elsewhere. We heard the rolling thump-thump-thump of a courting grouse, laughed at the bobbing, jerky movements of a woodcock, and marveled at the colors of the various warblers, blue jays, and rose-breasted grosbeaks on these spring walks. My father knew the common and Latin names of every tree, bush, and plant we passed. Between him and our successive dogs—Gypsy, Tuffy, and later Pepper—who had to sniff every growing thing in sight, our walks could be characterized as "deliberative."

The road through the woods wound past Dr. George Marcy's log house in its heart and the back of the Malicks' property, before linking up with a gravel road, leading out of the woods and through overgrown meadows of flowers and bushes to the parking area. My mother loved this route, and when I was very small, we often walked it together. When both my sister and I had birthday parties at the beach in April, this walk on the beach and through the woods was a highlight. My father taught me how to pop the seeds on the "touch-me-not" plants along the road in the late summer. Of course, he also taught me that the common name of this plant is Jewelweed, and that the Latin name is *impatiens capensis.*

We had fantastic birthday parties. I profited in many ways by being the youngest of three children. By the time I came along, my parents had mastered the most important, parenting skills, such as how to put on a great birthday party. My sister had several parties at the beach, when I was still having quite tame parties at home. Her parties usually involved a scavenger hunt or treasure hunt, with two or more teams of her friends, collecting the items on their team's list (a float, a fern, a frog, a shell, a feather, and an acorn were popular things to be scavenged) or following clues from point to point around the woods, beach, and cow pastures to find the next clues and finally the small treasures hidden by my parents and my brother. I watched and learned.

The party always included hotdogs and hamburgers, which my father cooked on the outdoor grill at the cabin, and potato chips, pickles, and soft drinks with, of course, birthday cake and ice cream. When it began to get dark, my sister and her friends would troop to the beach to roast marshmallows over a fire and to sing songs. Sometimes they also lit flares—red, yellow, and green—that my grandfather Schultz had brought from his work as a U.S. Customs officer in the train yards (he had a whole chest full of them). These had to be lit very carefully after being stuck in the sand, for they burned very intensely with a bright light. My father or brother usually did the honors.

My sister and her friends had wonderful fun at those beach parties, as well as at Chestnut Ridge Park near Buffalo, where they would roam to their hearts' content. I remember that, once, as my father drove a car full of girls back from a birthday party in Canada at the Kennels, one of my sister's friends, named Ginger, thought she would be cute with the American immigration officer at the bridge, who asked us all at the checkpoint where we had been born. Everyone said, "Buffalo" or "United States," except my father, who responded as always "Tonawanda," and Ginger, who said, in what she imagined to be a heavy Russian accent, "Russia." "Get out of the car," said the immigration officer sternly. She was hustled out of the car, and disappeared inside the Immigration Office. Only through the good graces and intervention of Grandpa Schultz—who as the former customs chief on the bridge still had influence—was Ginger finally able to go home with us.

When I was quite young, my birthday parties were usually held in our Buffalo backyard or in the attic of our house. We played Pin the Tail on the Donkey, Musical Chairs, and another game, in which each child followed a different, colored string of yarn up and down the stairs, in and under furniture, and back and forth throughout the house, winding it on a spoon, until they found a small prize at the end. Follow the Thread was usually a big hit and took at least half an hour to play. We also had peanut hunts, where we searched for peanuts hidden in the attic or in the backyard. Years later, I was still finding peanuts in the attic—mementos of former glory!

As I grew older, my birthday parties graduated to the beach, or to my grandparents' house at Lewiston, or to the park in Queenston, Canada, where we played the same games I had learned at my sister's birthday parties, plus baseball and Capture the Flag. There were old, earthen works, dating from the War of 1812, near Brock's Monument in Queenston, perfect for playing Capture the Flag. We also climbed the monument, which provided an outstanding view of the Niagara River's lower gorge and Lewiston on the American side of the river. I had about six boys and six girls at my parties until I was twelve. The usual group consisted of Ellen Warner, Tana Lee Stewart, Tina Haines, Dava Katz, Janine Hannel, Linda Smith, John Mooney, Enn Teivas, Mike Weinberg, Bruce Bleichfield, Richard Bassett, and me. Then the girls seemed to lose interest in baseball and other outdoor activities, preferring dance parties, Spin the Bottle (in which you sat in a group in a circle, with a bottle on its side in the middle that was spun by each participant; you took the person of the opposite sex that the bottle pointed closest to and kissed them), and so-called "necking" parties. But my pals and I preferred baseball at that age. And so we boys partied on without them.

My mother's birthday was May 17th. We celebrated usually with Grandma and Grandpa Schultz by having dinner at their house. My father and mother liked to go to a concert at Kleinhans Music Hall or to a play at the Studio Theater, afterwards. I remember missing my mother's birthday, when I was three, because I was in Children's Hospital to have my tonsils out. That's when I grabbed the nurse's hair net and pulled it off, as she was trying to hold me down on the operating table to put me to sleep for surgery. My mother brought me some ice cream from her party, but I couldn't eat any cake, because my throat hurt so much. After I got home several days later, I remember drinking lots of ginger ale and eating Jell-O, soup, and ice cream for a long time. I also remember that I vomited into one of the "registers," or heat vents, on the floor of the music room. Emily and Mom didn't appreciate my choice of a place to vomit. It was very difficult to clean up, and for years I could detect a faint smell of vomit, if I removed the register and put my head in the vent.

Three other events occurred in the spring, which I will always remember. When I was six, my brother John had a terrible accident in his sophomore year at high school in March. He and another student, Paul Schnatz, collided head-on in the swimming pool at Nichols. Paul had a headache afterwards. John fractured his skull and was in the hospital for two weeks and home for a month after that. My parents, my sister, and I were terribly upset. I thought John was going to die. He couldn't play football ever again, but later became a standout, long-distance runner on the track team, and a star soccer and squash player. I remember my mother telling me and Ceci, when John first

68

came downstairs after several weeks in bed upstairs, to be quiet and not to disturb him, as he sat up in a chair in the living room for the first time since his accident.

John, Mom, and me, 1959

Shortly after my brother's accident, I tripped and fell, head-over-heels, down the stairs at my grandparents' Lewiston home, breaking my right forearm in two places. I always blamed my sister for that, since she was chasing me at the time, but she really had nothing to do with it. John had a plate in his head, but I had a cast that I could wield as a convenient weapon against my sister and cousins, if necessary! In fact, I terrorized them with my cast. My mother also was in the hospital that month for minor surgery. It was a tough month for my parents. I vividly remember that spring, and especially the process of putting the cast in place on my right arm. Dr. Roswell Brown, my surgeon and orthopedic doctor, and his wife Dr. Enid Brown, who was my pediatrician, signed the cast in their offices on Delaware Avenue, across the street from the old Temple Beth Zion and next door to my grandfather Hobbie's office, where Dad worked. It was the first of several casts. In my childhood I broke my right wrist twice and my left ankle.

Breaking my arm was the only accident I ever had at Lewiston. Ceci also had a bad accident, when I was three and she was ten, in March 1948, crushing two fingers on her left hand in a corn-shucking machine in the barn at Red Bank Farm. I remember that incident, as clearly as I could always hear the dinner bell, which used to clang from outside the back door at my grandparents' house, calling us kids back home from the farm, riverbank, or fields at mealtime.

Ceci and I were in the barn. In March, our activities at the farm, where fields and orchards were still under snow, were pretty much limited to the barn, which was a fantastic refuge from boredom. One of the many machines stored in the main room of the barn, between the haymows, was a corn-shucker. This was a small, red machine, operated by turning a flywheel on one side. Ears of corn were fed into a hole at the front and, with a few hefty turns of the wheel, emerged on the other side, through three exit holes, in three parts: the corn shocks and kernels, respectively, which the machine had stripped off the ear, and the leftover corn cobs.

We were feeding ears of corn into the machine, when one got caught, and the flywheel wouldn't turn. My sister put her left hand into the hole in the machine to try to free the stuck ear. When she did so, the flywheel started to turn, and she started to scream. She had a good voice, too. The screams of both of us on this occasion rivaled the siren at the Lewiston firehouse that went off at noon every day. I remember running with her to the Morgan farmhouse's kitchen, where Aunt Mary Morgan wrapped the bloody hand in some white cloths and called my grandfather, who in turn called Lewiston's resident physician. Our family was in a terrible state. It turned out that my sister's two middle fingers were smashed. She could never bend them much after that, but it didn't seem to affect her piano playing. She was a gifted pianist. Years later, when she tried to take up the violin, she had to play on a left-handed violin.

Ceci playing the piano, 1952

Spring at Lewiston was a fairyland of blossoming orchards. As the snow melted, the frozen, dirt road on the farm, leading from the barns to the cow pastures, turned to mud. We would get up before dawn, as the mourning doves began to coo. I love that sound to this day, for it evokes those crisp mornings, when we would dress quickly, while the house was still silent, and run across the peach orchard in the dark to the barn, where Uncle Percy, Uncle Warren, and Bill Morgan would be preparing to milk the six cows.

The breath of the cows rose like frosty plumes in the milking room. Before the milking machine was hooked up, a pail of milk would be obtained by hand milking. This was for the spring calves, which had just been born, and for the barn cats. There were a dozen or so of them, with many kittens in the spring. Finding the newest batch of kittens, carefully hidden somewhere in the barn by their mother, was one of my specialties. If you listened very carefully, and screened out the sounds of the other animals, and of the wind wafting through the barn, you could hear the kittens, meowing very faintly in their secret, hiding place.

The orchards on Morgan's farm

As the cows were milked by the electric milking machine, we took turns with a pitchfork, cleaning out the manure from around each cow's stall. Each cow's head was confined between two curved bars, one on each side of the cow's neck, which kept the cow in the stall, when the bars were locked. Only a metal rail separated one stall from another. A depression in the floor behind each cow caught manure and urine, directing these towards the barnyard outside. When I was a little older, I learned to milk the cows by hand.

Once, when I was eight years old and at the barn with Ceci and some of her friends, they dared me to get on a cow's back. In fact, they "double dared" me, which was the severest kind of challenge to reputation. So I climbed on the cow's back, while it was in its stall. I think it was Mrs. Wiggins. Of course, Ceci couldn't resist giving Mrs. Wiggins a nudge with a prong of a pitchfork, so she bucked, and I fell off, narrowly missing the manure and urine trough. I was not happy.

With the milking done, we would help carry the four-gallon milk cans over to the Morgan's farmhouse, across the road on the riverbank. There we would help Aunt Mary Morgan pour the milk into the "separator" machine, watching as the milk whirled around in the machine, dividing into cream and milk. Then, the milk was heated, or pasteurized, and poured into bottles. The rich smell of the frothy milk and thick cream made us unbearably hungry.

Aunt Mary Morgan was a warm and grandmotherly woman. She was my Aunt Betty Hobbie's stepmother. Aunt Mary could twist her mouth into more funny shapes than anyone I ever saw. And she told us wonderful stories about a family of frogs, complete with the best imitations of different kinds of frogs you could imagine—especially the grandfather bullfrog.

As soon as the milk and cream were ready, we would carry several bottles back to my grandparents' house: two of milk, one of cream. A hearty breakfast waited, which was usually scrambled eggs and bacon with muffins. Then, after the ritual admonishment from my grandparents about the dangers of the riverbank and of the farm, we ran back to the barn to join the parade to the pastures.

The cows would be anxiously waiting to get out of their stalls. In turn, each was released from the neck bars, backed out of the stalls, and ambled out into the barnyard. At the far end of the barnyard was a gate, leading to the dirt lane that wound out through the orchards and still empty fields to the pastures, which were about three quarters of a mile from the barn. Usually, Bill Morgan would drive the tractor, an old Ford, following the cows down the lane at a very slow pace, and I would hop up to ride behind his seat, after opening and closing the barnyard gate. When I very young, there were several horses, which joined this procession. Later, after the horses had died and the tractor had taken over all their farm work, there were just the cows and us.

Bill Morgan, Uncle Warren's son, was a wonderful man, and a good friend. He was about twenty years older than I was, but treated me as an equal, told me all about his life (particularly a tragic love story), taught me how to operate the tractor and other farm machinery, and taught me how to milk and care for cows. I think he was lonely; he was always very glad to see my sister, John, or me, and our cousins or friends. Bill was kindness personified, and no matter what mischief we kids got into, he was never mad. Even when my sister drove the combine off the dirt lane into the ditch one autumn, Bill never showed the slightest anger or concern. He spent incredibly long hours, working in the orchards and fields. His hands were rough and callused. His neck and face were always sunburned. When he took off his farmer's cap, his bald pate was a brilliant white. He told me my head would be bald like his someday. I missed him terribly, when he later got sick and died quite young.

As we crawled down the lane on the tractor, or walked behind the cows with long sticks, we moved through drifts of pink, white, and red blossoms in the orchards. Hawks wheeled overhead. The cows swayed from side to side, as they walked. One of them wore a cowbell around its neck, which gently clanged. As we crossed the old railroad tracks across the road, marking the halfway point on the trip to the pasture, we often saw foxes or deer in the abandoned track way. The cows always knew the route, faithfully followed the road, and turned into the pasture on cue. Occasionally, a new one would bolt into the fields or orchards, and have to be shooed back onto the road. At the pasture, which had an electric fence around it, I would check the electric box to be sure the power was off, shoo the cows through the wire gate, close the gate, turn on the electricity, and climb back on the tractor. We then retraced our route to the barn, down the muddy lane. There was something new to see or do on every one of those trips. Riding, and later driving, a tractor on the Morgan farm was a highlight of my life, thanks to Bill.

Ceci at my grandparents' home, Lewiston, New York. Spring 1955

Although the official beginning of summer did not come for several more weeks, for me the end of spring was Memorial Day weekend, when most families moved over to the Kennels for the summer. Boats were wheeled through the cut, from the parking lot to the beach. Shutters came off the cabin windows. The grass around each cabin, by now almost waist high, was cut with a scythe. Everyone pitched in to help. The Sunday morning baseball games in the parking lot resumed. On Saturday evening there was a potluck dinner for all the families, usually held at the badminton courts. After dinner, the badminton games began on the two, lighted courts. The holiday weekend was an unforgettable beginning to summer every year. But I remember best my father's personal ritual that weekend.

My father was a strong swimmer. When he was in college at Cornell University, he once swam across the Niagara River, below Red Bank Farm.

The current pushed him several miles downstream. At the beach, his Memorial Day ritual was to go swimming in the still frigid waters of Lake Erie. He took pride every spring in being the first person at the Kennels to go in swimming. I remember his strong, sure strokes carrying him out into the waves. I later learned that he had won swimming medals in high school. I usually waited until late June to go swimming at the beach, when the water had warmed to a tolerable degree.

When I remember spring in my childhood, I think of beginnings: endless beds of crocuses, daffodils, and tulips, as the magnificent Canadian gardens at Niagara Falls sprang to life; opening day at Offerman Stadium; the eggs in the nest of a song sparrow, hidden in the climbing rose bush in the sumptuous gardens of my grandparents' Lewiston home; the piglets, chicks, kittens, and calves at the Morgan farm; the graduation of my sister from Campus School in 1952, when I gave her a frog for a present; and my father, pushing through the waves at Holloway Bay on Memorial Day, to inaugurate a new, summer season on Lake Erie.

Mom and Dad in my grandparents' backyard, Lewiston, New York, 1955

Chapter Three—
Childhood Summers 1945–1959

Dad and I, swimming at the beach, Holloway Bay, Ontario, summer 1953

Next to my grandparents' gardens at Lewiston, there was a tamarack tree, in the Elsons' backyard, which I climbed as often as I could. When I was seven, I was finally tall enough to be able to grab the lowest branch by jumping as high as I could. Once my hands were on that lowest branch, I could pull myself up and start to climb. The branches on that wonderful tree were spaced about eighteen inches apart, forming a perfect staircase, all the way to the top. Standing on the branch that was about three below the top most branches, I could poke my head out of the crown of the tree and see for miles, balancing myself, as the treetop swayed under my weight.

Summer in Western New York State was glorious in so many ways for a child. Trees and water were the primary natural elements of my joy then. Climbing upwards into friendly branches lifted me above the confines of my size and age. Erie, Ontario, and Niagara were awesome, beautiful, natural features, bounding my existence, and taken for granted. So much water, and such wind, storms, placidness, peace, coolness, color, and expansiveness were almost too much beauty to bear. Wherever I was outdoors as a child, I was conscious of the water nearby.

And there was always a gentle breeze from the lake. As the temperatures climbed into the eighties in July and August, our windows were open most of the time, allowing the movement of cooler, outside air through our stucco house, which kept the inside temperature bearable. Through the open windows came also the calls of the neighborhood kids, playing Kick-the-Can on the sidewalks, Giant Step on the driveways on either side of each house, or SPUD in backyards. Anthony, or "Anthoneeee," as his mother usually yelled at him, played a lulling, lazy saxophone on a back porch, sometimes echoed by Ernie Siegel's trumpet across the street. Sparrows in the vine on our house chirped off beat and off tune, occasionally upstaged by the rapturous, repeating calls of the cardinals in the solid green wall of mock orange bushes, cradling our summer backyard on two sides.

Our backyard was a lovely refuge. It was usually cooler in summer than our neighbors' backyards, because of the three, tall trees on the south side of our property, and because our neighbors' houses on both sides extended farther into their backyards than our house did, blocking the early morning, and late afternoon, summer sun from our back lawn and gardens. We spent much more time outside in our garden than our neighbors did. Dad had a constant war against the dandelions in the lawns, and both Mom and Dad loved to weed the garden beds. I recall a raspberry patch and a tomato patch, as well as dozens of rose bushes, all carefully tended. It was my job, from an early age, to cut the grass, edge the gardens, and roll the lawns in front and back with the heavy roller that was stored in the backyard (left over from the days, before I was born, when there had been a grass tennis court behind our house).

Looking west towards Lafayette High School from our backyard, July 1958

Summer was a season of daytime excursions in my grandfather Schultz's new, purple, 1949 Nash sedan, the seats of which folded down to make a delightful, flat, sleeping area. We often visited Niagara Falls, loving to drive north about thirty minutes along the Canadian side of the Niagara River, a route which is beautifully landscaped and was a favorite picnic spot. I liked the Falls, especially the cool mist at overlooks near them, which always produced a rainbow and relieved the heat. The Falls were truly awe-inspiring. You could hear them from a mile away. The sight of so much water, plunging over the edge, and the sheer majesty of the entire scene were humbling, fantastic, and frightening. In 1953, the water over a portion of the Horseshoe Falls, nearest the Table Rock Pavilion, was stopped by the building of a series of coffer dams to allow for remedial work to be done to the edge of the Falls. This was supposedly done to allow a more even water flow and to slow the rate of erosion. We went to see the Falls without water. The silence was deafening. Residents of Niagara Falls couldn't sleep at night without the sound of the Falls.

I preferred the Falls when the fullest volume of water crashed over the precipice, creating a thunderous roar. My parents told me that in the past, before the ugly power plants were built, the volume of water and its roar had been much greater. To generate power, a large part of the Niagara's flow was diverted to the plants, especially at night, when the reduction in water volume was not so noticeable.

Huge lights bathed the Falls at night in alternately white, and then red, yellow, green, blue, and purple light. Cars from all over the country provided an opportunity at the Falls to add to my list of license plates, as I tried to see plates from every state and territory. Guam and Hawaii cars never came to the Falls.

Dad, Ruth Culliton, and Mom in our backyard

We walked in the gardens at the Falls and particularly loved the rose gardens at the Niagara Parks' School of Horticulture, just north of the Falls. Canadians know how to garden! Later, when tall towers were built at Niagara Falls, I enjoyed whisking up to the top of the Seagrams Tower, with its incomparable view, almost as much as a trip on the *Maid of the Mist*, which cruises right up to the base of the Falls and gives you the feeling of being in a hurricane, with the choppy waves, driving mist, and thunderous roar of the water on all sides.

Other day trips that I loved were to the Devil's Hole State Park along the Niagara River, where Seneca Indian warriors massacred almost eighty British soldiers in 1763; the Iroquois National Wildlife Refuge east of Buffalo (which we called the "Alabama Swamps"), where I saw my first wood duck and bald eagle; Old Fort Erie, across the river from Buffalo, with its magnificent view of the city; the Welland Canal, where we watched huge ships raised and lowered through the lock system; and old Fort Niagara near Youngstown, which in the first half of the eighteenth century was probably the most important fort in North America.

My mother and I often walked around nearby Bidwell Parkway and Colonial Circle, when I was a toddler, in the shade of the elms. Later, I remember watching the unveiling of the huge statue of a Civil War general on horseback in the center of the circle: General Daniel Bidwell, a Buffalonian killed at the Battle of Cedar Creek, Virginia, in 1864. His grave lies close to the Hayes-Hobbie plots in Forest Lawn Cemetery. When we played baseball or football on the parkland near General Bidwell's statue, I wondered if he suspected, when he left Buffalo to fight, that he would never return alive.

On the same circle we walked around our lovely, Gothic-style church—
St. John's Episcopal—situated at the intersection of Bidwell Parkway and
Lafayette Avenue. My grandmother Schultz (her second marriage), my mother
and father, Fred Turner's sister Martha, and my sister and her husband, John
Pehle, were all married there. I saw half of those marriages. The grassy areas of
the circle and parkway beneath the elms witnessed thousands of touchdowns
and home runs in the 1950s and 1960s.

St. John's Episcopal Church, July 1956

As soon as I could ride a bike, I was free to visit friends' houses, such as
John Mooney's home at 785 Bird Avenue. John's neighborhood had a lot of
nice kids: Ann Jones, Mary Jean Digati, Richard Bassett, Kathy Ellis, Danny
Rumsey, and others my age, whose sisters or brothers had gone to school
with my sister and brother, or who were in our class at P.S. No. 56. I had a
tremendous crush in fourth grade on Mary Jean, who lived half a block away
from John's home.

I remember John's parents, Nina and Earl Mooney, and his two older
sisters, Pat and Joanne. Mrs. Mooney was the quintessential, Italian mother: an
attractive, warm-hearted woman with black hair and snapping dark eyes, who
always had cookies in the kitchen and a kind word. She was one of my favorites.
My mother liked her a lot, too. Mr. Mooney was a civil engineer with a hearty,
Irish laugh. I liked to talk with both of them, even though Mr. Mooney was
prone to talk about his health excessively. My parents tried for years to get the
Mooneys to rent a place at the Kennels. They never did, but John visited us
often there, where he had a girlfriend, Holly Henry, for several summers. The
Mooney home on Bird Avenue was a special place, always inviting.

John and I used to go to the movies at the Elmwood Theater, or at the
Grant Theater. Cowboy and Indian movies were our preferred choice, but

pirate movies were a close second. *The Charge at Feather River* was an all time favorite, especially because it was in "3-D," which required you to wear special glasses in the theater to get a "three dimensional" effect. It was great! The arrows and the lances seemed to pop right out of the screen at you, and I was weaving and ducking in my seat, as the Indians charged the cavalry across the river. Guy Madison was the star, and I liked the television program he also starred in: "The Adventures of Wild Bill Hickok." Another favorite movie was *The Crimson Pirate* with Burt Lancaster.

Whether on Bird Avenue or West Delavan Avenue or Colonial Circle, the huge elms kept our lawns and porches in shadow, during the day, and latticed the streaming twilight in the evenings, as the ting-a-ling of the ice cream man's cart, or the piercing, thin steam whistle on the popcorn man's yellow cart, signaled us to run to the curbside with our quarters. In the evening the west side adults adjourned to neighborhood bars and restaurants—one on almost every block, it seemed. Those who stayed home ate dinner on their porches, played cards, listened to Bill Mazur's broadcast of Bison baseball on WEBR, or laughed at George Burns and Gracie Allen, Jack Benny, or Edgar Bergen and Charlie McCarthy on the radio. Long, soft sunsets ended summer days on the Niagara Frontier.

Our backyard at 453 West Delavan Avenue, July 1959

As pleasant as the city was during the summer, with its neighborhood friends, familiar sounds and smells, vast parks, and alluring waterfront, I looked forward to summer escapes to the beaches of Canada or to the lawns, gardens, fields and orchards that lay beneath the tamarack tree at Lewiston. To the west, in the summer, my view from the top of the tamarack tree was of the incomparable Niagara River gorge, just beyond the roofs of my grandparents' house and the smaller, white house next door, belonging to my great Aunt Mabel and Uncle George Elson. Aunt Mabel was Grandpa Hobbie's sister.

The tamarack was on the Elsons' property. Between the river and me was the River Road, which followed an old, Indian trail from the Falls, down the river northwards to Fort Niagara. I imagined that I could see the handful of British survivors of the Devil's Hole massacre, several miles to the south, struggling northwards down the trail, along the east riverbank, towards the safety of the fort, as Seneca Indians attacked. Across the river in Canada lay the heavily wooded, western riverbank, with the golden fields of the farms beyond.

To the north was the Sage family's huge, white house, next door to the Hobbie house. The Sages had two children: Helen and Carlton. I recall that Helen married and then died at a relatively early age. Carlton became an Episcopal minister and then switched to enter a Roman Catholic Order. The garden behind the Sage house had lovely hedges and a small fish pool with gold fish, all clearly visible from my perch. Beyond the Sages' property were the Scovell house and several other imposing estates. The Scovells' granddaughter, Candi, was a cute girl, several years younger than me, who hung out with me, when I was about eleven. Beyond these neighboring estates lay the convent of the Sisters of St. Francis at Stella Niagara, whose bells on the hour lazily marked the passing of summer, wherever I roamed in Lewiston's fields and woods or on the Morgan farm.

Closer to my perch were the magnificent black walnut trees on my grandparents' lawn on two sides of the clay, tennis court. We sometimes played softball or tennis on the court, which had a tall fence at each end. With binoculars I could often see Baltimore orioles in those trees. From one of them hung a forty-foot swing, as I have previously mentioned. If you grabbed the seat of the swing and climbed onto the stonewall that separated the Sages' land from the Hobbie estate, you could get a wonderful, initial swoop on that swing. If you twisted the swing seat around and around, until the ropes were tightly twisted around each other, and then climbed on the swing and jumped off the wall, you got the "tornado" ride, with the fantastic, stomach-churning sensation of spinning, while flying. My cousins, friends, and I spent many afternoons, flying on that swing. It was the best swing I ever saw.

Just below the tamarack to the north were the several gardens belonging to my grandparents, laid out in a circle, like a doughnut, with a round lawn and a birdbath in the middle. In summer these were full of peonies, lilies, zinnias, English daisies, and other flowers of all kinds, including a lovely, rose garden. Next to the gardens closest to my grandparents' house was the old, apple tree with a tree house or platform in it, as I have mentioned. Even a young child could climb up the metal ladder, leading up about twenty feet to the platform, from which a stout defense could be made against marauding Indians, North Koreans, or even female cousins.

Looking east, in the distance, beyond the small creek at the eastern end of my grandparents' three acres of lawn and flower gardens, I could see more fields and woods, whirling with life. In the closest field was another old apple tree, just beyond an abandoned wagon with four, huge, wooden wheels. Countless, joyous hours on that wagon and in that apple tree—always keeping a watchful eye on the abandoned "haunted" house nearby at the back end of the property—saw us beat back many an Indian attack, as we crossed the plains and mountains of the American west, armed with my grandfather Hobbie's ancient BB rifle. Sometimes, if I was in my tamarack early in the morning, I could see deer through the mist that gently draped the meadows, beyond the wagon. On some days, the mist lay so close to the ground that all you could see of the deer was the occasional head that popped up through the mist, looked around warily, and then disappeared in the whiteness.

Aunt Kate and Dad play baseball, as Grandpa Schultz and Gypsy watch, Lewiston, 1953

But it was towards the south that I most often turned my eyes from the tamarack tree. The Morgan farm, with its huge, old barn, chicken coops, pigpen, storage sheds, and winding lane, leading out into the adventure of orchards and pastures, was my kingdom every summer of my early life, until it was sold in the late 1950s and became a housing development.

From the tamarack, I could see if Bill Morgan was out on the farm, plowing or planting the wheat and corn fields, spraying the fruit orchards, or spreading manure from the "honey wagon." Or I could spy his father, Uncle Warren Morgan, puttering around the equipment storage sheds. He was an engineer, who had helped build the Panama Canal and Holland Tunnel, contracted malaria, and retreated to farm life for health reasons. Uncle Warren walked with a very pronounced limp and wheezed when he breathed, but lived to be well over a hundred years old. He was quite deaf and shouted at you, as though you were deaf, too.

Or I could see Uncle Percy, with his walrus-like mustache, checking the weather station, near his vegetable garden, between the road and the riverbank, next to the Morgan house. He was an attorney, who, like his brother Warren, had decided to farm instead of pursuing his profession. Any of the Morgans' activities guaranteed adventure. Having identified a promising target, I climbed down as fast as I could, dropping from the bottom limb onto the ground.

Just east of the tamarack tree, and between it and the old abandoned wagon in the outlying field, was a small white house belonging to Aunt Mabel and Uncle George's daughter, Gladys McConnell, and her husband, Charlie, who was usually cutting the grass in the summer. I liked the McConnells, who always asked about my parents and siblings. They had two daughters, my second cousins, Susan and Sheila McConnell. I often dropped by their house to see if either of them wanted to join me in my escapades. They had a lovely Springer Spaniel, named Toby, who was my constant companion and the first dog I ever had as a close friend, until Gypsy arrived.

My brother, sister, cousins, and I would head for the farm whenever possible, usually with Toby shadowing us. As I grew older, I sometimes was accompanied by only Toby. We played hide and seek in the tall grass in the fields. Toby taught me the value of being perfectly still in the grass for a few minutes and allowing the birds, rabbits, woodchucks, and occasional deer to forget that we were there. I remember the pungent smell of wet grass and the taste of dirt and the peacefulness of lying on your back, with a dog next to you, watching the summer sky, clouds, and hawks, wheeling above.

Uncle Percy Morgan was my Aunt Betty's father. His second wife, Aunt Mary, was Aunt Betty's stepmother. Uncle Warren's wife was named Blanche, and they had two children: my friend and "cousin" Bill and a very pretty daughter named Sue. They were all my family by virtue of my Uncle Tom's marriage to Betty, his next-door neighbor. As I have mentioned, I had two Aunt Bettys and loved them both dearly: Aunt Betty Hobbie (married to Uncle Tom) and Aunt Betty Craig (my father's sister), married to Uncle Bob Craig.

One of my favorite stories came from Uncle Percy, who once told me about my Aunt Betty's marriage to Uncle Tom. The marriage was in 1934 in Lewiston, and there was a reception at the farmhouse afterwards. In those days, the Morgans had a farmhand, who was like one of the family, but not known for his agility of mind. He asked what he could do to help with the reception and was told by Uncle Percy that he could stand by the road to direct the guests, as they arrived up the River Road from Lewiston, to park in the fields next to the orchards, and then to walk over to the reception at the farmhouse on the riverbank, a distance of several hundred yards.

All went well until at some point, during the reception, a state policeman approached Uncle Percy and asked him what in the world was going on. Uncle Percy explained about the reception and then accompanied the policeman, across the road, to the farm and its fields, where *every* vehicle—trucks, buses, and cars—that had come down River Road in the past two hours was parked in the fields, with some pretty distraught drivers.

My father often told a story about a wedding and reception in his past, and a contribution to the bliss of the honeymoon. As the story went, someone tied a piece of Lindberger cheese to the radiator of the groom's escape car, so that as the engine heated up, en route to the honeymoon destination, the cheese melted and perfumed the air. I never heard this confirmed, but I always suspected that the escape car was Uncle Tom's.

Linking up with one of the Morgans at the farm, on any of my daily excursions there, usually led to some hard work. I learned how to change the oil in the tractor, drive a straight line in plowing a field, shovel manure into a manure spreader, throw manure onto the fields from the spreader, shovel out chicken poop from the chicken coops (which is the worst smell in the world), mow hay, bale hay, pick fruit, sort fruit, drive a combine to harvest wheat and oats, feed horses, pigs, cows, and calves, milk cows by hand or machine, and handle a host of other farm chores, including making and recording weather observations. Grandfather Hobbie, who tried to interest me in cutting the grass or weeding garden beds or the clay tennis court on the Hobbie property, was pretty frustrated that I preferred the harder, dirtier, and smellier farm chores next door. Returning from the farm for dinner, exhausted after a day of farm work, I was required to take a bath and change my clothes, which reeked of delicious, farm odors.

My grandparents' house on River Road, Lewiston, New York, 1956

One summer day in the early 1950s, accompanied by a Buffalo friend, I was walking down the lane, at the far eastern end of the Morgan farm, and spied a strange contraption in what was usually a horse pasture of a neighboring farm. There was often a beautiful Palomino horse in that pasture. When we investigated what looked like several trucks with rockets mounted on the back, we were confronted by a soldier with a rifle, who told us to leave immediately and to keep quiet about what we had seen. Of course, we spent the next couple of days, creeping about in the nearby woods and watching the military activity, and the two dozen soldiers, through my grandfather's binoculars, telling everybody in the neighborhood about our discovery.

We later heard that these were mobile "Nike" missiles, supposed to target any air strikes launched against the United States from Canada or over Canada from the north. We were, of course, at war against North Korea then, and while, on my last visit to the beach, Canada still seemed friendly, and was fighting as an ally in Korea, it was possible that it could change its mind and target Lewiston, as the British did in 1812. It also seemed quite plausible that the North Korean air force could sneak across Canada and try to bomb the Morgan Farm. Several years later, I wished that I had had some of those missiles to target the developers who bulldozed the farm into oblivion.

Another summer, when a different Buffalo classmate was visiting Lewiston with me, we went over to the barn for milking, early one morning, and discovered that a cow—I think it was Mrs. Wogus—had squeezed through the door of the milking room into the silo and then squeezed through the narrow opening of the silo, becoming stuck in the silo. The Morgans were trying to figure out how to get Mrs. Wogus out, and she was pretty unhappy, as her bellowing indicated. It seemed impossible that such a big cow could have gotten through the narrow, silo opening.

What fun we had! Bill Morgan greased Mrs. Wogus with a thick, machine grease and then pulled her halter, with Uncle Percy and Uncle Warren, pushing and jabbing her with a pitchfork from behind, until finally she got the idea and pushed her way out. The yelling and mooing were frightful! It was one of the best days I ever had at the farm.

Several times each summer, my grandparents would have a picnic for family or friends in their gardens. Saw horses were pulled out from the carriage house at the end of the driveway, and 4x8 foot sheets of wood were mounted on them to form long tables. These were covered by white tablecloths, and the six, five-foot long, green garden benches were pulled up to the tables for seats. On hot days the tables were grouped in the shade, under the apple tree or under the huge wisteria vines that grew on the nearby icehouse and tumbled over the driveway to supporting trellises, forming a tunnel of blossoms in early summer—more like an incredibly fragrant tree than vines.

With my sister, brother, and cousins, I helped Grandma Hobbie prepare for these picnics by shucking corn, shelling peas, and preparing salads of fresh lettuce, cucumbers, and huge tomatoes from the vegetable garden. When the time came to cook hamburgers and hotdogs, I helped Grandpa Hobbie light the charcoal in the barbecue and cook the meat. He had a big, wire, handheld, two section grill, which had hinged surfaces. You placed the meat or corn on one part of the grill, and the other part folded over to hold everything being cooked in place. The stone barbecue was located next to the icehouse and near several Smokebush shrubs, which I thought appropriate.

With the lemonade, ice tea, salads, fresh corn, hamburgers, hot dogs, and pies, those picnics were feasts! Usually, the children were allowed to take their paper plates of food and drinks up to the tree house in the apple tree. From there we looked down on the sea of adults below: my Hobbie grandparents, parents, Grandpa Schultz, uncles and aunts, Wellesley classmates of my grandmother's, the Morgans, McConnells, and Sages from next door, my elderly Aunt Reba from North Tonawanda, and the Elsons. If we had peas, it was fun to shoot peas down at them, through straws, to try to get Aunt Reba—my grandmother's kind but dour sister—to crack a smile. When she did, the little hairs on her chin, which tickled your face when you kissed her, jiggled delightfully.

On these picnic days, some attendees would sneak out behind the wisteria on the icehouse for a smoke, screened by the Smokebush shrubs. My grandparents on both sides did not like cigarette smoking. My father, mother, Uncle Bob Craig, and Aunt Betty Craig were smokers. One or more of them often sidled out past the gardens to sneak a smoke.

Grandpa Hobbie and Grandpa Schultz at Lewiston, 1953

Uncle Bob Craig was one of my two godfathers. A former naval officer, he was handsome and had crinkly, laughing eyes. In the war, he liked to say, he had spent years learning Japanese pretty fluently, and then in customary military efficiency had been assigned to duty in Italy. As I have already said, he and my Aunt Betty had twin girls, several years younger than me. When they visited Lewiston from New York City, I liked to pull the twins around the gardens in a small wagon. If I went fast, Molly would cry, and Kitty would purse her lips, determined not to. In later years, the Craigs moved to Lewiston and occupied the little, white house on River Road, next to my grandparents' house to the south. Although they were girls, the twins were good natured and fun cousins to play with and talk to, whenever I visited Lewiston, and I loved them like sisters.

Uncle Bob and Aunt Betty were favorites of mine. They smoked and drank, while none of the other Hobbies did (except Mom and Dad). And they talked about New York City's social scene, poetry, and *avant-garde* writers. I remember them both, with cocktail glasses and cigarettes in their hands at Lewiston—years after my grandparents had died. I was eternally grateful to Aunt Betty and Uncle Bob for suggesting that I wear his naval uniform and Commander's hat to a costume ball in Buffalo, when I was fourteen. Boy, did I feel good in that uniform.

Aunt Betty Craig had been a good friend of my mother's at the Buffalo Seminary, where both went to high school. It was through that friendship that my parents met and married. Aunt Betty had a wonderful, wild streak, which my mother loved. My grandfather Hobbie once told me that he had been driving past the Buffalo Seminary, one school day in the 1920s on Bidwell Parkway, when he looked up at the distinguished school building to see my Aunt Betty, dangling from one of the windows on some sort of rope. She climbed down the rope and set off towards Elmwood Avenue, with my grandfather following in his car at a distance. Aunt Betty visited a candy store on the corner of the parkway and then started back towards the school, whereupon my grandfather stopped the car and offered her a lift. At the school, she got out of the car and climbed back up the rope, presumably laden with goodies. I suspect that my grandfather didn't approve of this escapade, but in telling me about it, he obviously considered it a fond memory, which he relished.

On another occasion in the 1920s, Aunt Betty invited my mother and other Seminary classmates to Lewiston for a weekend sleepover. The high school girls were hidden in the bushes on the riverbank in a group, gossiping and smoking, and unaware that my grandmother had invited the high school's strict headmistress, Gertrude Angell, to visit that afternoon. Of course, when my grandmother and Miss Angell strolled down towards the river (as all visitors invariably did), the cloud of smoke, wafting up from the bushes on the riverbank, gave the girls away. They were all suspended from school for three days for smoking. Neither my grandmother nor Miss Angell ever found out that the girls had been smoking hemp, according to my mother.

Aunt Betty scared the daylights out of me once, when I was about six. I was staying at Lewiston, when Aunt Betty, Uncle Bob, and the twins were visiting, one very hot, summer night. I got up in the middle of the night to go to the bathroom at the far end of the long hall, wary as always for any ghost that might appear in that old house. On the way back to the "blue room," where I usually slept at Lewiston, suddenly I heard the floorboards creak, and a formidable, white figure appeared in the hallway ahead of me in the dark—seemingly a naked ghost—coming towards me. I silently ducked into one of the closets along the hallway, shaking with fear, until it passed. Then, I ran as quietly as possible for my bed, where I trembled all night. The next morning Aunt Betty said that she hoped she hadn't frightened me.

I remember those summer picnics in my grandparents' gardens well. Surrounded by beds of roses, lilies, asters, peonies, and dozens of other flowers, the tables of happily chatting people made you forget every care in the world. After we finished eating, if it was an especially hot day, my grandfather would hook up several hoses to the water spigots in the gardens, and the kids would run back and forth through the plumes of water. Or, sometimes, we would play tennis or baseball on the court between the Hobbie and Sage houses, or stroll along the riverbank next to the road.

In the tennis games we often had half a dozen people or so on each side of the net, ranging in age from five years old to eighty. Uncle Bob's sister, Marian Craig, was undoubtedly the best tennis player in the family, even well into her seventies. I made the mistake of challenging "Aunt May" to a table tennis match once, when she was about sixty and I was a teenager. She "cleaned my clock," standing about five feet behind the ping-pong table and rifling volley after volley back across the net. She did the same thing on the Lewiston tennis court in my younger days against all the males of the family. Aunt May had been a finalist in the women's doubles division of the national public parks' tennis championships in the 1920s, with her partner from Cleveland, Edna Smith, I later learned. She had a great, comfortable laugh and was an art teacher in Cleveland for many years, before she retired to Rockport, Massachusetts. Once, Aunt May frightened me, during dinner at her little house on Country Club Lane in Rockport, by suddenly, and without warning, picking up a sizable dart from under the table and hurling it across the table at a target she had hanging on the back of the dining room door. She was full of nice surprises. I remember her and her wonderful dog Muffin—a handsome Springer Spaniel— very fondly.

On the riverbank strolls, we passed the fruit and vegetable stand, at which the Morgans sold every kind of produce imaginable, during the summer.

Occasionally, we helped man the stand. I learned to count money on those hot days, selling fruit and vegetables. A little farther up the river was the Morgan's farmhouse, which was really a huge, old house, divided into two residences. The Percy Morgans lived in the south wing, and the Warren Morgans lived in the north wing. A small door in one of the bedrooms upstairs connected the two sides on the second floor, and a door between the living rooms in the wings connected the two sides on the first floor. I liked that arrangement. Both wings had back verandas, with gorgeous views of the Niagara River below.

There was an American chestnut tree of enormous girth in Percy Morgan's front yard, which lingered long after the chestnut blight had taken every other chestnut tree I knew. I made it a point to visit that tree, whenever I was at Lewiston. It provided beautiful chestnuts, which I saved in a bowl in my room for many years. In the pantheon of my favorite trees, that chestnut tree is at the top, with the cedar on the riverbank and the tamarack, although I never climbed it. We played a game with chestnuts called Kingers. You selected the roundest, biggest chestnut that you could find, drilled a small hole, right through the middle, and tied an eighteen-inch piece of string to it. This was swung at the "kinger" held by your opponent. With practice we became pretty good at hitting each other's chestnuts. The strongest chestnuts withstood even direct hits from other kingers. If your chestnut broke, or came loose from the string, your opponent won whatever other chestnuts had been bet.

A picnic at Lewiston on the Fourth of July was especially exciting, because Grandpa Hobbie had an old, small cannon, which made a terrific noise when fired in celebration of the day. After the firing of the cannon, out by the barn at the back end of the property—which we could watch but were never allowed to get very close to—sparklers were passed out at dusk to everyone.

Sometimes, we drove up the River Road to town on the Fourth, which took about ten minutes by car. The town of Lewiston set off fireworks at the river's edge, at the bottom of the steep gorge, just downstream from the suspension bridge connecting Queenston with Lewiston, We sat in my grandfather's green, Pontiac sedan, and later a black Chevrolet, always with the same New York license—1MD 279—barely able to keep awake, watching the balls of fire arc above the river and imagining that the Battle of Queenston Heights was happening again on that very spot.

On a couple of Independence Days, we visited my Uncle Tom's family in Sodus, New York, just the other side of Rochester. My six cousins were usually involved in the Fourth of July parade down Main Street—U.S. Route 104—in front of my uncle's lovely, old, brick house (one of only two in Sodus) with its wraparound porch. Sodus also had super Memorial Day parades. I fondly remember those small town parades, where everyone seemed to know everyone else, and the whole town was involved. Usually, at least two of my cousins were marching. Sodus was the "Cherry Capitol" of the world, and the parade was heavy on cherries.

Uncle Tom was the town doctor. He had delivered virtually everyone in town under the age of forty, recognized everyone in the parade, and knew everything that was going on in Sodus. People called him "Doc," just as old timers in Lewiston called my grandfather "Doc." In later years, when I met people in Korea or Washington, who had grown up in or near Sodus, they invariably knew Doc Hobbie and his girls.

I liked visiting Sodus. My cousins kept me occupied every minute and maintained a constant stream of gossip about Sodus and their neighbors. After all, there were seven females in the Sodus Hobbie family. I admired my Aunt Betty for keeping my cousins all in line with a sure, gentle manner. I never heard her lose her temper. She was a kind, wise, and loving person. We corresponded throughout my life. During these visits, I got to know my cousins' friends pretty well, too, especially my cousin Kate's best friend, Jan, who had a sweet laugh and liked to embarrass me by telling stories about the neighborhood boys and what they did to girls in Sodus.

My uncle's office was on the first floor, to the right of the front door, as you walked in. It smelled like a doctor's office—of alcohol and disinfectant. Just outside the office was the waiting area for patients, in the vestibule. On the left in the vestibule were the stairs to the second floor. Under the stairs was a bathroom. I was told to use the backstairs on my visits there, so that patients sitting in the vestibule would not be disturbed. The steep backstairs, which were off the dining room behind a door that looked like a closet, led to a storage area on the second floor and opened on the bedrooms. At the top of the stairs were several loose floorboards. My cousins kept forbidden treasures under those loose boards, in a little space, such as the comic books and magazines they were not permitted to buy or read. I once saw some cigarettes there, too. I think my uncle and aunt knew about the hiding place, but had decided long ago that their girls needed a place to hide secrets.

At the end of the driveway was an old barn, which my uncle used as a garage. On the second floor, in what used to be a haymow, was a large, open space with a basketball hoop. On the side of the room facing the driveway was a large, sliding, wooden door, probably used in the past to load hay through into the haymow. When open in the summer, that door provided daylight and a cool breeze onto the barn's upstairs basketball court, where I spent many hours, shooting baskets with my cousins or alone. I often wondered for which of my cousins my uncle had put that hoop up.

Outside of Sodus was a sheep farm, belonging to friends of my uncle and aunt. I visited it late one spring. The hundreds of bouncing lambs surprised me! I had never seen lambs close up before, and to this day I have never seen a more joyous sight than spring lambs, leaping and cavorting in the sunshine.

My cousins were all very musical. Each played an instrument, and all played the piano and sang pretty well. A highlight of my early childhood was a Sodus High School production of "Oklahoma," in which several of them starred. Just off the living room was a kind of music alcove, with an upright piano and a record player. One of my cousins was usually practicing. Along one wall was a built-in bench with comfortable cushions. If no one was practicing, that was a great place to lie and listen to records. I remember hearing Brahms' *Double Concerto for Violin and Cello* for the first time there and thinking that it was one of the most beautiful, musical pieces I had ever heard. That nook was one of my favorite places. A succession of Tom Hobbie dogs over the years—Duffer, Frieda, and Aly—joined me there in comfortable bliss.

In my childhood, my two oldest cousins were married in the Sodus Presbyterian Church, during the summer. The church was on Main Street about two blocks from my uncle's home. Those were among the first weddings I ever attended. I was an usher in both weddings, and my sister and brother were also in the bridal parties. I remember how hot the weather was for the first wedding, which was my cousin Beth's, although she was the third oldest in my generation. On the morning of the wedding, Uncle Tom asked me to accompany him to pick up the wedding cake from a bakery, about a half hour's drive from Sodus. On the way back to Sodus, I sat in the front seat, balancing the wedding cake on my lap. The heat, however, caused the cake's icing to melt, and one by one the roses and other decorations, around the top of the cake, plopped off, to my great dismay. My uncle said not to worry. Sure enough, my Aunt Betty managed to put all back together, and the wedding cake was lovely again by the time it was cut. That cake epitomizes my earliest impression of weddings; preparations seem to lurch from crisis to crisis, but in the end the icing on the cake is just fine.

My uncle provided free, medical care to the African-American, migrant workers who came to Sodus from the South to pick fruit. He once showed me the broken-down barns and other dilapidated buildings, where the workers were housed for the picking season. One summer, a migrant worker and her very young daughter came to the house after office hours. I still remember how scared the woman looked. The child was very sick, very thin, and was carried by her mother. My uncle treated the child for an intestinal parasite. He later told me the parasite he removed from the child was a worm over four feet long. That night in 1953, I first became aware of the poverty and discrimination that permeated the fringes of the world of my childhood, mostly out of sight and out of mind.

On the evening of the Fourth, my cousins took me to Sodus Point, on nearby Lake Ontario, where the town celebrated with fireworks. Years later, their family had a comfortable little cabin there. I stayed at the cabin on several occasions, when the house on Main Street was overflowing with guests on special occasions, such as my uncle and aunt's fiftieth wedding anniversary celebration in 1984, and on the celebration of "Tom Hobbie Day," which the town of Sodus arranged in 1985, as a surprise, to thank Uncle Tom for his work over fifty years, as the town doctor. Only it wasn't a surprise, as he admitted later, because he had found a discarded invitation to his "surprise" celebration weeks earlier, when he was rummaging through junk at the town dump.

His visits to the town dump may explain why Uncle Tom seemed to know so much about what went on in people's lives in Sodus. He also had a reputation for predicting accurately the gender of the hundreds of babies he had delivered over the years. He once told me about an obstetrician he knew, from Cornell, who always knew in advance the gender of the baby he was going to deliver. This doctor would examine a woman and then tell her what the baby's gender would be, for example, a girl. In so doing the doctor would tell the woman that he was writing this gender on a piece of paper and putting the paper in a sealed envelope in the woman's records. But he would say one thing—"girl"—and write the other gender—"boy"—on the paper, without showing the woman. If the gender turned out to be different than what he had stated, the mother would be shown the paper—with the correct gender written on it—and believe that she had not remembered correctly what had been said. The doctor's reputation for infallibility would be preserved. I wondered if Uncle Tom was that doctor, but he wouldn't say.

My uncle died in 1986 from an infection he got from a patient. I remember his memorial service at the Presbyterian Church on Main Street, where my cousins had been married, and how unhappy my father was at the death of his twin. I felt like hugging Dad every time I looked at him, he seemed so forlorn. Several months after his death, I had a strange experience involving Uncle Tom.

My daughter, Amy was five years old then. My wife, Young, our children, and I were living in a townhouse at 285 Gundry Drive in Falls Church, Virginia. Uncle Tom had died in May. One July evening, Amy was quite sick, with a very high temperature. I read her a story and then sat with her in her room, until we both fell asleep. Suddenly, Uncle Tom was in the room with his black bag. He put his hand on Amy's forehead and took her pulse. He said that she would be fine in several days and not to worry. She had the flu, he said. Then, Uncle Tom said not to worry about him, that he was fine where he was. Only he was perturbed that his autopsy results had misreported the real cause of his death, which had been kidney failure, he said. Then he was gone. I went to our bedroom and woke Young, telling her what had happened. To this day, I am sure that Uncle Tom visited Amy and me that night.

On other Independence Days, our family celebrated at the beach at Holloway Bay. We got together with the Halbins, Turners, Sloans, or other families for a picnic in the evening, and then the whole Kennels' community, of thirty or so families, congregated on the beach at dusk for a huge bonfire and fireworks. When you looked around the bay from the beach, you saw dozens of bonfires and fireworks everywhere, while the regular, sweeping flash of the lighthouse, at the tip of Point Abino, provided its own spectacular, light show.

Fireworks were illegal in Buffalo, but as soon as you crossed the Peace Bridge into Canada in the summer, there were roadside booths, selling fireworks, everywhere. Each family had their own roman candles, sparklers, and other fireworks, but the community association provided a spectacular display of skyrockets. We sat on towels or blankets, on the cooling sand around the bonfire, and oohed and aahed. The only members of the community who didn't have a great time on the Fourth were our dogs. As we went to the beach for the noisy celebration over a twenty-five year period, Gypsy, Tuffy, or Pepper—my childhood best friends—would already be whimpering under the double bed, where my parents slept in the cabin.

Ceci, me, Mom, and Dad at the beach, 1953

Some years, on July Fourth we would attend the Ridgeway Firemen's Carnival on the Main Street in Ridgeway, Ontario, which was the town closest to the beach. Canadians didn't celebrate July Fourth, of course, but our northern neighbors were outnumbered by Americans during the summer in Ridgeway and helped us celebrate. I learned to gamble at the Ridgeway Carnival, where, among hundreds of booths, hawking games and food of all kinds, there was a roulette wheel. You put down a quarter and guessed a color—red or black—or a number—even or odd or a specific number—and, depending on what you chose to bet on, you could double or triple your money. On one magical Fourth of July night at the roulette wheel, Heidi Marquis, whom I knew from the west side neighborhood in Buffalo, and I won ten dollars in quarters! I looked forward to the experience of that roulette wheel every summer and always hoped to meet Heidi there again. I never did.

My grandparents celebrated their fiftieth wedding anniversary in 1953 with a grand party at Lewiston. I was eight years old. I remember that there were hundreds of people there, including all my first cousins. My Uncle Tom's youngest daughter, Ellen, was young enough to be held in the arms of my cousin Kitty, who was about six then, for the formal family picture. Grandpa Hobbie held little Ellen's hand in his in the picture, I noticed. I had to wear a bow tie that day, which I didn't like very much. There was a lot of food. I especially liked the pastel pink and green mints, about the size of a half dollar, which were among the many goodies on the dining room table.

**The Hobbies at Lewiston in 1953 during my grandparents'
fiftieth wedding anniversary**

In 1949 our black cat "Inky" had a litter of three kittens. One was pure black, from head to toe. My brother, sister, and I chose to keep him and named him "Jinx," after the black cat in Walter R. Brooks' *Freddy the Pig* books. Jinx was a good cat. But one romantic, summer night at the beach, he met and danced with a skunk. I remember the discussion among the adults about how to get rid of the skunk smell on Jinx, who stank royally from that pungent skunk spray, and was determined to come into the cabin for the night. Eventually, it was agreed that a bath in tomato juice was necessary. What a struggle ensued with Jinx! We never let him out of the cabin at the beach again.

Years later Jinx developed the "mange," which was a kind of nasty, skin condition in the summer that he scratched, until most of his hair was gone. My mother spent hours, coating Jinx with medicinal cream, which he quickly licked off. I wondered if the skunk's spray or the tomato juice had caused the mange. Jinx lived to be fifteen years old, despite his hairless summers, giving the hope of longevity to the men in our family, who were also becoming hairless.

Jinx was joined at our house in 1952 by my first dog, Gypsy, whom we got as a puppy—a beautiful black spaniel and terrier mix. They always got along very well together. Gypsy was a spirited, friendly dog. I loved taking her for walks around the neighborhood. I was admonished to clean up after her poop and to keep her tightly leashed. One summer day—Gypsy was two—my friend, Enn Teivas, and I were walking Gypsy around Colonial Circle, when I decided that she would be happier if she was off the leash and free to run a little. As we walked past St. John's Church, a car, coming around the circle, blasted its horn at another car, spooking Gypsy. She started to run for home, with Enn and I in pursuit. I saw the car that hit Gypsy seconds before the impact. The driver never stopped. She made it about half a block and collapsed in the front yard of Bob Gerace's house. I got to her, just as she died. Enn ran to get my mother. John came to get Gypsy and carry her home. I have never cried so hard in my life, nor felt so terribly guilty. I remember Gypsy, whenever I pass the Gerace's old house on Richmond Avenue. She is one of the six beloved pets buried in the backyard at 453.

In my early childhood visits to the beach, my sister and brother led me through the woods of spruce and white pine, and through the fields of wild flowers and grasses taller than my head, on trails fragrant with earth, pine needles, and golden rod. I used to dream about those trails, usually running with Ceci and John and getting lost in the sumptuous vegetation, until they found me.

Later, I dreamed that I could elevate myself above the high grasses and thistles by moving my arms up and down rapidly, like a bird, but also using a circular motion. Over many years, my arm technique improved to the point where I could reach in my flights the lower branches of trees, then the tops of trees, and, finally, well above the forest canopy. Some of my very best dreams were of flights I took, always alone, inspecting tree tops from above or examining the friezes at the tops of buildings. I was careful to avoid telephone and power lines. These dreams continued well into my adult life. I was often surprised in downtown Buffalo, and even later in Washington, D.C., to look up and see a detail on a building façade, which I recognized as a detail seen before in one of my night flights.

I remember my first real flight. One of our beach neighbors, appropriately named Mr. Dare, worked for the Bell Helicopter Company in Niagara Falls, New York. On a Sunday afternoon in 1953, a three-passenger helicopter descended from the sky into the cow pasture we used as a baseball diamond. We were all treated to several brief flights, around Holloway Bay and its environs. I was amazed at the totally different perspective one had of the beach community, and of its woods and fields, from a height of several thousand feet, and at how the streams, roads, and fields below were all laid out in a discernible pattern. Most of all, I recall the tremendous exhilaration I felt, as I swept over the woods and fields, with the wind tousling my hair in the open, bubble cockpit.

My sister and brother led me into the sand dunes separating the beach from the parking lot and the Kennels' community. The dunes were covered with wild grape vines and stunted trees, providing an endless source of lookouts, hide-and-seek spots, and ambush sites. They taught me to avoid the hated poison ivy and to open the pods of the milkweed, with its seeds and silken parachutes, ready to be blown from the tops of the dunes.

John and his friends set off cherry bombs in the dunes. If you dug out a cave in the sand, about three feet wide, in the side of a dune (preferably facing inland), and then lit a cherry bomb placed at the very back of the cave, the blast was deafening and would bring adults running from the cabins. Of course, John, his friends, and I were long gone and hidden in the dunes' vines by the time anyone arrived. In later years, my own friends and I committed the same atrocities in the dunes.

Just outside the screen porch at our cabin, my father strung an army hammock between two pine trees. The hammock had a canvas roof, with mosquito netting that connected the roof with the canvas bottom. A zipper, which was operated from either the outside or the inside of the netting, allowed me to zip myself into mosquito-free bliss in the shade of the pines, catching the summer breezes and reading or napping to my heart's content. I spent many hours in the hammock, which was a refuge from the crowded cabin.

The beach on Holloway Bay, looking east towards Point Abino

Our neighbors at the beach, the Sloans, had a great tent, which they pitched on a platform, behind their cabin, for their boys—Buddy, Ricky, and Johnny—to sleep in. Sometimes I would join John, Ceci, and the Sloan boys in a sleepover in that huge tent. On the first of those occasions, I saw trembling lights, flickering on and off in the bushes and grasses surrounding the tent. From that night on, catching fireflies and holding them in bottles for several hours (before releasing them unharmed) was a favorite evening activity, even more fun than catching frogs in the bog near the Dare house.

Near the tent, one summer, the Sloans kept several cages of black and white rabbits. When I was five, I worried that the caged rabbits didn't seem to have as much fun as their wild counterparts, which hopped around our community by the dozens. So one evening, I opened the cages and let the six rabbits out. My altruism was discovered in the morning. Despite the efforts of dozens of searchers, no black and white rabbit was ever found. Mrs. Sloan explained to me that I didn't do the rabbits any favors by releasing them, because they were tame rabbits and not used to the dangers of the woods. But the Sloans understood that I had acted with good intentions. I liked Ruth and Jack Sloan.

Jack Sloan also had a large sailboat. As his boys grew up and came to the beach less and less often, he let me crew for him. We never had a boat, but since the Sloans, Halbins, Turners, or Benzows always needed a crewman on their boats, I spent many sunny hours in sailboats on Lake Erie. I liked the stillness of sailing, with the only sounds the rush of the water past the boat, the snapping of the lines, and the wind in the sails. There are few things as peaceful. I also remember the sense of urgency that arose when storm clouds appeared, and how an uneasy, prickly feeling on my neck was engendered by a dark sky with a suddenly fierce wind. Terrible storms came up quickly on the lake. We would race to the beach, ground the boat as the waves rose, and join the others, pulling boats across the sand, as high on the beach as possible, before the storm hit. On the Great Lakes we had squalls with ten or fifteen-foot high waves and ferocious winds, that would suddenly appear, devastate anything in their path, and then vanish just as suddenly.

The Halbins had one son—Peter—who was my brother's age, and one daughter—Gretchen—who was my sister's age. Our families did a lot together, and the kids often played tricks on each other. Peter Halbin usually slept in his underwear. One night, for some reason, he was sleeping on the porch of what was the Henrys' cabin that summer, at the base of the cut to the beach, while they were away. This cabin was located several hundred yards from the Halbins' cabin, which was next door to ours. John and Fred Turner, with Gretchen and Ceci, sneaked over to the Henrys' cabin during the night and stole all of Peter's clothes. When Peter awoke the next morning and couldn't find any clothes, his yells could be heard from our cabin. All the kids, or course, had been told of the prank and were prepared to cheer Peter on, when he wrapped a sheet around himself and legged it back home. That made a big impression on me.

On another summer night, when I was about ten years old, Gretchen was staying the night with Ceci at our house in Buffalo. They were sleeping in the front bedroom, which had two big windows, looking out over the porch roof to the West Delavan Avenue side. Next to the street was a street lamp that shone brightly into that front bedroom, requiring that shades be pulled down on the windows, if you hoped to get any sleep at all. The gently sloping roof was accessible from the windows of the adjoining front bedroom. My friend, Mike Weinberg, and I dressed in some long jackets, and each pulled on one of my father's hats, before quietly easing onto the roof and inching over in front of the windows of the room, where Ceci and Gretchen were chattering away. As we stood up on the roof and our shadows hit the shaded windows, the chattering inside stopped suddenly. There was a sweet silence, and then some muffled murmuring, before the bedroom door slammed and feet pounded down the stairs to the living room, where my father was reading. We managed to get off the roof and out of our disguises, before my father was persuaded by the girls to come up to investigate.

Almost every evening at the beach, the adults and kids would meet at the two, lighted badminton courts on the north edge of the Kennels. From dark until midnight, we played badminton, usually with four on a team, and four teams playing at any given time. As the summer progressed, we got better and better. Players were grouped by age and gender and by singles or doubles into brackets. Almost everyone participated. The "ladder" of players and teams was posted on the community bulletin board. If you challenged the person or team just above you on the ladder, and won, you moved up. When I was twelve, I won the boys' singles title with a lucky swat against Alden Harwood.

The next year, Christine Benzow and I teamed up to win the 13-14 year olds' mixed doubles championship. She was a great player and a good friend from P.S. No. 56. I still remember her red hair, funny laugh, and white bathing suit. Chris was a neighbor of Heidi's on Ashland Avenue in Buffalo—two lovely girls on one block.

There were a lot of swats on those badminton courts in the evenings. Most of them were aimed at the ravenous mosquitoes that descended on the players, as soon as the evening breeze off the lake died down. Several times each summer, Hilda Forester, the owner of the Kennels and landlord of all of our community, arranged for an exterminator to "fog" the entire community with DDT to kill the mosquitoes. My parents called us inside, as soon as they heard the sound of the fogger's jeep. A device at the back of the jeep put out a tremendous cloud of DDT, as the jeep drove up and down the roads and around the badminton courts and parking lot. For weeks after each fogging, the mosquitoes disappeared. But they always came back with a vengeance.

In 1955, several of the adults at the beach got together and built what we called the "tripod"—a teepee-like structure with three twenty-five-foot long poles, joined at the top and linked at the foot by connecting boards, with a triangular floor of boards, forming a platform, placed about half way up. On one side was a ladder. When the "tripod" was placed in the water at a depth of about six feet, and the feet of the tripod anchored on the bottom with concrete blocks, we had a fantastic diving platform about five feet above the water. The only problem was that, in the course of the summer, storms would tip over the tripod and repeatedly wash it into shore. The tripod lasted three summers, before the adults got tired of towing it out and resetting it after every storm, but while it lasted, it was our jewel.

The Children's Fair Day at the beach in late August saw several dozen "booths" set up in the parking area and manned by the Kennels' residents, such as the Bean Bag Throw, the Water Dunking booth, Apple Bobbing, pony rides, and the Wheel of Fortune. Free tickets were given out for these activities. When I was five, I ran the Wheel of Fortune with the Millers. A child would present a ticket and spin a huge spinner, winning the prize that the spinner pointed to. My sister won the prize that year for the prettiest booth, where she was selling sponges.

We had the Kennels' hay ride in late August, following the Children's Fair. Horses pulled about thirty of us kids on a local farmer's wagon for an hour-long trip, up the Holloway Bay Road and back. I loved the clop, clop, clop of the horses' shoes on the road and the sweet smell of the hay in the wagon. Later, a tractor pulled our hay wagon, but it was still tremendous fun, singing and shouting as we went. When I was six years old, we arrived late for the start of the hayride. I ran like crazy to catch the wagon, as it was pulling away, and just as I was about to reach the extended hands at the back of the wagon, I tripped over a dog and fell, hitting my forehead and chin on the back of the wagon. There was lots of blood. But I was carried to the wagon by Johnny Sloan and Fred Turner and, with my face wiped clean of blood, was able to continue.

Another Kennels' event very dear to my heart was the Sunday morning baseball game in the parking lot. Almost everyone—husbands and wives, and kids of all ages—participated. We sometimes had twenty people on each team. As soon as Kennels' residents had eaten breakfast, bought their Sunday newspapers at the Triangle Store, lingered with their morning cups of coffee over the paper on the cabins' porches, and cleaned up the breakfast dishes, several of us would go cabin to cabin to remind people to come to the parking lot for the baseball game.

When I was eight years old, I got a book of baseball's rules for my birthday. Our Kennels' neighbors were extremely tolerant of my efforts to ensure that every play was strictly in accordance with that rulebook. Later, as I got bigger and better as a ballplayer, I was usually one of the team captains.

I particularly remember one game, in which the score was tied in the bottom of the ninth inning. Fred Turner's father, Mark Turner, got a hit, advanced to third on a single, and was perched on third base. My father came to bat and hit a towering, fly ball to short center field. Mr. Turner, who was then about fifty-five years old, waited, until the ball had been caught, and then ran for home. Woody Smith—a Dartmouth grad, who was about thirty-five years old and a gifted, pretty hefty athlete—was the catcher. My friend, Enn Teivas, playing center field, threw a strike to Woody, who waited to tag Mr. Turner out. Somewhere between third base and home plate, Mark Turner left his feet in a spectacular dive, covering about thirty feet in the air and crashing into Woody, knocking the ball loose. Everyone was shocked into silence at this incredible display of prowess and spirit by Mr. Turner, who was usually a quiet, unassuming man. When Mark and Woody finally came to their senses, and Mark had been duly congratulated for winning the game, he admitted, laughingly, that he had tripped over a stone.

Enn Teivas with Tuffy, 1957

Mark Turner and his wife, Anna, were a wonderful couple and best of friends with my parents. Their three children—Martha, Anne, and Fred—were three of my favorite people. Martha Turner's wedding at St. John's Church was the first wedding that I ever remember and one of the loveliest. Martha was a beautiful girl. Anne, her sister, had been injured at birth and had difficulty moving and talking. She was one of the few people I knew as a child with any kind of disability, but I soon learned that she was extremely smart, kind, and just like anyone else, even if I had difficulty understanding her speech. She always participated in any event that her family attended. My mother told me that, after Anne's birth, the attending doctor had never told the Turners about her birth injury, and that it was not until much later that they discovered Anne's disability. I watched the entire Turner family love Anne and care for her, with no thought of placing her in an institution—which was a common practice in the 1950s and 1960s for a disabled child.

Our whole family admired the Turners. Mark Turner was our family attorney. Anna Turner, my mother often remarked, was the kindest person we knew. Fred was my brother's best friend, attended Nichols High School and Dartmouth College one year behind John, and later was my camp counselor. One evening, when we were at the Turners' house for dinner, Mr. Turner suggested that I might enjoy listening to his new record of Pablo Casals, playing Dvorak's *Cello Concerto*. I remember lying on the floor with some headphones and wondering at the beauty of Dvorak's music, which that night became one of my favorite classical pieces. Years later, I heard Casals play the same piece at Marlboro, Vermont. His humming was sometimes louder than the cello. I always think of Mark Turner, when I hear the *Cello Concerto*.

At least once each summer our family visited Crystal Beach, which lay one bay to the east. Crystal Beach was a child's paradise and my first amusement park experience. Built in 1888, it had the look and feel of the nineteenth century. I remember the magnificent roller coaster called the "Giant," which was built entirely of wood and rattled and banged, as the cars swooped up and down and around. I think that it was purposely constructed of wood to be noisy and give you the feeling that it was about to collapse at any moment. There were also the "Magic Carpet Funhouse," the "Laff in the Dark," a beautiful carousel, a midway, a terrifying ride called the "Wild Mouse," a boat ride called the "Old Mill," and a large Ferris wheel, from the top of which you could see the lighthouse at Point Abino. The crowning glory of the park's attractions was a huge roller coaster called the "Comet," which I was not allowed to go on until I was about eight years old.

The Comet was tightly built of steel supports and had a tremendous hill at the beginning of the ride. The cars would slowly climb, clackety-clack, clackety-clack, up this hill, and then the front of the train of cars would inch over the summit until half of the cars were over the top, and then whoosh.... The track went out over Lake Erie at one point, and I thought that, if the coaster went off track, I would prefer to be over the water when it happened. On some days, I preferred the speed of the Comet to the shaking of the Giant. On other days, it was more terrifying to imagine that the Giant was about to disintegrate from its vibration.

When I was quite young and riding the "kiddie coaster," I remember that my hat came off and fell to the ground, below the slightly elevated tracks. I was not happy about that and didn't repress my feelings. I also remember with delight that my sister took great offense at the blasts of air from the hidden floor holes in the Magic Carpet Funhouse, which sent skirts and dresses flying upwards, revealing underwear.

In seventh and eighth grades, students were selected to be on the "safety patrol." As a safety patrol member, you wore a white belt at an angle across your front. The belt had a marvelous, silver badge on it. One eighth grader, who was chosen to be the "captain," wore a badge that had a blue background. Three students were "lieutenants," with red backgrounds on the badge. I was a lieutenant for two years. Ronnie Hoover was the captain our last year. (I was disappointed not to be chosen.) The job of the safety patrol was to maintain order on the playground and to stand at the major intersections to ensure that kids coming to school crossed safely. For two years, with Joel Lippes, who lived close by, I was the safety patrol on the corner of Chapin Parkway and West Delavan Avenue, with a lovely lady, Mrs. Titchler, our longtime, crossing guard there. Every morning, as I walked the one half mile up West Delavan Avenue to P.S. No. 56 from our house, I passed the intersection of

Elmwood Avenue and West Delavan Avenue, where another great lady, Mary Langford, was the guard.

The Buffalo school system treated all of its safety patrol members, every year, to a day at Crystal Beach with free tickets. Several of our teachers and the adult crossing guards accompanied us. It was blissful event, and we looked forward to the day for months. I still remember being astonished when Mary—the lady who was the crossing guard at the intersection of Elmwood and Delavan Avenues for my ten elementary school years—stood up in the front seat on the Comet at the top of the hill, with her arms in the air (violating all the rules), and yelled joyously at the top of her voice. I was equally astonished, later the same day, when my friend Ron Carey (or "Ricon" as we called him), who was riding with me in our two-person car on the Wild Mouse, threw up.

Until the mid 1950s, you could take the ferryboat to Crystal Beach from Buffalo. I recall several trips with my family on the two steamboats: the *Americana* and the *Canadiana*. Dad told me that he had commuted back and forth to work in Buffalo on several occasions from the beach by walking the three miles to Crystal Beach, on the shoreline and on a road which cut through Point Abino, and taking the ferryboat back and forth from Buffalo to Canada.

Ceci's graduation picture, Buffalo Seminary, 1956

When I was four, my brother started leaving home for parts of the summer and then for the whole summer, first to scout camp at "Scouthaven" for several weeks in the late 1940s, and then, in 1951, to work for the Appalachian Mountain Club, or "AMC," at Pinkham Notch in the Presidential Range of the White Mountains in New Hampshire. My sister started to attend summer camp for several weeks when I was six—Camp

Gohadogo in the Allegheny Mountains in 1951—and then followed John to work for the AMC at Pinkham Notch in New Hampshire, in 1955, when she was seventeen.

The AMC maintains a string of "huts" or hostels, for hikers, spaced about one day's hike from each other in the White Mountains. These huts are located on the shoulders of the Presidential Range's peaks or in notches between adjacent mountains. Sleeping between twenty and ninety hikers, the huts in the 1950s were manned by crews of high school and college boys, who cooked, cleaned the huts, packed in supplies on their backs up (or sometimes down) "pack trails," maintained the huts and connecting trails, served as rescue or search parties for injured and lost hikers, and otherwise engaged in the wildest, best parties and creative adventures you ever saw. *Animal House* (the movie) is tame by comparison to what went on in the huts.

The headquarters of the Hut System is at Pinkham Notch, at the base of Tuckerman Ravine on Mount Washington, where the AMC has long had a lodge for hikers to stay at and get meals. The Pinkham lodge crew was comprised of first year boys, who usually trained for one year there before being assigned to a hut, and girls, who in the 1950s could not work in the huts, but manned Pinkham. Wherever you worked in the Hut System, the pay was poor and there were no benefits, but the experience and the fun were incomparable.

I first came to know the AMC and its huts when my parents and I took my brother, and later my sister, back and forth to their summer jobs. As I recall, in 1951 I had the measles and had to stay at Lewiston with my grandparents, while the rest of the family made the first of these trips in 1951. My first long car trip was in 1953, when I was eight. In subsequent years we went to New Hampshire almost every year, until I graduated from Dartmouth College in 1967. In the 1950s, it took about eighteen hours by car to get to Mt. Washington from Buffalo, so it was a two day trip, east on Route 5 to Herkimer, then on Route 29 to its end at Route 22, then north up to Route 4, with a stopover at a motel near the New York-Vermont boarder. Sometimes, we took, instead, the southern route across Vermont on Route 9 to the Connecticut River, then north up the river to Route 4.

On those trips in our old Chevrolet sedan, or in my grandparents' old Pontiac, we played games to pass the time. A favorite was the Alphabet Game, in which passengers on the right side of the car formed one team and passengers on the left were the other team. Each team's objective was to see all of the letters of the alphabet, in order, in signs on your side of the road. As you saw each letter, you called it out, so that it could be verified by the other team. Whichever team saw all twenty-six letters first, won the round. The letters "Q" and "Z" were extremely hard to spot. I used to get puzzled looks from strangers at rest stops, who wondered why an eight-year-old was asking if there were liquor stores ahead. Fortunately, there was a sufficient number of "Zion" churches and temples in the small towns, and no passing "zones" along the road, to allow these games to be completed in a reasonable amount of time. Our best time was sixteen minutes. Several games went on for hours, when we drove through tee totaling counties.

Another game was counting cows. The objective was to see which side of the car could count one hundred cows first. If you passed a cemetery on your side of the car, you had to start all over again. We got to know where all the cemeteries were along the route!

And we laughed at the Burma-Shave signs, advertising a popular men's shaving cream, which typically consisted of five or six small, red and white signs, spaced about fifty feet from each other along the road, each carrying several words of a funny poem: "Burma-Shave / Was such a boom / They passed / The bride / And kissed the groom." Or another favorite: "To kiss / A mug / That's like a cactus / Takes more nerve / Than it does practice / Burma-Shave."

We also sang songs. Some of my favorites were "Ain't Gonna Grieve My Lord No More," "On Top of Old Smokey," "Oh Suzanna," "Clementine" (and to the same tune, "Found A Peanut"), "Green Grow the Rushes, Ho," "I've Been Workin' on de Railroad," "Red River Valley," "Alouette" (my sister's favorite), "She'll Be Comin' Round the Mountain," "Home on the Range," "Dixie," and "Battle Hymn of the Republic." I also liked to sing Christmas carols, especially "Twelve Days of Christmas." Most of these songs also had off color variations in the lyrics, which my brother and sister had learned at summer camps, designed to cause consternation for my parents.

The night before leaving on one of the initial trips to New England, we went to a drive-in movie theater on Sheridan Drive. I think it was called the "Sheridan." We saw *The Phantom From Outer Space*, which was a terrifying movie, with very scary and eerie music, about an invisible alien from another world, who terrorized a community, murdering people. I was very scared after seeing that movie. When we stopped on our trip to stay the night at a motel in the countryside on the New York-Vermont line, I became aware for the first time in my life of the tremendous number of stars in the sky above that motel. And I thought of the huge probability that, at any second, an alien from one of those star systems was zooming towards earth. To make matters worse, just before we went into the motel, we saw several shooting stars in the dark sky. I lay awake all night worrying about the "phantom" and whether or not I would be a victim that night.

John's graduation picture, Nichols High School, 1953

In 1954, portions of the New York Thruway (I-90) opened, cutting the time to Vermont in half. Other interstate highways quickly followed, which reduced the time further. As great as it was to have a shorter trip on those four lane highways, I missed the old landmarks along the two lane state highways: the small towns, cemeteries, Burma-Shave signs, schools, churches, liquor stores, and occasional monumental trees, which had become familiar mileposts, and which I would probably never see again. Somehow, the car games and the singing were also left behind in the fields, woods, and towns, which the interstate highways bypassed.

I still remember the first time I saw the grand old mountains of New England, when we crossed the border into Vermont: the Green Mountains first in Vermont and then New Hampshire's magnificent White Mountains on the horizon beyond. They captured my heart. I had never seen mountains before. The rolling hills of western Vermont gave way in the distance to purple ridges that stretched as far as the horizon, in wave after wave, across New Hampshire. Wisps of clouds lingered just below the summits and spilled over the notches between peaks. In the valleys along the roads were endless banks of ferns, bordering forests of tremendous white pine, balsam, fir, and spruce, mixed with the hardwood trees—maple, elm, oak, chestnut, and hickory—with which I was most familiar. Interspersed among these giants were the incandescent white birches, which I had not seen before. My father rolled down the windows in the car for the first few miles after we crossed into New England so that we could all breathe the pine and balsam scent and relish the cool, clean air. On the hundreds of trips to New Hampshire since that first one, upon crossing from New York State into New England I never fail to recall the wonder of those initial childhood impressions.

When we dropped off or picked up my brother or sister in the White

Mountains, we stayed a few days to hike. In the summers of 1952, 1953, and 1954, after spending his first summer at Pinkham Notch Camp in 1951, my brother worked at Lakes of the Clouds Hut, situated on a shoulder of Mt. Washington. His good friend, Fred Turner, worked at the Carter Notch Hut during the summers of 1954 and 1955, and Ceci worked at Pinkham during the summers of 1955 and 1956. Among them, they provided plenty of opportunities for our family to visit and to hike in the Presidential Range in the 1950s and introduced me to the joy of hiking, especially above tree line.

Tuckerman Ravine is a fantastic glacial cirque on the southeast side of Mt. Washington—a gigantic bowl slashed on the flank of the highest mountain in the northeastern United States. Massive amounts of snow linger in the ravine even until late July. The Pinkham Notch Camp was several miles farther down the mountain from the bottom of Tuckerman.

To get to the Lakes of the Clouds Hut from Pinkham Notch Camp, you climb straight up the Tuckerman Ravine Trail from the camp, at an elevation of about two thousand feet, to the hut, at an elevation of about five thousand feet—a steep, roughly three-thousand-foot ascent. This was the first trail I remember climbing with my family. It was 1953, and we were hiking up to visit my brother at the hut. There is a beautiful falls, called Crystal Cascade, about one quarter mile up the trail from the Pinkham Lodge. I often visited the falls, when we stayed at Pinkham. From Crystal Cascade to the floor of the ravine is about a two-hour hike, passing the small Hermit Lake and the Tuckerman Ravine Shelter. To the ravine's floor, the trail is a series of gentle switchbacks, winding through a forest of spruce and pine. As you climbed higher and higher, the trees and bushes got smaller and smaller and the rubble of loose rocks more pronounced. Finally, you came to the toughest part of the trail—from the base of the ravine's headwall to its top. You have to scramble up a steep slope of rocky debris, on which snow persists through the early summer, sometimes forming an amazing, but dangerous, snow arch.

As you climb up the headwall or skirt it on another trail, you realize that the trees and bushes are disappearing and that you are suddenly exposed to the wind, with an incredible view of the neighboring Wildcat Ridge and Wildcat Mountain. It is almost too beautiful to bear. On that first climb there were clouds in the notch below me as we climbed, which overwhelmed me with the feeling that I was higher than I had ever been in my flying dreams, high above the tamarack tree at Lewiston, and in a place where I wanted to be.

From the top of the headwall of the ravine, we hiked up a grassy, ledge-filled slope to a trail junction, called Tuckerman Junction, marked by several, weathered signposts that pointed to the various trails leading from the junction to the summit or to other points on Mt. Washington. After leaving the headwall of the ravine, to this point and beyond we were on, or near, the top of a treeless ridge, leading to the cone of the summit. The trail up here was guarded by cairns—piles of grey stones, spotted with greenish lichens, about three feet high, marking the trail at intervals of approximately fifty feet. At the junction we turned onto another trail, called the Tuckerman Crossover, and were quickly enveloped in a cool wind and a cloud. It only lasted a few minutes, but I saw that the trail had magically disappeared in the swirling curtains of the cloud, along with my sister and my parents. For a brief moment, I felt alone and lost in a fog, high in the sky. I remember a prickly sensation on the back of my neck and a second of panic. Then, I saw a cairn, and as I moved towards it, I saw beyond it the dark outlines of the rest of the family in the cloud. Suddenly, I was in bright sunshine and the cloud was gone, trailing a dark shadow on the alpine meadows, covering the mountain's shoulder. I was still on the trail, more nervous than I had been before and much more appreciative of the work someone had performed, probably a century before, building those cairns.

The Tuckerman Crossover trail soon joins the Crawford Path. It leads to the hut. About fifteen minutes later, we came to the two, small lakes, sitting on the shoulder of the mountain, between the summit cone and its neighboring peak, Mt. Monroe, and at the foot of the latter. Fifty yards west of the larger of the two lakes lies the Lakes of the Clouds Hut. My brother welcomed us to the stone structure, with its five rooms—two bunkrooms for guests, a large dining room with eight long tables, kitchen, and crew's bunkroom—and magnificent view. I was delighted to see that the men's bunkroom had *four* levels of bunk beds and slept about forty-eight. The women's bunkroom seemed about the same size. With its large windows on three sides, the "croo" called it the "goldfish bowl."

John and Carl Hoagland ("Hoagie") at the summit of Mt. Washington, packing supplies, 1953

The crew in 1953 was comprised of Roger Smith, Al Starkey, Bob Monahan, Larry Eldredge, Carl Hoagland, John, and Lindsey Rice. They treated me wonderfully. "Starkey," "Hoagie," and Bob were my favorites. The seven-man crew, I learned, alternated packing supplies from the summit (which was accessible by supply trucks via the Mt. Washington Carriage Road) down to the hut on their backs, in one hundred twenty pound loads, cooking for the guests, cleaning and maintaining the hut, and rescuing hikers in distress. There were often close to a hundred guests for meals, so cooking was an all day affair for one of the crew. (I recall that one morning, after John returned home from his first summer of packing and cooking at Lakes of the Clouds Hut, he cooked breakfast for our family and made enough oatmeal and pancakes to last us a month!) There were about eighty-five guests for the three days we stayed. We helped set tables, wash and dry dishes, and make bunks. We sang and played cards in the evenings, as the wind howled around the hut. I took a quick swim in the larger of the lakes, which was icy cold, but bearable, and had a great time, exploring the nearby summit and ledges of Mt. Monroe. In short, it was paradise!

John had some days off, when we visited, and hiked with us up to the summit of Mt. Washington, about one and a quarter miles from the hut. He had just set a record for the time to make the round trip from the hut to the summit and back. I think it still stands, some fifty years later. On the summit were the weather observatory and a hotel, as well as an Air Force facility for testing jet engines. I remember that the wind was so strong that it almost blew me over. Besides being the highest peak in the northeastern United States. (6,288 feet above sea level), the mountain has some of the planet's most severe weather, and retains the world record for wind speed: 231 miles per hour.

When I was nine years old, I had surgery for a hernia at Children's Hospital. I was there for several days and recovered quickly, but my family was planning to visit the White Mountains, and I was distraught that I could not go, because I was forbidden to exercise for a month, following the surgery. My brother, however, volunteered to carry me on his back, wherever we went. So in the summer of 1954, sitting backwards on an empty, five-gallon gas can, that was strapped to a pack board on John's back, I was carried up the Tuckerman Ravine Trail to Lakes of the Clouds Hut and then down the Ammonoosuc Trail from the hut to the Cog Railway Base Station, and later into Lonesome Lake Hut on the Lonesome Lake Trail. On that trip I learned how scary it is to go up a trail backwards, particularly a trail with cliffs on each side, and especially when you are perched at shoulder level on someone's back, who occasionally lurches his pack board onto a boulder to rest, or purposely stumbles a bit. I remember being pleased to find out that

Lonesome Lake used to be called Tamarack Pond, probably in honor of my climbing tree at Lewiston.

On other visits in other summers, my parents and I, and sometimes Ceci and I, hiked to two smaller huts, located below tree line, which each accommodated only about twenty to thirty hikers: a second visit to Lonesome Lake Hut, next to the beautiful, isolated, mountain lake that was Lonesome Lake (Tamarack Pond), and to Zealand Falls Hut, nestled near a stunning waterfall. I remember my parents arguing with my sister about her dangerous habit of hiking alone, even to these readily accessible huts below tree line. Sure enough, on one trip with her, down the Ammonoosuc Ravine trail, on the west side of Mt. Washington, she sprained her ankle. It took us hours to hobble down to the bottom, and I learned that an accident could happen to anyone at anytime, just like it happened to Gypsy.

Even seemingly minor accidents can be very dangerous, especially on a mountain where the weather changes in a minute, dropping the temperature by fifty degrees, and where over two hundred people have died of exposure. Perhaps because of the ever-present threat of danger in the mountains, at whatever hut we visited we found a warm welcome from the crew and friendly hikers staying at the hut. I cherish the memories of White Mountain hikes with my family.

In the mid 1950s, I started attending camp for at least one week each summer. At Point Abino Day Camp, located in Canada not far from the Kennels, the 9 AM – 3 PM day camp was run by a genial man, named Weyland. My counselor was a Colgate student, named Bob Kreuger. Day campers spent many happy days on the huge, Pt. Abino estate of William Baird, whose family claimed ownership of the Peace Bridge as one of its financial interests. Bob played end on the Colgate football team. I once saw him recover a fumble to win a game against Cornell and then met him, the same afternoon, on the train from Ithaca, as my family returned to Buffalo. He was black and blue from the pounding of the game, but greeted me like a brother. Besides being a football star for Colgate, he was very good at organizing young boys into teams to play baseball, touch football, and Capture the Flag. The Baird estate had stables, a swimming pool, tennis courts, and acres of fields and woods—perfect for day camp fun.

Later, I spent one week, during each of two summers, at the YMCA Camp Weona, which was a boys' camp near Warsaw, New York, about an hour's drive from Buffalo. I have hazy memories of that first week of summer camp away from home, but recall swimming in the small lake, the tiny, log cabin in the so-called "Iroquois Village," where six of us slept on bunks with a counselor, and a huge old barn, where we did crafts and watched movies. We took turns waiting on tables at mealtimes in the large dining hall—my first of many experiences as a waiter. I remember the "bug juice" (red cool aid), softball games, volleyball games, scavenger hunts, playing Capture the Flag, and the campfires. Despite the activities, it was hard to be at camp the first summer. I didn't know anyone else. I was lonely. The second summer was much more fun, as I knew many of the returning campers.

After my second summer at Camp Weona, and just after my sister had received her driver's license, Ceci and I spent three, wonderful days together at Letchworth State Park, southeast of Buffalo, on the Genesee River. We stayed at a cabin in the park, where we had stayed several times with our parents before. I remember that we hiked for miles along the incredible gorge—the "Grand Canyon of the East," with its four hundred-foot cliffs and magnificent series of three waterfalls. I saw my first rattlesnake, not far from the middle falls. We climbed up to the railroad bridge that spans the gorge, above the upper falls, and put pennies on the track to be flattened by the freight trains that regularly crossed. I also recall visiting the log cabin home of Mary Jemison, an eighteenth century settler, who was kidnapped by Indians in a raid that killed her family, and chose to remain with her captors on land that later became part of the park. Letchworth is still one of my favorite places in New York, always evoking fond memories of that brief visit with my sister.

My next camp experience was totally different. At Camp Jobildunc in New Hampshire, which was a boys' camp run by Dartmouth College at Dartmouth's Moosilauke Ravine Lodge, the camp counselors were all Dartmouth students. Dartmouth students also served as the crew at the lodge, working for the college. I spent two weeks during each of the summers of 1956 and 1957 at Jobildunc, hiking, canoeing, and camping in the White Mountains, which had already claimed my soul on earlier visits with my family.

My brother was a crewmember at the Ravine Lodge during the summer of 1956, between his junior and senior years at Dartmouth. I remember him cooking in the kitchen for crowds of one hundred people, as he had at Lakes of the Clouds Hut in past years, and yelling at people to get out of the kitchen, while he brandished a ferocious, kitchen knife in mock rage. About half of the time, the twenty or so Jobildunc campers ate our meals at the lodge and slept in a bunkhouse, a little ways from the lodge. My bunkmate was Terry Ruggles, who became a good friend. The rest of the time we were hiking around northern New Hampshire and Maine, or camping on Mt. Moosilauke's heavily wooded slopes, amidst crystal streams, century old trails, and soft winds, which kept the mosquitoes away and blew pine fragrances through our tents.

One summer, the Jobildunc campers went camping and canoeing in Maine on the Rangeley Lakes. My arms ached from the paddling for the entire week, but otherwise I loved canoeing on those incredibly peaceful and lovely lakes. I will never forget the sight of Fred Turner, who was a camp counselor in 1957, frantically paddling a canoe towards an island in the middle of Mooselookmeguntick Lake, during a tremendous storm that blew up suddenly, and finally being swamped by waves, which sank the canoe, including my sleeping bag! Fred was a great counselor, but even he could not dry out that sleeping bag. I remember how horrible sleeping in a wet sleeping bag was.

On another trip, the camp visited the Dartmouth College Grant in northeastern New Hampshire, which is a wilderness area near the Diamond Peaks. I panned for gold in the Swift Diamond River and found a few flakes. We stayed in several of Dartmouth College's shelters on the Grant, visited timbering operations, and ate with rough lumberjacks at a logging camp kitchen, with magnificent food in tremendous quantities. The apple and cherry pies were especially incredible!

At the College Grant we were taught how to build a firebreak in the path of a forest fire. We labored for a week with picks, scythes, axes, and shovels to clear an area about three hundred yards by thirty yards to protect a cabin from the likely route of a fire. The work was backbreaking and hot. I imagined how horrible it must be to construct a firebreak with an actual fire bearing down on you.

When we stayed near the Moosilauke Ravine Lodge, in the evenings after dinner, when the temperature dropped, there was a fire in the lodge's huge fireplace. Just after dark, the campers gathered before the hearth in comfortable chairs and listened to the story of old Doc Benton. Doc Benton was a vampire-like village doctor from the early nineteenth century, who lived in the town of Benton on the north side of the mountain, had discovered the secret of everlasting life, while studying in Germany, and still roamed the Mt. Moosilauke area, preying on animals and people alike. The tale lasted over an hour and was punctuated throughout, at appropriate moments, by sound effects from the crew, such as muffled moans, clanking chains, and horrific screams, calculated to scare the pants off any listeners. I was terrified, but loved that story, which I probably heard at least a dozen times. (Years later, before the same, massive, stone fireplace at the lodge, I had the great satisfaction of watching my nephew, Lawrence, levitate about four feet in the air, when the first, muffled scream in the course of the story of Doc Benton pierced the calm of a Moosilauke Ravine Lodge evening.)

The heads of the camp, during my two summers there, were Dartmouth outdoorsmen: Brad Leonard, the first summer, and then Dick Sanders. With the Dartmouth students who ran the camp, they taught us how to chop wood, build fires without matches, construct shelters in the woods, cook simple meals, and otherwise survive on our own. We learned first aid and orienteering with a compass and contour maps. Our counselors taught us that hiking above tree line in a storm is extremely dangerous. "Lightning, wind, and hypothermia are the enemies," they drilled into our heads. "Get down into the woods for cover during storms." Before the end of the camp, each of us had to stay by ourselves in the woods and survive for two days, with nothing more than a sleeping bag, ax, two sandwiches, and a candy bar. I learned a lot.

The Dartmouth counselors made Mt. Moosilauke come alive for us. Through them, we came to know its trails intimately: the Beaver Brook Trail, Benton Trail, Gorge Brook Trail, Ridge Trail, Asquamchumauke Trail, and the Carriage Road. We learned to track Mt. Moosilauke's animals and recognize its birds. And we came to understand its moods—sultry on a hot, clear, summer day; exuberant on a clear, cold night with thousands of stars above; mysterious in the morning with clouds cloaking the summit and high shoulders; and chillingly dangerous below storm clouds and rising wind. On the windswept summit of the mountain there is now an inscription in memory of Dick Sanders, which any devout outdoorsman would covet: "The still North remembers him; the hill winds know his name; and the granite of New Hampshire keeps a record of his fame." All of those Dartmouth student counselors deserve a like epitaph.

Ceci and Patsy Runk at their graduation from the Buffalo Seminary, 1956

I was blessed to have childhood summers geographically etched by my Buffalo neighborhood, Lewiston, Holloway Bay, and New Hampshire, and spiritually nourished by my parents, brother, sister, relatives, and Buffalo friends. There is an inscription in my windswept memory of June as a season of graduations: my brother's graduation from Nichols High School in 1953, when he was honored as the class president, and my sister's graduation from the Buffalo Seminary in 1956, when she looked gorgeous in a beautiful white dress, and afterwards stood in our garden with her two best friends, Pat Zimdahl and Patsy Runk, also dressed in white, amidst mounds of golf ball size hailstones that had fallen from the heavens in her honor. July is inscribed as Independence Day and family picnics; August is camp month. Early September is football and school.

As each summer ended, I regretted that another season of flowering, whirling life was drifting away with the wind. My childhood summers were far too short. They almost didn't provide enough time to grow up. Lake Erie's ever-present breezes open summer in June by blowing the dandelion fluff, from the west side parks' carpets of dandelions, into inches-deep, gossamer heaps of white, along the curbs of adjacent avenues. Several days later, it seemed, in late September the wind rustles the green from the trees and kindles autumn's burning leaves on the streets of Buffalo.

Chapter Four—
Childhood Autumns 1945–1959

Mrs. Kelman's second grade class at Public School No. 56, 1952–53

On Labor Day weekend, my mother took me to the barber for a haircut. Of course, we went regularly throughout the year, also, but I remember the early September trip to Charlie's Barber Shop on Bryant Street, near Elmwood Avenue, as a part of the ritual preparations for the start of school. The barbershop had a red, white, and blue barber's pole outside the main entrance. Charlie had a red face and white hair, when I first went to his barbershop. He said the blue was for his mood sometimes. His nephew, Nicky Locisero, lived on Ardmore Street in the house behind ours. There were three, imposing, barber chairs in the shop. Charlie's chair was the closest to the large, front window, from which you could see the church across the street. For the first five years or so at Charlie's, I sat in a booster seat, craning my head often to keep an eye on the closet door in the back of the shop, where Charlie kept a psychotic monkey.

Charlie told all his young customers about that monkey. If you behaved yourself during your haircut, he promised to show you his monkey. If, on the other hand, you fidgeted, cried, or otherwise behaved badly, the monkey might get angry and come busting out of that closet. I was always pretty well behaved, but that monkey worried me. I knew another monkey, who lived at the Buffalo zoo—a chimpanzee named Eddie, who used to bare his teeth and spit at visitors. Eddie was pretty big and mean looking, although he had a reputation for having been a favorite of many visitors. I envisioned Charlie's monkey as twice as big as Eddie and probably twice as mean looking. I didn't want to meet Charlie's monkey, but I was curious.

Every time that my good behavior merited a peek at the monkey, Charlie checked first to see if the monkey was awake. (He hated to be awakened and could be especially vicious if he was in a bad mood.) Charlie opened the closet door a crack and peered inside, and then quickly closed the door, reporting that the monkey was asleep and should not be disturbed. After several years, I began to doubt that there was a monkey in that closet.

At the height of my disbelief, however, once when Charlie cracked open the door, there was a tremendous commotion in that closet, and something swung out in a flash. I remember that it was brown and quick, but I didn't get a good look at it, as I high-tailed it for the front door. When I peered back into the shop through the front window, it appeared as though Charlie was pushing something back into the closet. Later, Charlie said that the monkey that day was even more angry than usual at being disturbed. I never asked to see the monkey again.

My father and brother went to Charlie's Barber Shop, too. After Charlie died, a barber named Tom—who had always worked at the middle chair— took over the shop and moved up to Charlie's chair. He kept the name of the shop the same, even though Charlie was gone. Tom was a thin, Italian man with a pencil mustache and curly, black hair. He looked rather severe, and had been very quiet when Charlie was alive, but, with Charlie gone, Tom became very friendly and talkative. We talked a lot about people we both knew, problems at school, and life in Buffalo, in general. Austin Fox—a revered English teacher at Nichols High School—was another of Tom's customers. I often saw him at the barbershop. Tom never failed to ask about my father and my brother. The monkey died with Charlie.

Tom loved opera. If I went to have my hair cut on Saturday afternoon, Tom and I would listen, without talking, to the Texaco opera broadcast on his old radio. Tom taught me about opera. His favorite was Puccini's *Madame Butterfly*, which became my favorite. Tom always finished a haircut by giving your head a vigorous massage with his finger tips, "to keep baldness away." I went to have my hair cut by Tom for over twenty years, listened to portions of dozens of operas in his shop, and was devastated, when Tom finally hung up his scissors. Without those head massages, I started to become bald in my late twenties.

Septembers started with a haircut and the beginning of school after Labor Day and ended with the elms beginning to shed their golden leaves. When the winds off Lake Erie began to have an autumn bite, the first leaves would float down like feathers onto the roofs, gutters, and lawns of Buffalo's west side. There was a sugar maple in a neighboring backyard, across the back fence. It was the first tree to burst into stunning, burning reds and oranges each year, and the first to lose its leaves. It amazed me that such a display of incredible beauty could so quickly fade away. The rows of elms in my childhood neighborhood took about a month to assume their winter, leafless silhouettes. Leaves piled up everywhere. We raked them to the edge of the curbs on West Delavan Avenue, and piled them high into inviting mounds. Every house had several huge mountains of leaves. When we had exhausted our urge to run and flop onto the piles, my father raked them into the street and burned them there.

Burning leaves have a delicious smell that permeated the west side in late September. The blue-gray smoke drifted high into the branches of the elms, edged into our homes, and obscured the autumn skies. It was a smoke of nostalgia, as summer memories drifted to the heavens and gave way to the World Series, football season, and the stress of school.

Charlie—the barber—reassured me, when I was four years old, that I would like school. He was right. I remember registering for kindergarten in 1949 with my mother, my childhood friend, April Lee Haydon, and April's mother and grandmother at Public School No. 56. We entered the old, red brick, school building at 716 West Delavan Avenue, through the front door in the middle of the school on the first floor. P.S. No. 56 was on the north side of West Delavan Avenue, facing south and occupying almost half a block, between Brantford Road and Chapin Parkway. Boys entered the school through the entrance on the west side of the building. The girls came in through the east entrance. The side entrances on the west and east faced onto narrow, paved driveways, which connected the large, paved playground at the rear of the school to West Delavan Avenue. There was a flagpole to the left of the walk, as you came up the sidewalk to the main entrance in front. A four-foot high hedge edged the center sidewalk, leading to this entrance, on both sides, and separated the front lawn of the school from the sidewalk on West Delavan Avenue and from the driveways at each end. Nobody went on that lawn, except to pick up trash or to put up the flag.

We waited in a long line in the hallway of the first floor. The line moved quickly. P.S. No. 56 was run efficiently and compassionately. As soon as we registered, we entered the Principal's Office to meet her. The principal was a distinguished, German lady named Elizabeth Fritz Strauss, whom I came to love. Her assistant was Mrs. Young, also a kind and competent person. My kindergarten teachers were Miss Mulligan and Miss Kick. Miss Mulligan was elderly, wore glasses, and shuffled when she walked. Miss Kick was young, attractive, and a bit impatient.

In kindergarten I met many of the children who would be my classmates for the next ten years: Mike Weinberg, Richard Bassett, Ellen Warner, Tina Haines, Linda Smith, Carol Magavero, Joann Cippola, Ann Jones, Joel Lippes, and dozens of others. Several of them—Bob Rosenthal, Cal Brainard, John Mooney and Bob Jacobs—would be classmates of mine at Nichols High School, as well. That first year of elementary school I met the first girl, besides Gigi Gucker, whom I ever wanted to marry before I was five: Joanne Cippola, who lived on Potomac Avenue, two houses towards Elmwood Avenue from Larry Marshall's house. I was invited to Joann's birthday party, when she turned five. Her family lived in the top floor of a duplex, which was the usual type of home in our west side neighborhood. She was a dark-haired, Italian bombshell, with lovely big eyes and long eyelashes. And her mother made fantastic baked apples! Her house was the center of my attention for a long time thereafter. Many years later my godmother, Ruth Culliton, moved across the street from the Cipollas, and I still felt my eyes drawn to Joann's home, whenever I visited Ruth.

The kindergarten room was in the northeast corner of the school, on the first floor. When the heat was on, the radiators in the classrooms got pretty hot and banged and rattled, as the steam filled the pipes. Someone got burned, it seemed, almost every day. I liked the snack time in kindergarten. We had cool aid or milk and small cookies in the mid morning and again around 2:15 PM.

School began at 9:00 AM and ended at 3:00 PM, with a lunch break from noon until 1:00. My mother, or the Haydons, picked me up at school promptly at noon, and we walked the seven blocks home—about one half mile—where I usually had a sandwich and milk for lunch. I liked peanut butter and jelly, tuna fish, or ground up pickle-ham sandwiches best. I used to help my mother make the delicious mix of ground pickles and ham by helping her cut the ham and pickles into small pieces and then feed them into the hand grinder, which went round and round, as I turned the handle.

After lunch we walked back to school at 12:45, where the dreaded naptime awaited, from 2:30 until 3:00. During naptime, each child was supposed to lie down on a small mat or rug that was brought from home at the beginning of the year. No one ever really slept. It was a time when nerves seemed to be most frayed, as all of us thought about getting home and watched the slow, big hand of the clock on the wall, as it agonizingly inched its way up towards twelve.

At the end of my first week of kindergarten, my family went to Toronto, Canada, by boat to visit the Toronto Fair. I think we went on a Saturday. I remember embarking from the old dock at Queenston, Ontario, on the *SS Cayuga,* sailing down the Niagara River past Red Bank Farm and my grandparents' property, and steaming by Fort Niagara. This was my first trip on a big ship and the first time that I saw the Morgan Farm and Hobbie house from the middle of the Niagara River. It was lots of fun. When we got out onto Lake Ontario, the trip became even more interesting, as there were high waves and lots of people vomiting over the rail from seasickness.

We made it safely to Toronto, and the Toronto Fair was my first experience with amusement rides, towers, and bustling people, whose eyes shone with fairground excitement. I remember, especially, the enormous Ferris wheel, which was much taller than the one at Crystal Beach. And there was also a fine, miniature train ride around all the various exhibits. The trip back in the evening was calm and beautiful. We saw a gorgeous sunset over Lake Ontario en route, and arrived at Queenston well after dark. The week following our trip to Toronto, another steamship—the *SS Noronic*—caught fire and burned in Toronto's harbor. Over one hundred twenty people died. My father and mother said over and over again how lucky we were that nothing so dangerous happened on our trip.

On Dava Katz's fifth birthday, her mother brought cupcakes and little paper cups of ice cream for a birthday party at school. Besides being a cheerful, pretty girl and a good friend, Dava had a reputation for toughness, based on her having survived a fall—without a scratch—from the attic window of her house on Brantford Avenue, when she was three years old. Dava's family lived just up the street from David Shire, who was my sister's age, and whose father,

Irving, was an exceptional musician and friend of our family's. David later became a well-known, Grammy-winning composer. Dava's mother's cupcakes were fantastic—the first and best I ever ate at school. (When I was recognized by Dava's parents on a plane over California, almost twenty years later, I told Mrs. Katz that I still remembered those delicious cupcakes.) Dava's party at school was the first of dozens I enjoyed.

In kindergarten I remember coloring a lot with crayons. Each child brought a box of crayons to school on the first day, along with a nap rug. Crayons came in different size boxes of twelve, twenty-four, or thirty-six. I soon learned that the size of your crayon box marked your status. My kindergarten year I had a small box of twelve crayons and felt ashamed, until for Christmas I got a box of twenty-four, as a present. Later, I realized that, of the twenty-four crayons, you only used the basic, eight colors. Those colors were worn to nubs by the end of the year, while the other colors—various shades of red, green, blue, purple, and gray—stayed pointed and unused in the box. They were pretty to look at, but were useless and discarded at the end of the year, without being used (you couldn't have any old crayons in your new box each year). I felt sorry for those unused crayons. Nevertheless, I wasn't really satisfied until I had a new box of thirty-six crayons at the beginning of school each year. I still try to buy new crayons every year.

My second year of elementary school, I attended something called "pre-primer" with most of the children from my kindergarten class. A couple of children went directly to first grade, but we languished for another year with Miss Angel, crayons, and nap rugs. I liked her, but I didn't like the way she took us in groups to the *girls'* bathroom, which was the closest to our classroom, directly across the hall from the kindergarten room. You were required to go to the bathroom in these groups, even if you said that you didn't need to go. And I didn't like having all the kids in line behind you—boys and girls—as you did your business. After pre-primer, I learned to plan my bathroom needs, so that I could use the toilet at home at lunch or after school. I never went to the bathroom again at P.S. No. 56 after that year. I think my teachers thought my bladder was the size of a basketball.

Another place I avoided at school was the nurse's office, located next door to Miss Angel's pre-primer classroom. The school nurse was a very large, red-faced woman with a loud voice. Her name was Miss Brick. The only time I went to her, because I wasn't feeling well, she took my temperature rectally. That was it. I never went back, no matter how sick I was.

That second year of school was the year I saw "The Lone Ranger" on television for the first time, at Mike Weinberg's house, in 1950. It was every bit as good as the hundreds of programs I had listened to on the radio for the past three or more years. I was especially interested to see the "faithful Indian companion" Tonto. Often, it was Tonto, who tracked the criminal or rescued the Lone Ranger, and I liked the name of Tonto's horse: Scout. Tonto often said, "Giddy-up Scout." Each program ended, after a heroic deed by Tonto and the Lone Ranger, with people wondering whom the masked man on the white horse was. "Who was that masked man? He rides a white stallion named Silver and has silver bullets! Silver bullets? He must be the Long Ranger!" (In the distance, over the sound of hooves and a crescendo of the *William Tell Overture*) "Hi-yo Silver, away!"

In first grade our classroom was still on the first floor, but in the northwest corner of the building. My teacher was a very kind woman, who loved children. You could tell. Mrs. Kelman read to us, drilled us in arithmetic, and taught us how to read. Most importantly, for the World Series between the Yankees and the Giants, she let any of us, who wanted to, listen to the afternoon games. The Yankees won in six games, but thanks to Mrs. Kelman, I witnessed, via the radio, the start of Willie Mays' and Mickey Mantel's World Series careers, and Joe DiMaggio's last game. I can never thank her enough. I liked first grade a lot.

I was very apprehensive, when I heard that my second grade teacher was someone new to the school. No one knew much about her, but she seemed pleasant enough, and we liked her. Then, one day she was gone, and was replaced by Mrs. Kelman, to the great joy of those of us who had been taught by her in first grade and loved her. Mrs. Kelman's daughter was a beginning teacher and helped her mother with our class, as she practiced her teaching. I don't recall her name—it may have been Beth—but I remember that Mrs. Kelman's daughter was a good teacher, just like her mother. Mrs. Kelman was very proud of her.

When the World Series came around in October, 1952, Mrs. Kelman arranged for a television to be brought into the room—a large, black and white conduit to the thrills of the battle between my beloved Brooklyn Dodgers and the hated New York Yankees, who won the series four games to three. My friends and I were sure that no better teacher and no better woman existed in the entire world than Mrs. Kelman. She was the first of many, excellent teachers whom I experienced at P.S. No. 56, but she was the only one who shared my love of baseball.

In Mrs. Kelman's second grade class in 1952, we started to have air raid drills, in addition to the fire drills that we had undergone periodically, since kindergarten. For fire drills, which were signaled by a continuous ringing of the school bell system, we formed into lines with a partner and followed our teacher, two-by-two, down the hallway, down the east steps, out the east doors of the school, and down the east driveway to the main sidewalk in front of the school. There we waited, until several short bursts of ringing told us that it was all right to reenter the building. We never had a real fire situation in the ten years I was in elementary school.

There were two kinds of air raid drills. For the first and scariest kind, the school bell rang in short bursts of five rings, for a total of fifteen, short rings. It seemed as though the ringing went on forever. That was the signal for all of us to get under our desks, on our hands and knees and face down, with our hands and arms protecting our heads. The shades in the classroom were pulled down, the lights were turned off, and the row of children, sitting closest to the windows, quickly moved into, and knelt in, the aisle between the wall and the row of desks farthest from the windows. We waited in hushed silence for about ten minutes or so, expecting bombs to burst onto the school at any moment from North Korean planes. This plan was supposed to be the best protection against a surprise, aerial attack on Buffalo, with no time to seek better shelter.

I preferred the second kind of air raid drill, which lasted a lot longer and gave us a chance to move around the school and see the other classes in close proximity. In the second type of air raid drill, the bells rang in bursts of about fifteen seconds each. We formed into our two-by-two lines and quickly walked down the east steps to the long hallway in the basement of the building. In the basement, we sat on the floor, all jammed together, and quietly waited for the attack.

The school basement was interesting during those drills in that, depending on where you were sitting on the floor, the basement smelled quite different. The overall, basement smell was mildly mildewy, and the air was a bit dank. At the east end of the long hallway, which ran the length of the basement, where we sat in second grade, there was also a strong smell of sawdust and glue, since the industrial arts room was nearby. As you moved towards the center of the building, that smell gave way to the smell of sweaty clothes and sneakers in the locker room near the gymnasium, which was located in the basement's east wing, under half of the auditorium. Moving further down the hallway into the basement's west wing, the smell was first of chlorine, from the room where the pool was located, next to the gym, and then of furnace fuel, as you passed the boiler room. All of these interestingly smelly places were off limits to second graders. Not until fourth grade did we get to use the gym, pool, and industrial arts room. In the meantime, only during air raids did we have the chance to sniff the basement air. I looked forward to going into the basement. To my knowledge, between 1949 and 1959 there were neither sneak attacks nor attacks with prior notice by the North Koreans, Indians, or anyone else, but we faithfully practiced, just in case.

Besides air raid drills, I also liked what we called "assembly," in which all the school's classes—except for the kindergarten—participated. P.S. No.

56 had a large auditorium, with a fine stage. There were heavy, dark green curtains on the stage, with a flag of the United States standing on the right of the stage (on the left as you faced the stage) and the New York State flag standing on the left. There were about twenty rows of seats with twenty-two seats in a row. A wide, middle aisle divided the auditorium into two halves. The pre-primer, first, second, and third grades sat in the front half of the auditorium, with the lower grades in front of the higher grades.

After forming rows of students by class in the outside hallway, classes filed into the auditorium with great precision and order. Mrs. Strauss played stately marches on the piano in the front of the auditorium, or the school orchestra played, as the classes filed in. Our principal was an excellent piano player and clearly loved to play. Her father had composed the various marches she played.

During assembly programs, each classroom teacher occupied a middle aisle seat, next to her class. The boys' gym teacher (Mr. Brown), swimming teacher (Mr. Burke), and industrial arts teacher (Mr. Werick) usually sat together in the last row. There were in all about thirty, classroom teachers. All the classroom teachers were women, until in the mid 1950s, Elmer Schamber—a fantastic seventh grade teacher—joined the teaching staff.

The auditorium seats were wooden and dark-stained. Each seat moved up, when not in use, and down, when needed as a seat for a student. In either direction the moving seat squeaked, so that, as the four hundred forty seats were occupied, the squeaking created a terrible din. Miss Erna Soell, a strict but much-loved fourth grade teacher, was in charge of the processions into and out of the auditorium. She stalked the aisles, making sure that each class moved swiftly and silently—except for the squeaking of the seats—into place. I marveled at the efficiency of the process of filling the seats in that auditorium. It was like a huge, squeaky army, occupying a field of battle with practiced precision. No one dared to attract attention from the field commander, Miss Soell.

Assemblies began with two students carrying in the U.S. flag and the New York State flag, climbing the steps to the stage, and placing the flags in their holders on the edge of the stage. Then we recited the pledge of allegiance to the flag, followed by the singing of "The Star-Spangled Banner." As an eighth grader, I led the school in both, standing on the stage and feeling very important. In 1954, after five years of reciting one version of the pledge of allegiance, someone had the bright idea of changing it to include the words "under God." This caused all kinds of confusion in reciting the pledge, as some kids forgot to insert the new words, or inserted them in the wrong place.

I remember complaining about the addition of the new words at the dinner table. My father agreed that it was unnecessary, and blamed the

Catholic Church for the change. He didn't often blame anyone for anything. When he did fix blame, he usually pinned it on Notre Dame, which he disliked intensely. (I think the football rivalry between Dad's alma mater—Cornell University—and Notre Dame, during his student days in the 1920s, when each university had national championship football teams (although they never played each other), had permanently fixed an anti-Notre Dame passion that occasionally prompted an uncharacteristic, anti-Catholic remark.) As it turned out, the Knights of Columbus *were* partially responsible, I learned years later.

Except for Notre Dame, my grandmother Schultz at times, and President Roosevelt, my father was an extremely tolerant, understanding, and congenial person, although he could get very angry, especially when he was driving. I don't think that he ever met a person whom he didn't like or want to talk with. And he didn't have a prejudiced bone in his body. For years he was the president of the Equality Club in Buffalo, which my grandfather Hobbie had helped to found in the early part of the twentieth century. It was a men's club, comprised of men of all nationalities, color, and religion, which met for lunch once a month at the downtown YMCA. Sometimes, they had a big dinner or other outing, to which all their family members were invited. I remember going to several picnics, attending an African-American church on several occasions, and being entertained by a wonderful magician at a couple of Equality Club parties. Members of the Equality Club, whom I remember, include Mark Turner (who was Fred Turner's father, an attorney, my godfather, and a good friend of my father's, as I have mentioned before); Frederic Marshall, a well known local photographer (father of my early elementary school classmate and friend, Larry); Reverend Foster, a black, Baptist minister and friend of my father's; Dr. Robert Montgomery, our family dentist; and Dr. Joseph Manch, Superintendent of the Buffalo Public Schools.

I also recall that Dad was a member of a bowling league for several years, which, like the Equality Club, included a highly diverse group of men: African-Americans, Polish, Italian, Jewish, and Catholics, as well as Protestants. The league bowled at the Lafayette Presbyterian Church lanes on the corner of Elmwood Avenue and Lafayette Avenue, every Wednesday night. Dad once came close to bowling a perfect game, when I was about five years old.

Dad's acceptance of people of other faiths and color extended to the gay community. I never heard him say a bad thing about gay men or women. When I was very young, in the late 1950s, the choir director, who was also the organist, at St. John's Church was gay. At some point his sexual orientation became known to the parishioners. As a result, at the next meeting of the St. John's vestry, a motion was advanced to fire the individual. My father, who was a member of the vestry, spoke long and eloquently in defense of the right of the man to be gay, without retaliation or effect on his position. The man was ultimately fired over Dad's strong objection, but forty years afterwards, at Dad's funeral service in 1992, I was first told of this by the church's organist, who stated that he was still grateful for Dad's "legendary," early defense of gay rights.

At P.S. No. 56 there was a wide variety of assembly programs. Every class had an annual play. I played major roles in some of the early plays, which my class put on. Most of these plays were insufferable, but one musical about a tailor was pretty good. It starred Mary Jean Digati, Carol Magavero, and Richard Bassett, as I recall. I was the stage manager. My major contribution was catching a ball thrown by the hero, played by Richard, on stage into the wings. Throwing a ball so far that it never hit the ground was a demonstration in the script of the hero's strength, so it was important that the ball be caught without a sound. Richard Bassett and I practiced that for hours (he was an erratic thrower), and the scene came off without a problem.

At other assemblies there were speech contests. My mother and father often laughed at the dinner table in the evening, when I launched into a lengthy description of the day's activities, and talked and talked. They both said I should pursue a career that involved interminable talking and arguing, such as law. My first formal speaking happened in fifth grade. I recall having to memorize a *Readers' Digest* article entitled "Our Lives, Our Fortunes, and Our Sacred Honor" (about the *Declaration of Independence*) one year and the *Gettysburg Address* another year. If you were a finalist in your grade, you had to recite your speech in front of the entire school at the annual speech contest assembly. That was an extremely stressful event for the speakers and an equally distressing event for the audience, which was bored almost to tears. I recall entering in the fifth and six grades, and winning the boys' competition. Our principal, Mrs. Strauss, stalked around the back of the auditorium, cupping her hand to her ear to signal the speaker that she couldn't hear and that the speaker should raise the volume. If you didn't speak loudly enough or slowly enough, Mrs. Strauss would interrupt you and make you say it again. I learned to watch her from the stage, over the lights, and to keep my speaking slow and loud, as she coached from the rear of the auditorium. (Decades later, when I argued before panels of judges in various appellate courtrooms, I sensed that Mrs. Strauss was there with her hand signals.)

The best assemblies were the movies, which were the first Wednesday of every month. I recall seeing *The Birth of a Nation*, *Black Beauty*, several Laurel and Hardy movies, Ma and Pa Kettle movies, cartoons such as *Bugs Bunny*, Disney's *Song of the South* and *Fantasia*, and several Audubon or nature movies, among many others. I loved *Fantasia*.

The second best assemblies were the "sing-alongs." The words of songs were flashed on the big screen on the stage, while either Mrs. Strauss or Mrs. Mitchell (my fifth grade teacher, who played the piano almost as well as Mrs. Strauss) played the piano. Another teacher used a light pointer to help us keep up with the words on the screen. Most of the songs were patriotic: "It's A Grand Old Flag," "America the Beautiful," "My Country Tis of Thee," and "The Battle Hymn of the Republic" were favorites. We also sang a lot of Stephen Foster's songs, such as "Oh Susanna," "De Camptown Races," "Jeannie with the Light Brown Hair," and "Old Folks at Home." Others I recall were "She'll Be Comin' Round the Mountain," "Red River Valley," "I've Been Workin' on de Railroad," and "The Erie Canal." I really enjoyed singing in a big group like that!

In second grade, I went to the dentist for the first time. My father's cousin, Dr. Bill Foster, was an extremely old dentist in North Tonawanda, with very ancient, dental equipment. His elderly wife, Mary, was his dental hygienist, although she was very near-sighted. Cousin Bill did not believe in Novocain or gas, apparently. His dental drills were belt driven and pretty slow. The first cavities that I had filled were excruciatingly painful. I gripped the arms of the dental chair, as though my life depended on it, as soon as the nasty whine of the drill started. Happily, he retired after I had been going to him for about a year. We switched to another cousin, Dr. Robert Montgomery, in Buffalo, who had modern equipment, loaded you up with Novocain before he even checked your teeth, and had a pretty, dental assistant, named Ginger. Dr. Bob was a great dentist, and his fillings have lasted fifty years, to the great disappointment of my current dentist.

My third grade teacher was Mrs. Ann Henry, who was a short, pretty woman. She was a new teacher at P.S. No. 56 and often consulted with the other third grade teacher, Miss Tillotson, who had reddish hair, tied up in a bun, wire rim glasses, and a very delicate way of moving around the classroom, as though she were afraid of breaking something. The third grade classrooms were on the second floor, with the big kids—the fourth and fifth graders. I enjoyed third grade, because we left the "Dick, Jane, and Spot" thrillers behind and started to read more advanced books. Besides reading, we studied spelling, arithmetic, writing (which was really printing), music, and drawing. Mrs. Henry, however, did not particularly like baseball. In the fall of 1953, I gazed wistfully at Mrs. Kelman's room, whenever I walked by it.

As third grade started, my brother was starting his freshman year at Dartmouth. The house seemed lonely without him, and I missed the Nichols High School sports, activities, and news that he had brought home to our family. Ceci was starting her second year at the Buffalo Seminary. I recall her discussions at the dinner table about dates, the high school intramural teams at "Sem" called the Yellow Jackets and the Hornets and why there was no "Wasps" team (they were all WASP teams), and the new headmaster, who had gigantic shoes to fill, in following the fifty-year tenure of Miss Gertrude Angell. Her escapades with her girl friends, Pat Zimdahl, Patsy Runk (or "Ratsy Punk" as I affectionately called her), and Pat Curtis, filled the news void created by John's departure to New Hampshire.

In third grade, we started to have a weekly, art class with Miss Diadata and a weekly, music class with Miss Millward, both of whom I appreciated enormously for the totally new information their classes provided, for their enthusiasm, and for the sheer fun of art and musical creations. Frankly, after four years of elementary school through second grade, I was getting tired of school, slightly bored, and ready to move on with life. Happily, I didn't know at the time that I would attend school for another twenty years. Moving to the second floor and having some different kinds of classes was the boost I needed.

We also started to take field trips in third grade—wonderful, eye-opening field trips, which highlighted the next six years! We visited the Buffalo Museum of Science, Erie County Historical Museum on Delaware Park Lake, Niagara Falls, Buffalo Zoo, General Mills' cereal plant, Hershey's chocolate factory, and Albright Knox Art Gallery. We attended children's concerts with the Buffalo Philharmonic at Kleinhans Music Hall (where I got to show off my violin teacher, Harry Taub) and visited Old Fort Erie, across the river in Canada. Each field trip was exquisite in a different way. I deeply appreciated them all.

Perhaps the most surprising aspect of any of these trips was the horrible smell in the chocolate factory, where I expected to have my olfactory senses dazzled by exposure to so much of the food I loved. Instead, the aroma of cooking chocolate turned out to be an odor so bad that I swore off eating chocolate for a full two days afterwards.

A close second in the surprise category during those field trips was the huge, smelly wad of spit from Eddie, the chimp at the zoo, which traveled about fifty feet through the air before landing on my jacket. I didn't blame Eddie. Although I loved the zoo, I would be spitting at people too, if I had to live in the monkey house, which smelled almost as bad as the chocolate factory.

One day in third grade we were told—along with our parents—that we had the opportunity to be pioneers in a very important medical test. A doctor by the name of Salk had developed a vaccine for polio. It had to be tested on children. So one day my classmates and I, and the first and second graders, stood in long lines to enter the auditorium, class by class. We sat nervously in the squeaky seats, and row by row were called up to the front of the auditorium, where a nurse gave us a shot. Some of us, we were told, were being given the real vaccine. Others were being given a "placebo," which was not the real thing, but hurt just as much going in. I recall that we were called back weeks later and given a booster shot. No one was told who had received what. There was a lot of speculation as to which of us had the real thing and which did not. We were given little pins for bravery, and our teachers called us "polio pioneers." I never did find out what I got. No one got polio.

The classrooms at P.S. No. 56 were pretty uniform in size and appearance, no matter what the grade. All had windows along the left side of the classroom, above the clanking radiators. In the front and on the right wall were blackboards, extending the entire width of the walls. The classroom monitors, who rotated among all the students and were assigned each week, were responsible for such tasks as wiping the blackboards clean at the end of each school day. On the front wall there was usually a round clock above the blackboards—the single, most carefully observed thing in the entire classroom. In one of the front corners of the classroom there was an American flag. Almost all the classrooms had desks, with attached chairs, in five rows of seven desks each.

Student art works or other projects were taped to the unused blackboards or tacked to the walls, above the blackboards. Some teachers had short poems or pithy sayings on the walls. Miss Soell, my fourth grade teacher, had one above the blackboard, in her perfect script, which read: "Good, better, best; never let it rest. 'Till your good is better and your better is best!" Mrs. Morganstern, the other fourth grade teacher, had a lot of pictures of different kinds of dogs and puppies on her walls. Miss Plumley, our wonderful upper grade art teacher, had prints of paintings of famous artists, such as Monet and Renoir, on her classroom walls, as well as every kind of artwork, in every art medium, possible.

Above the blackboards in the music room, Miss Millward had prints depicting every instrument in the orchestra. She would drill us on these pictures of instruments every week, rearranging the order of the prints from time to time to make sure that no one could just memorize the order. I particularly was interested in the English horn, since my maternal grandparents were English. It looked like a clarinet with a black bulb at the end. I never could distinguish its sound from a clarinet or oboe.

In my third grade year my friends and I started to have paper wad fights. For ammunition, you folded a one-inch square piece of paper repeatedly, until you created a small projectile, which, when bent into a V shape, could be launched with surprising accuracy and velocity by a rubber band, held between your thumb and first finger. Mrs. Henry put a stop to these immediately at school, so we took our fights to the Hobbie attic on the third floor of our house at 453 West Delavan Avenue.

My grandfather Schultz had renovated our attic, when I was about five years old, in 1950. I remember watching him work. He was an excellent carpenter, electrician, and tiler. I think he had worked in construction for many years, when he was a very young immigrant, in the early years of the twentieth century, before he became a customs officer. I recall that he tiled the bathrooms, kitchen, and part of the basement at his house at 715 Richmond Avenue, as well as the laundry room in our basement. Grandpa Schultz put special tiles, depicting deer and flowers, among the wall tiles. He was a bit gruff, and called me "boy," instead of using my name, which was what they did in Germany, he told me.

He also told me how he had been the first of his family to come to America, when he was just a boy himself. He came alone. He had brought his brother and sisters over from Germany, one by one, until they were all settled in Western New York. We used to visit his brother's family—Uncle Fred and Aunt Emily Schultz—at their farm near Ransomville, New York, and his sister, Aunt Emma, in Tonawanda. When my Grandmother Bray was living on the second floor at 208 Bird Avenue, during the First World War, she took in a boarder to help make ends meet. Several years later the boarder—Charles Schultz—married her on June 5, 1919.

I helped him as much as a five-year-old boy could with the attic project, not knowing that the bright and clean room he created out of a dusty and dark third floor would become one of my favorite childhood rooms at 453. The attic consisted of a large room, running east to west the length of the house—about thirty-five feet long and about sixteen feet wide—with a ceiling that was seven feet high in the middle third of the room, but sloped off into eaves on each side—eaves that were accessible only by low doors in the middle of each wall. My grandfather had framed in the eaves, plastered the ceiling and walls, installed three ceiling lights, and painted the room a light blue. There was a large window at each end of this room, which let in light and opened in the summer to cool off the attic.

Those two attic windows were major problems, twice a year. In the spring, we had to take off the storm windows on all of the house's windows and carry them to the basement for storage, replacing them with screens. In the fall, about the time school started, the process was reversed. The storm windows and screens for the attic windows had to be raised and lowered from each window by rope, which was a Herculean task, especially from the third floor, attic windows.

In the northwest corner of the attic, next to where the chimney came up from the living room fireplace, there was an old gas stove, which provided sufficient heat in the fall, winter, and spring to permit use of the attic, even during colder weather. I was not allowed to light the stove by myself, until I was about ten. I remember that to light it you first made sure that at least one window was cracked open and that the gas was completely off; then, you lit a match and placed it on the bed of ceramic "coals" inside the stove's two small doors. Next, you carefully and slowly turned on the gas by a valve on a small pipe, which connected the stove to a larger gas pipe hidden in the wall. There would be a "whoosh," or sometimes a more ominous "whump," as the gas caught fire. Finally, you closed the small doors and turned the door handles to fasten the doors tightly shut. Within minutes the "coals" would turn a satisfying red, and give off prodigious amounts of heat. It was very important to turn off the stove and close the window, when you left the attic, I was told repeatedly by my parents.

Our attic had an interesting history from the time of the First World War. My mother told me the story. Our house had been built and owned by an English couple, Pop and Elizabeth Cooling, who was called Tante. They operated a grocery store on Grant Street, near Bird Avenue, for many years. My grandmother Schultz, who was then Margaret Bray, worked in the grocery store and got to know the Coolings well. The Coolings raised their two sons, Wilfred and Reginald, in the house at 453. My grandfather, Arthur Bray, worked in a machine shop with Mrs. Cooling's cousin, Cecil Clarkson, also from England, before Grandpa Bray died of tuberculosis in 1916. After Pop Cooling died, cousin Cecil moved into the house at 453 and lived with Tante, who died on Christmas morning, 1943. I never knew her except by my family's fond references to her exploits, including having severed a squirrel's tail with a knife, while chasing it from her raspberry patch in the backyard.

After Tante's death in 1943, my parents bought the house at 453 from Cecil Clarkson and the Cooling family, with the understanding that he would live with us, and be cared for by my mother, until he died. I knew him as "Uncle" Cecil, and my sister was named for him. He smoked cigars and gave me rides in a wheelbarrow around the backyard, until he died in 1948.

The story involved a German family named Doenitz, who lived across the street from 453. Mr. Doenitz was a photographer. During the First World War, in the anti-German frenzy, the Doenitz family and their daughter Dorothy, who was a little older than my mother, came into hard times and lost their business and house. The English Coolings invited the German Doenitz family to live in the attic, which they did for several years, until the Doenitz family recovered its life and fortunes after the war. My mother and Dorothy became close friends at that time, and Dorothy, who was an elementary school art teacher, was still a good friend of our family during my childhood.

Paper wad fights in the attic involved two forts, constructed of sheets or blankets thrown over card tables or chairs at opposite ends of the attic. Each fort's garrison would spend perhaps thirty minutes, making a large number of paper wads, and then the fighting began, with paper wads zinging and zipping back and forth across the attic. We used thick rubber bands. When you got stung the third time, you were out of the battle. The fighting ended only when the supply of wads, accessible from the cover of the fort, had been exhausted. Then we declared a truce, gathered up the "spent" wads, and started all over again. It was lots of fun!

On other days in the attic, we built forts and castles of wooden blocks (which my grandfather Schultz had made), and lined up toy soldiers on the ramparts. Then, from a distance of about twenty feet, we picked off the soldiers with our paper wads. Between my brother's collection of little, lead, Roman soldiers, gathered in the 1940s, and my collection of little, lead, British soldiers, with their bearskin hats, together with my collection of plastic, modern, American soldiers in various battle poses, there were perhaps two hundred fifty soldiers, so this endeavor sometimes occupied us for several hours.

The paper wad wars evolved over time into the "BB gun" wars. My parents never found out about the latter. I always wanted a BB gun for myself, after I found my grandfather Hobbie's BB gun, in the closet off of the kitchen in the house at Lewiston. That was an old rifle, which you cocked before each shot. My friends John Mooney, Mike Weinberg, Bruce Bleichfield, and Enn Teivas and I practiced shooting at targets—usually tin cans—in the Lewiston fields, carefully following my grandfather's admonition to be very, very careful. There was a weather vane, on top of a telephone pole on the property line between my grandparents' gardens and the Elsons' property next door, which was a favorite target. I recall Mike Weinberg hitting that vane with a lucky shot, making a nice, pinging sound. Once, however, I shot at a sparrow, when I was eight years old, and to my horror, killed the little bird. I took it to my grandfather, who was very understanding and considered this a regrettable "learning experience." I never shot at a bird or animal again with that BB gun. But our interest in target practice slowly evolved into a more radical interest: taking turns at shooting at each other with that rifle, always from a sufficient distance to assure that no one would get hit by a BB. I didn't mention this game to any adult. Fortunately, no one ever got hurt. I never got my own real gun, of any kind.

In third grade, when I was nine, my friends and I started to play football in Bidwell Parkway or on Colonial Circle, under the glare of the "No ball playing" signs. We played tackle football, as opposed to touch or flag football. Each year, we got a little better and a little bigger. Each of us had a helmet and shoulder pads. We threw, caught, tackled, and blocked, from the end of the World Series until the fields were covered with snow, around Halloween. We thought that we were pretty good. Usually, we divided up our group into two, evenly matched teams of about seven players on a side. Each game took about two hours. The elms were our sideline markers and goal posts. Sometimes, we played teams from other neighborhoods. My friends and I were deceptively small, at least until I began to grow rapidly in fifth grade. We were often challenged to games by groups of older, bigger boys from other neighborhoods. To the great surprise of the older teams, we usually won, for we were fast, tough, and had played together for a long time.

Mrs. Ann Henry's third grade class at Public School No. 56, 1953-54

Fourth grade was perhaps my favorite grade. I think I peaked academically, when I was ten years old. We started to learn geography. Our wonderful, fourth grade teacher, Miss Soell, ordered a huge globe, which had the outlines of continents, rivers, mountain ranges, and countries, but no names. She formed teams, and we had a competition among the teams to see which team could identify a geographical feature fastest. It was like a quiz show with teams. Usually, the teams were established by rows. With Miss Soell almost everything became a game. We had great fun.

Another favorite game involving geography was called the *Game of the States*. Miss Soell would hold up a card, on which there was a map of the United States, but no state names. One state was blackened, and it had a white dot, representing the capital. The competing teams had to identify the state and the capital city. Later, this game was expanded, as we all became experts on the location of each state and each state's capital, to include state flowers, state birds, state songs, and each state's best-known feature or product. Mary Jean Digati, Tina Haines, Carol Magavero, John Mooney, and I were the best in our class at naming states and state capitals. We had a constant battle to gain an edge over one another.

Mary Jean was a cute, little, Italian girl, whom I adored for several years. I used to ride my bicycle by her house on Bird Avenue and pretend to fall off and hurt myself, so that she would come out to talk. Tina was a lovely, tall, graceful girl, whose father was a doctor at the State Insane Asylum on the corner of Elmwood Avenue and Forest Avenue. Tina lived on the grounds of the asylum. I had several crushes on her over the years, and wished that I could spend more time with her, but her house was not very accessible.

My father used to tell me the story of his encounter with an inmate of the asylum. One day, when he was driving by the asylum on Forest Avenue, near Tina's house, his car had a flat tire. Dad pulled over to the curb, stopped his car near a group of inmates, who were cutting grass on the other side of the fence that encircled the asylum, and began to change the flat tire. At some point, he unscrewed the lug nuts, holding the tire in place, placed them on the street near a sewer grate, and removed the flat tire. As he stood up, he accidentally kicked the lug nuts through the grate into the sewer. By this time the asylum inmates had gathered to watch his efforts and observe his predicament: he couldn't reach the lug nuts under the sewer grate, which he needed to fasten the spare tire in place.

Dad called to one of the watching inmates and asked if there was a telephone nearby. The inmate responded that there was no need to call for help. All Dad had to do was remove one of the four lug nuts, holding each of the other three tires in place, and use the three lug nuts to fasten the spare tire in place, until he could buy new lug nuts. Dad thanked the inmate, and then said to him: "That is very good advice. You don't seem as though you should be in this place."

The inmate responded: "I may be crazy, but I'm not stupid."

In Miss Soell's class even arithmetic had a game. Miss Soell wrote the numbers 1 to 100 on the blackboard. Then, in a competition between two teams, each team's representative held a pointer and stood next to the blackboard. Miss Soell called out an equation, such as two plus two minus one, or ten times nine plus two minus three, and the first child to point to the correct answer won a point for his or her team.

Another favorite game of mine was the *Dictionary Game*. In fourth grade each student had a dictionary. Miss Soell would give us a word, and as soon as you found the page on which the word was listed, you raised your hand. The first row with all hands raised won. Class monitors checked each student's page to be sure that each student had the correct page. After we all became quick as thieves in looking up words, Miss Soell would give us a word and ask for what part of speech it was, its root, or a synonym or antonym, its plural form, or alternate definitions. In this way we learned about words—definitions, spelling, parts of speech, roots, past tense form, and the like.

Of course, for all these games one student was designated as a scorekeeper, and results were tabulated on a blackboard at the back of the room. On a weekly basis, the team with the most points was rewarded with some honor, such as being the first to leave the room at dismissal, during the next week, or the first to enter the auditorium for assembly. It was amazing how fast we could learn virtually anything, when a game was involved.

At 9:00 AM sharp Miss Soell would move her chair to the center of the front of the room, facing the class, and, after taking attendance, start to read. She would read for about fifteen minutes; if she were in a good mood, she would read until 9:30. What fantastic books she introduced us to! I remember well the first book she read: *The Black Stallion* by Walter Farley. *Son of the Black Stallion* was the next book she read to us. Later, she read us *Lad: A Dog* and *Bruce,* by Albert Payson Terhune. I actually looked forward to going to school just to relish those precious minutes at the beginning of the school day. As a reward, if the entire class had been good, she would read again late in the afternoon.

There was one boy in our class who didn't get along very well with Miss Soell. Danny Rumsey just could not keep quiet or still for more than a few minutes at a time. I always thought that Danny had a good heart—he was never mean or obnoxious to anyone. But he spent a lot of time under Miss Soell's desk (which was where recalcitrant students abided). I always felt very sorry for him. It was the only thing that Miss Soell ever did that I did not approve of.

Me at Lewiston, 1955

Fourth grade was also where we learned to write. Miss Soell taught us to write in careful, round script, following the outlines of the letters in our writing book. The book had double lines, about half an inch apart, between which you were supposed to write letters. The most difficult letters were the capital forms of "B," "D," "F," "G," "P," "R," and "S." Especially hard was planning each letter, so that the small letters took up only half the space between the lines and the capital letters did not extend above the top line. Miss Soell could write perfectly. She never went under or over the lines.

Each desk had an inkwell in the upper right hand corner. Each student had a pen, which had to be dipped into the inkwell for just the right amount of time to load up the pen with ink, but not too much, or the ink would blot on the paper. The classroom weekly monitors were in charge of keeping the inkwells full. Miss Soell warned us to be sure not to spill any ink. I remember that my hands shook the first time I was responsible for disbursing ink as a monitor. The inkwell was the size of a fifty-cent piece, and the ink container was pretty heavy. Almost always, the ink monitor spilled a few drops on each desk, until you mastered the tipping and pouring. You had to quickly wipe these drops up with a cloth, before they stained the desk.

Another task in fourth grade, which I liked better, was to police the neighborhood around the school, picking up whatever paper or other trash you found within a four block radius of the school. The so-called trash monitors were permitted to be up to ten minutes late for school in the morning and to leave school ten minutes early in the afternoon. That privilege was a very big deal! The positions of trash monitors were highly valued. The eight or so fourth grade monitors each carried a bag, in which you placed the trash you found. Before reporting to class, you emptied the bag into a big trashcan in Mr. Schwartz's office in the boiler room. On the route to his office, you could walk up and down the length of the basement hall several times—forbidden territory to all grades under the fourth.

In the spring of my fourth grade year, Miss Soell and our class were invited to be on television. This was a momentous event! No one from P.S. No. 56 had ever been on television before. So one day, we were all bused to the studio of WBEN Channel 4, which was located on the top of the Statler Building. I remember walking through the lobby of the Statler Hotel and going up to the top floor by elevator. It was the first time I had been so high up in a building. The view of Lake Erie and of the Niagara River was magnificent! The studio had arranged a classroom that was very similar to our fourth grade room at P.S. No. 56. Miss Soell taught us in the studio classroom, just as though we were back at P.S. No. 56. The only difference was that there were all sorts of strange cameras on all sides of the room, which we were told not to look at.

I remember very bright lights, but not much else. It was a live show, but a recording was made, so that later we all saw ourselves on television.

Perhaps the best single thing about fourth grade was swimming. P.S. No. 56 had the first swimming pool of any elementary school in the city. By the time I attended P.S. No. 56, there were many other schools with swimming pools. Having the first pool, however, apparently meant that at P.S. No. 56 we had a reputation of excellence in swimming to maintain. The boys' swimming teacher, Mr. Burke, never let us forget that. Also driving us to a swimming obsession was the requirement in the Buffalo schools that, in order to graduate from eighth grade, each student had to know how to swim at least two lengths of the pool.

I clearly recall the first day we had swimming class. We each had a towel from home. The boys in Miss Soell's class assembled in the swimming pool locker room, and Mr. Burke told us to take off our clothes, take a shower, and then get into the pool. Some of the boys were pretty modest and acted as though they had never been naked with other boys before. That didn't bother me, but I was apprehensive that the outer door to the basement hall, at the far end of the pool, might open unexpectedly at any minute, letting a hoard of our female classmates into our private sanctuary.

I was surprised that some of the boys did not know how to swim. I guess that years of summers at the beach, at day camp, and at summer camp had taught me how to swim well already. Mr. Burke was a good teacher. Each boy was assigned a partner. Your partner was responsible for making sure that you didn't drown. Mike Weinberg, John Mooney, Richard Bassett, and Enn Teivas were usually my partners in the pool. Richard was one of the boys who did not know how to swim at first. But he picked it up fast. We spent a lot of time in the shallow end of the pool, holding onto the wall and practicing our crawl kick. Then, we flipped over and practiced our backstroke kicks, still holding onto the wall with our hands over our shoulders. By the end of the first month of fourth grade, all of us could kick across the width of the pool and back, holding onto a buoyant board. Even those of us who already could swim were required to go through all the steps, helping those in the class who could not swim.

The next thing we learned was how to breathe properly, with your face in the water, holding onto the board at the end of your outstretched arms and turning your face to the side, every fourth kick, to get air. After we had all mastered kicking and breathing, so that we could kick perhaps forty widths or so with the board, we graduated to the deep end, and started to kick dozens of laps with the board. Over time, we abandoned the boards and kicked laps with our arms stretched out in front of us in the water, and then floating on our backs. Finally, we added the crawl stroke and the backstroke to our kicks. By the end of grade four, we were all swimming dozens of laps on our stomachs and on our backs, using the crawl and backstroke.

When everybody could swim at least a little, we were able to play water games, such as water polo or dodge ball. Subsequently, we learned how to dive from the edge of the pool and swim to the other side. We also learned the frog kick and breaststroke. Jimmy Huntington perfected the breaststroke and frog kick in a few months, while the rest of us struggled with these unfamiliar strokes and kicks. Even worse was the butterfly stroke and kick, which were becoming popular. Mr. Burke was as unfamiliar with these as we were, I suspect. I never really learned how to coordinate the butterfly stroke with what he called the dolphin kick. Enn Teivas got very good at the butterfly.

We had swimming class for forty-five minutes each week in fourth grade. The pool was only seventy feet long and about twenty-five feet wide. There were six rows of lights on the ceiling of the poolroom, so if you were swimming the backstroke, you could tell when you came to the end of the pool by counting the lights. Mr. Burke taught us flip turns, for reversing direction at the end of each lap. I spent many happy hours in that pool, and became the fastest freestyle and backstroke swimmer in my class. Enn Teivas was a close second, and sometimes beat me in backstroke. Jimmy Huntington could kill all of us in the breaststroke.

Each week in fourth grade, we also had forty-five minutes of gym class. The gym was quite small, with a ceiling that was only fourteen feet high. On the right side of the gym, as you entered, was a row of windows, covered with a wire mesh. On the other side was a series of wide, wooden, ladder-like rungs in four-foot sections. Hanging from the ceiling were half a dozen or so gymnastic rings and some climbing ropes, which all could be raised or lowered. There was a basketball backboard and hoop at each end of an area on the floor, with lines delineating the court, about sixty-five feet long by thirty feet wide. Stored at one end of the gym were several gymnastic horses in front of half a dozen gym mats, which were hung on big hooks on the wall. I seem to remember that there was an old, upright piano near the door, as well. The gym looked and felt old. Our gym teacher for fourth, fifth, and sixth grades—Mr. Brown—was also old. While the boys had gym class, the girls had swimming class, and vice versa.

I have a hazy recollection of learning square dancing in the gym with the girls in my class, sometime before the fourth grade. We must have had some dance classes of this type in the gym in the first years at P.S. No. 56. Occasionally, when the swimming teacher was absent, the boys and girls in our class would combine to have gym together. I don't recall that we ever had swimming class together, until the big challenge in eighth grade, when the girls dared the boys to race them. One girl in particular, Marcia Fry, was an excellent, fast swimmer, and several other girls were known to be very good.

Whether we would accept the challenge was the subject of much debate among the boys in eighth grade. All agreed it would be fun to have a swimming meet with the girls. However, the prospect of losing to Marcia, or to some other girl, was not a happy one. Also, we were used to swimming without suits. Were we supposed to be naked with the girls? Declining the challenge, on the other hand, was unthinkable, as it would be interpreted as our being fearful of losing (which we were).

In the end, the swimming meet was held, with all participants fully clothed in bathing suits. Thankfully for the male egos, the boys won every event, despite some scary moments. The girls beat some of us. Marcia and I swam against each other in the freestyle and backstroke sprints. The pool record for the freestyle, one length sprint, which I set that day, still stood thirty years later, I heard. I really churned up the pool, I guess. Fear is a powerful motivator. If we had swum a race of more than four lengths, Marcia would have won, I know, for she was very strong, with better endurance and faster turns than me.

I liked the gym class a lot. We played dodge ball and basketball, ran laps, learned how to vault the "horses" and how to do pull ups and somersaults on the rings, and climbed ropes, among other activities. I recall that, as I grew older and became a lot taller than my classmates, I had a distinct advantage in basketball, and liked it more and more each year. The gym's low ceiling, however, was a big problem; any shot from more than about fifteen feet from the basket always hit the lights, rings, or other equipment, hanging from the ceiling. So I learned to shoot without an arc, which didn't help me much in larger gyms, especially when, in later years, my height advantage had evaporated.

Our Industrial Arts teacher, Mr. Werick, was an elderly, German man, with little, round glasses and a lot of patience. We all liked him a lot. Under his kind tutelage, the boys in our class learned to identify and work with every kind of hand tool you could think of, to cut and sand wood, to stain and paint, to operate electrical saws and drills, to wire electrical appliances, and to do just about anything you might need to do around the house with hardware. I remember making a cutting board for my mother, as one of my first projects. One of my last projects was a wood, table lamp in the shape of a water pump, with an inlaid base. The pump handle turned the light off and on, as you raised or lowered it. That lamp stood on the telephone table in the dining room for over three decades, after I presented it to my parents in seventh grade.

While we were in Industrial Arts class, the girls were in Home Economics class, where they learned to sew, cook, and keep records of household expenses. They didn't seem to like the class very much, and envied the boys' woodworking and metalworking projects. In eighth grade Mr. Werick retired towards the end of the year. The boys in grades four through eight collected about ninety dollars and gave him a retirement watch. I was in charge of getting the watch, and Enn Teivas—who was one of Mr. Werick's favorite students—made the presentation at an assembly. I recall that Mr. Werick cried a lot.

As I mentioned earlier, in 1953 and 1954 my family took vacation trips to the White Mountains to drop off John for his summer jobs with the Appalachian Mountain Club. My brother was always a prodigious picture taker. He had hundreds of slides of the White Mountains. Mom suggested that perhaps my fourth grade class would like to see slides of the mountains. With Miss Soell's approval, I prepared a one-hour presentation of slides about the huts and hiking in New Hampshire. This was the first time I had ever attempted to talk before a group. I was extremely nervous, but the program went off without a hitch, and I ended up showing John's pictures to Mrs. Morganstern's class (the other fourth grade class), as well. I thoroughly enjoyed talking with my classmates about the White Mountains, and learned that this was something I did well.

About half way through our fourth grade year, some of us decided to form a club, with its headquarters in the Hobbie attic. We might have named it the "paper wad" club, since paper wad fights were a primary activity in the attic, but we decided to call ourselves the "White Eagles," mainly because the P.S. No. 56 sweatshirts and T-shirts were white with a red emblem over the heart, displaying the number "56" in a circle, with the torch of learning separating the two numbers. The "56" shirts were convenient uniforms. Founding members of the club were Ellen Warner, Linda Smith, Tina Haines, Janine Hannel, Dava Katz, Tana Lee Stewart, Enn Teivas, Joel Lippes, Mike Weinberg, Bruce Bleichfield, John Mooney, Richard Bassett, and I. Other classmates joined later. Dues were ten cents a month.

Besides the paper wad fights, in the attic clubhouse we played pool on my family's old pool table; ping pong on the same table, which had a removable table top; flashlight tag in the dark, which could be pretty scary, if the eaves were within limits; card games, such as Hearts and Poker and Canasta; and pillow fights. We sometimes set up obstacle courses made from overturned chairs and tables and cardboard boxes. You had to crawl on your hands and knees, slide on your stomach, wiggle on your back, and climb step ladders to get through the course. The toughest part of the obstacle course was walking the attic railing.

My grandfather had constructed a railing about three feet high, made from two by fours, on three sides of the stairwell containing the attic stairs.

The railing was to prevent falls into the stairwell. We used it as a balance beam. It was about ten feet long on each side with a four-foot connecting rail at the top end. If you fell one way, towards the attic floor, it was a mere three feet; the other way the fall could be as much as ten feet into the stairwell. I once slipped and fell ten feet onto the bottom stair, knocking the breath out of myself. Mike Weinberg and John Mooney carried me into the front bedroom and lay me on the bed. I thought I was dying, as I couldn't breathe. My mother came running. She thought I was already dead. After what seemed like an eternity, I managed to catch my breath and gasped. I still remember the faces of my mother, Mike, and John, peering anxiously at me. We stopped using that part of the obstacle course, after my fall.

Some of the White Eagles in 1956: Mike Weinberg, Linda Smith, Ellen Warner, Enn Teivas, Bruce Bleichfield, Janine Hannel, John Mooney, Tana Lee Stewart, me, and Richard Bassett

There were several, old mattresses in the attic, as well, which we formed into a kind of ring, where we played a game, pitting two kids against each other, each with a different color paper, pinned to his or her back, the object of which was to keep the other player from seeing your color. No touching was allowed, but you had to stay in the ring on the mattresses. This game got quite lively.

Over time, the no touching rule was eased, and the game metamorphosed into wrestling matches. Linda Smith was a particularly difficult quarry to pin, although she was one of the smallest of our group. We also planned parties and expeditions to such destinations as the zoo, Delaware Park, Brock's Monument, Chestnut Ridge Park, and summer homes, such as our cabin at the Kennels. I recall that on one of these expeditions, with seven kids packed into our old Chevrolet, and my father driving us back to Buffalo along the Niagara Parkway on the Canadian riverside from a visit to Niagara Falls, we heard a song on the car radio called "Hound Dog," sung by a new pop star, named Elvis Presley. Janine Hannel taught us all the words. We eleven-year-olds thought the song was great! The White Eagles lasted about two years, through fifth grade, when the girls began to wear sweaters, makeup, and bras, and were reluctant to wrestle anymore with the boys.

Our fifth grade teacher was Mrs. Mitchell, who was a wonderful piano player and an excellent teacher. That year, Miss Millward, our music teacher, formed a school orchestra, consisting of about twenty students of all ages. Richard Bassett played the trumpet, Danny Fraustino and I played the violin, Mark Vail played the viola, Barbara Wolfson played the cello, and other students played flutes, clarinets, French horn, drums, and trombone. Miss Millward was a fine teacher, and with Mrs. Mitchell's help on the piano, we managed to play pretty well. For the next four years, our orchestra played at every assembly, as the classes marched in, and as a part of each musical program. My favorite piece of our repertoire was an adaptation of the fourth (adagio) movement of Brahms' *Symphony No. 1*, which has a lush, string passage.

Danny, Barbara, Mark, and I formed a quartet, and competed in eighth grade in a string ensemble competition at Kleinhans Music Hall. We played an adaptation of Saint-Saens' *Danse Macabre*, which was fast-paced, nerve-wracking, but fun. Although I think we played well, we didn't win. Later the same year, the four of us played in the Buffalo Youth Symphony's annual concert. I think we were rehearsing Haydn's *Surprise Symphony*, when the conductor, Josef Krips, threw his baton at us, as I have mentioned. We also played Strauss' *Overture to Die Fledermaus*.

Mrs. Mitchell taught us about elections and prompted us to elect class officers. I decided to run for class president. My parents, Ceci, and friends helped me cut out little rocking horses from colored cardboard paper, or "Hobbie horses." The rocking horse became my campaign symbol. "Rock with Hobbie." The symbol and slogan were my sister's idea. I ended up winning. Carol Magavero was elected Vice President. We stayed a team that was re-elected every year, until we graduated. Carol was a short, attractive girl, who also lived on West Delavan Avenue, but closer to school—between Ashland Avenue and Elmwood Avenue. She was very smart, kind, and trustworthy—a good, political partner and friend.

In fifth grade I recall cheating in a spelling test—the only time I cheated in school that I can remember. I arrived late one morning to school—I think I had a doctor's appointment—to find the class engaged in a surprise, spelling test, for which I was totally unprepared. My great, long-time friend, Tina Haines, who sat behind me and was a special person, secretly passed me a note, as soon as I sat down, with the correct spellings of the most difficult words.

All I needed was a glance, and the deed was done. As far as I know, only Tina and I ever knew about this incident. I felt guilty all year.

I remember being very content with life in fifth grade. By the end of that year, my classmates and I had been together for seven years. Several of my friends—Bob Jacobs, Bob Rosenthal, Cal Brainard, and John Mooney—left P.S. No. 56 at the end of fourth grade. John entered fifth grade at the Campus School, and Cal and the two Bobs entered fifth grade in Nichols' Lower School. A handful of new classmates had joined us over the years, but by and large, the Class of 1959 had stayed pretty much intact. I knew almost all of the sixty or so students in fifth grade, and got along with virtually everyone.

Ceci wrote me in January 1957, to tell me about her freshman year at Mt. Holyoke College. She wrote that John and I made her furious with our "A+ averages." She also mentioned, as she often did, her latest boyfriends, Phil and Duncan. I liked getting letters from Ceci.

At P.S. No. 56 there was a group of about five, older, Italian boys, who, perhaps because of language or family difficulties, did not perform well enough to advance with their classes, and they eventually joined our class in fourth and fifth grades. Some of them were fourteen or fifteen years old, while most of us were ten or eleven. They smoked cigarettes, wore black leather jackets, and combed a gel into their hair, which gave it a shiny look. I had observed in second and third grades that this group sometimes chased and roughed up the younger students on the routes to and from school.

At an early age, I decided that alertness and speed were the twin strategies best designed to avoid problems with this group. So I was ever watchful, wherever I traveled on foot or by bike on the west side. When I saw what looked like trouble ahead, I either turned and ran, or used one of the alternative escape routes I had planned in advance, such as the backyards and garages of acquaintances in our neighborhood. It was actually kind of fun for a while, pretending that I was an Indian or scout, dealing with hostile forces.

The playground at P.S. No. 56 was neutral territory, so if I made it to there, I usually felt safe. The school custodian, Mr. Schwartz, who lived on the school grounds, made sure that there were no incidents or any smoking near the school. And he didn't hesitate to call the police to enforce his rules. One evening, however, several members of the leather jacket group trapped Enn Teivas and me at the playground. We couldn't reach our bikes and were not about to abandon them. Mr. Schwartz was not around. So we turned and fought briefly with three or four of the older boys. One of them pulled out a switchblade. In the struggle the first finger on my left hand was cut. At the first sign of blood, the group retreated, and Enn and I grabbed our bikes and took off. I still have a small scar on my finger from that slash, which greatly alarmed Harry Taub, my violin teacher. After that incident, I never had another problem with that group, mainly because I started to grow rapidly in fifth grade and became physically bigger, stronger, and faster than any of them. By the time I turned fourteen, I was friends with most of them.

Enn was a good friend and athletic rival. He and his mother had emigrated from Estonia. Mrs. Teivas worked for the Brainard family on Lafayette Avenue, and Enn and his mother lived in an apartment on the upper floor of the Brainard home. Calvin Brainard, as I have mentioned, was a classmate at P.S. No. 56 for several years and later a classmate for four years at Nichols High School. Mrs. Teivas was very nice, had blond hair and blue eyes, and spoke with a lovely, lilting, Baltic accent. Enn was also blond with blue eyes, had a quick temper, and was a very good athlete. He could do anything well in sports. His father had been killed in the war.

Our sixth grade teacher, another Mrs. Henry, but this time Phyllis Henry, turned out to be the new teacher who had left so suddenly in second grade—to get married. She was young, enthusiastic, and smart. She was actually our homeroom teacher, but taught social studies to all the sixth through the eighth grades. We liked her immensely. She treated us like adults. She taught us, for the first time, how to take and to organize notes in classes. I am forever in her debt for that. Sixth grade brought major changes. Classes were on the third floor with the school's elite. Our class moved from room to room for each subject.

Another gem of a teacher was Miss Elinor Plumley. She was my homeroom teacher for seventh and eighth grades. Miss Plumley challenged us to be aware of current events, discussed philosophy with us, and encouraged all of us to engage more in art and music. She was a great teacher. I thought she looked a little like a kind lioness. Besides Miss Plumley, who took over the art classes from Miss Diadata, and Miss Millward, whose excellent music classes continued, Miss Poole (who smoked a lot and smelled of cigarettes) taught science, Miss Zuppo (who had bright, flashing dark eyes and stuttered when she got excited or angry) taught mathematics, Miss Mundt (who was a close friend of Miss Soell's and introduced us to Robert Frost's poetry) taught English, and the newest addition to the staff—a wonderful, young teacher, named Elmer Schamber—taught us history. Mr. Schamber and Mrs. Henry were breaths of fresh air at P.S. No. 56, and I often saw them plotting together.

Thanks to Mrs. Henry and Mr. Schamber, I suspect, our combined sixth grade classes went to see the newest, movie sensation called *This Is Cinerama*. The movie was projected onto a curved screen at Loew's Teck Theater. We had the cheap seats in the first three rows, so the picture was all around us. The noise was deafening. There was a wild, roller coaster ride at some point in the movie, I recall. With the movie projected on three sides of me, I felt as though I really was on the Comet! The girl behind me, Tana Lee Stewart (a member of the White Eagles), threw up over my left shoulder about half way through, missing me, fortunately. It was one of the best movie experiences of my life!

In the spring of my sixth grade year in 1957, my family attended my brother's graduation from Dartmouth College. We stayed with a family in Etna, New Hampshire, which is a small town a little east of Hanover, where the college is located. Hanover is such a small town that in 1957 it had only the Hanover Inn for accommodations. Townspeople there and in surrounding towns opened their homes to accommodate guests, during major college events. The mountain foothills around the house, where we stayed, were filled with wildflowers in June. The White Mountains were visible from the house's porch. We went canoeing in the Connecticut River and climbed Balch's Hill near Hanover.

John and his roommates taught me a new game called Frisbee, which you played by flinging a plate-like plastic object between players, standing about sixty feet from each other, who tried to catch the "Frisbee" before it touched the ground. I learned how to throw the Frisbee at an angle to make it curve in flight or to keep it level for a straight flight of greater distance. I loved that game! As soon as I got home, I taught my west end buddies in Buffalo how to play.

P.S. No. 30 was an elementary school, with classes through grade six, located on Elmwood Avenue between Highland and West Ferry, across from the post office. I always knew that P.S. No. 30 was connected to P.S. No. 56, but somehow it never dawned on me that after grade six those students would be coming to P.S. No. 56. Come they did: about thirty-two new students. So starting in seventh grade, we had new friends to socialize with and rivals to contend with. Happily, there were many more of the former than the latter. And a very pretty red head, Chris Benzow, whom I knew from the beach, was among them.

Elmer Schamber played the trumpet, particularly jazz. During our history classes, he sometimes played for us. He also cracked a lot of jokes and made history come alive, especially Civil War history. I read Bruce Catton's Pulitzer Prize winning book, *A Stillness At Appomattox*, at his urging, and was hooked on Civil War history forever afterwards. For one of my history projects, I made a relief map of the United States out of flour, water, and vegetable dyes, identifying the key states and their roles in the civil war by color. He liked it so much that he hung it in his classroom for years. He let us call him Elmer. He was one of the best teachers at P.S. No. 56.

Three events during seventh grade were especially important to me. In October, at the International Institute, my mother accompanied me in my fourth violin recital as a student of Harry Taub. We played the *Concertino Opus 25* by Oscar Reiding. I was very relieved when it was over.

In December 1957, I was in a confirmation class at St. John's Episcopal Church. A visiting bishop from Asia officiated. The Right Reverend Quentin Huang, retired Bishop of the Burma Road, was the first Asian person I ever met. I was pleased to be confirmed by someone from another country. Our regular bishop, Bishop Scaife, was a good friend of my father's and someone I also liked, although he had a wild daughter, Cindy. I recall attending one of Cindy's parties at the Scaife's house on Lincoln Parkway, several years later, where we stacked empty beer cans in a pyramid next to the front door, so that her father would knock them over, when he came home that night with a visiting bishop.

The Twersky Science Essay Contest, sponsored by the Buffalo Museum of Science, was held in the spring of 1958. "Exploring Space in Our Solar System" was the title of the essay, which seventh graders throughout the city were required to write. JeNien Chesley, who was a classmate, living at 595 West Delavan Avenue, just up the street from our house, and I, won third place and second place, respectively. There was an elaborate reception one evening at the Museum in honor of the winners. JeNien was a very quiet girl throughout elementary school at P.S. No. 56, and went largely unnoticed, until suddenly in fifth grade, she blossomed into a stunning beauty, with brains.

Another wonderful man joined the teaching staff during our seventh grade year, as our boys' gym and swimming teacher. Charlie Dingboom was a short, stocky man in his late twenties, with blue eyes and blond hair, who had starred in football as a lineman for the University of Buffalo. He had a great sense of humor, and we thought he was a wonderful teacher, because he joined in our practices and games. During gym class, we often formed two teams and played basketball—Charlie, me (the tallest kid), and the shorter, slower boys in our class against Enn Teivas, Ron Hoover, Ron Carey, Mike Weinberg, Joel Lippes, Danny Fraustino, and the other athletes. Charlie's team usually won. He was a superb athlete. Elmer, Charlie, and Mr. Schwartz could always be found together in the boiler room at lunch and on their breaks. They played cards and talked sports constantly. That was the best time to ask any of them for a favor.

Among the new kids in our seventh grade class were the Carey brothers— Ronnie and Tim, Ronnie Hoover, Jim McGibbon, Lucy Peale, Kedra Dubrindt, and Joy Telech. The Careys became good friends. Ronnie Carey was quite small, but quick and athletic—the best basketball player in our class. Ronnie Hoover had been the president of his class at P.S. No. 30, so he was a rival at first, but later became a friend. Jim, who was extremely smart, became a close friend and was a classmate at Nichols High School. He replaced me as the number two student in our class, behind Ann Melzer, who was a genius. Lucy was the niece of a famous minister and writer, Norman Vincent Peale, author of *The Power of Positive Thinking*. Kedra was a lovely, sweet Dutch girl, whom I liked a lot. I had a huge crush on Joy.

Mrs. Phyllis Henry's seventh grade class at Public School No. 56, 1957–58

Towards the end of sixth grade, we began to have dance parties, which usually ended up in the game of Spin the Bottle, with a variation. Instead of kissing the girl whom a spin of the bottle selected for you, the bottle determined who your "necking" partner would be. I was very slow getting into this game and nervous about French kissing and otherwise fondling my classmates. In fact, my partners, such as Tina Haines, who taught me how to French kiss (she of the spelling test cheating), and others may have thought me socially retarded, which I was in this area of our sixth and seventh grade culture.

The best parties were at Ann Jones' house, in her attic in seventh grade. Ann's parents were both doctors, and they were seldom at home on weekend evenings. We brought our 45-rpm records, cokes, chips, and other munchies to Ann's house almost every weekend for at least a year. Slow dancing under low lights gradually led to pairing off for necking in almost total darkness. Every week we seemed to have different partners. The girls were very kind to me, teaching me a lot about "necking." One girl, with alluring, shoulder length, tawny hair, and a gentle voice, reassured me that she didn't mind if I touched her breasts. She placed my hand under her sweater and loosened her bra. After my initial shock, I was befuddled and bewitched for weeks afterwards. Breasts took on new importance. I wondered how I had failed to notice them until that night—sort of like a magnificent building or tree that you pass every day without noticing and then suddenly, and shockingly, there it is, and you kick yourself for not seeing it sooner. I look back on those parties at the Jones' house as my initiation into the world of innocent sexual foreplay, with kind, patient, and helpful friends as teachers.

In the seventh and eighth grades, our boys' swimming team began to compete in earnest under coach Dingboom, winning our league title both years and coming in second in the city in 1958. In 1959 we won the city championship. In the individual citywide competitions, Jimmy Huntington won gold medals in breaststroke every year, and Enn Teivas won a gold medal in the butterfly and a silver medal in the backstroke in 1959. There was one boy from P.S. No. 52 whom I never could beat in freestyle. So both in seventh and eighth grades, I won silver medals in that event. In the medley relay, in which I swam anchor, we took the gold medal each year. In backstroke a new boy in our class, Tom Pelosci, and I traded winning. He was very fast. I won a silver medal and a gold, finally. We had a good team.

My mother was full of suggestions on how I could improve my life. One of many such suggestions was to change Boy Scout troops. I had joined Cub Scouts in second grade, joining the pack at St. John's Church, with Richard Bassett, Enn Teivas, Cal Brainard, and John Mooney, but never much liked the crafts and unexciting activities that Cub Scouts involved. At St. John's, there was a small Boy Scout Troop, which Richard, John, Cal, and I joined in fourth grade. The Scout Leader was William McLean, a member of the church choir, who was very kind and had a younger son, named Billie. But the relatively small troop did not undertake the exciting trips and projects that my brother had been a part of in another troop, where he had loved scouting and become an Eagle Scout. So after several years, my mother got me into a troop at the Kenmore Presbyterian Church, where the son of a friend of hers was apparently a happy scout.

The new, much larger troop was big into saluting and flag ceremonies. I lasted about six months. I still remember the first camping trip I went on with the troop in the Boston Hills, outside of Buffalo. It rained, and all the adult troop leaders stayed at a motel, while the scouts suffered in the cold and rain. By that time, I had two summers at Camp Jobildunc under my belt, with wilderness camping and skilled outdoor leadership from Dartmouth students, so I said that I had had enough with scouting. I only attained the rank of Life Scout.

Another of my mother's suggestions was that I should go to dance school. I barely had words to express to her how utterly ridiculous this idea seemed to me in sixth grade. She kept trying to persuade me for an entire year, and I finally broke down in seventh grade, agreeing to try dance school for one month at most. I still remember vividly how upset I was, and how foolish I felt in a dark suit and tie, when my father dropped me off at the Unitarian

Church, on the corner of West Ferry Street and Elmwood Avenue, on that first Saturday. Miss Mabel Elias' Dance School was located there.

Miss Elias was an attractive, tall, slender, vivacious woman, with silver-blond hair. She seemed a class act from the beginning. You name it—she could dance it and dance it well, as she showed us in the first class. Her co-teacher, Mrs. Kenner, was also a great dancer. They both had a sense of humor and a nice way of goading young men onto the dance floor. There were about twenty boys and twenty girls. Most of my friends in school were in the class. The girls were all dressed in their best clothes and looked pretty good.

I recall that Miss Elias had us form two circles—boys on the outside circle and girls on the inside circle. Then, as the music played, the circles walked in opposite directions past each other, until the music stopped. The girl opposite you, when the music stopped, was your partner for the next several dances. Miss Elias and her partner would demonstrate the position of your legs, arms, and hands for each kind of dance, and then teach us the dance step, transitions into steps, and a succession of steps. We followed. It was a slow process, but a very easy way to get to know a lot of girls in a short time! The first time we walked our circles and the music stopped, Heidi Marquis was next to me. I thought that was a good sign.

I think I first met Heidi at the beach, when she had visited her Buffalo neighbor, Chris Benzow. It was in sixth grade. I was twelve. Shortly after that meeting, someone started to call me in the evenings on the telephone. When I answered, there would be no sound, except that of someone breathing. This went on for weeks, piquing my curiosity. At first, I thought it was one of my friends, playing a trick on me. But all convincingly denied it. I think that Mike Weinberg first suggested that it might be a girl. This idea seemed very implausible, but my neighbor, Bruce Bleichfield, and I decided to investigate. I made a list of all the girls we knew and their telephone numbers. Bruce lived on Richmond Avenue, about eight houses from 453, but within sight. From the top floor of each house we could see each other's hand signals with binoculars and communicate by a walkie-talkie. When I received the mysterious telephone call, I would alert Bruce by walkie-talkie and then go to our upstairs phone, from which I could see Bruce's house. Bruce, armed with the list of girls and telephone numbers, called each girl in turn, while the mystery caller was on the phone with me. Then, he reported by signals which girls' telephones were not busy, slowly eliminating all the girls I knew well. When we finally added Heidi's name to the list and her telephone was busy—bingo. After that, Heidi, with her shy smile, short brunette hair, and brown eyes, was a special person for me.

Heidi was one of the gentlest, nicest girls I knew in Buffalo. She was a terrific dancer, too, and later invited me to a school dance at Nardin's Academy in seventh grade and to her eighth grade prom, which was held at the Buffalo Yacht Club. The dance at Nardin's Academy was my first experience with a social event at a girls' catholic school. I had expected that the nuns, who were part of the teaching staff, would closely supervise the dance. I was, therefore, extremely surprised, when Heidi took me on a tour of the school, late in the evening. We entered the darkened library to find dozens of couples, engaged in what we called "necking" or "petting," in every imaginable position and in every nook and cranny of the library. I didn't know what Heidi expected of me, and was so surprised by what I saw that I retreated in confusion, pulling Heidi out of the room. I was pretty stupid in seventh grade.

Heidi's prom the next year was wonderful. I recall that there was a great dance band, that we walked together on the docks of the Yacht Club under a full moon, that we were invited for a drink onto one of the yachts tied up at the Club, that Heidi was beautiful in her prom dress, and that I was very nervous and awkward about kissing her, when I was fourteen.

After the first series of dances with Heidi on the first evening of dance school, I began to relax and enjoy meeting, and dancing with, the other girls. Suffice to say that, after two or three dance classes, I started to think that the sensation of having a pretty girl in your arms, who smelled of lavender or gardenia, with good dance music playing, more than made up for any initial feelings of embarrassment or awkwardness. Slowly—horror of horrors—I started to really like dancing and look forward to the class, although I wouldn't admit this to anyone. I noticed that my male friends—expert in avoiding something they didn't like—also came to every class. We learned the waltz, foxtrot, cha-cha-cha, rumba, samba, and tango. I liked the waltz best. I learned to hold myself straight, but relaxed enough to be comfortable, and to dance on the balls of my feet, for the most part. I wished that we could have learned the jitterbug, but we didn't.

One night after dance class was over, several of us were waiting for our rides home, when we heard screams, coming from the second floor of the Unitarian church building. We rushed upstairs to find a lady from the church, writhing on the floor, and several of our dance school classmates screaming. I remember that Ann Jones took charge, announced that the lady was having an epileptic seizure, and forced open the lady's mouth to grab her tongue, as we held her head and arms. Ann was afraid that the lady might swallow her tongue, during the seizure, and choke. One of us called an ambulance. After a few minutes, the lady's seizure stopped, and she came out of it. The ambulance arrived and took her away, but not before one of the medics said that Ann had saved the lady's life. Although I had always liked Ann, I had a new respect for her after that and told her so. "Well," she said, "after all, I am the daughter of two doctors."

At the conclusion of the first year of dancing school, we had dance competitions. Ann and I competed in the tango contest and won. Tina Haines—who was the best dancer in our class—and I teamed up to win the waltz competition. I remember that we had a wonderful, end-of-year dance, for which Irving Shire's dance band played. Harriet Parker was chosen "queen," and I was "king." By the end of our second year of dance school, when we were all in eighth grade, we were getting to be pretty fair dancers!

At the end of our second year, Miss Elias announced that there would be a costume ball to conclude the two-year dance school. I had no idea what costume I should wear, and was beginning to get frustrated, when Aunt Betty Craig suggested that I try on Uncle Bob's naval uniform. I did, and it fit perfectly. Even the commander hat fit. I was a naval commander in full regalia for one night, and I blessed my aunt and uncle a thousand times for their idea. The ball was one of the most fun nights of my life, dancing again to Irving Shire's great music.

Uncle Bob's uniform, 1958

In seventh grade I wrote a letter to the former principal of P.S. No. 56, Ms. Frances A. Riches. Upon Ms. Riches' retirement after more than thirty years at P.S. No. 56, her successor—Mrs. Strauss—established the "Frances A. Richey Award," which was given to a boy and girl in the seventh grade annually for outstanding leadership. Winners had to write to Ms. Richey. In my letter, I told her that the thing I liked best about P.S. No. 56 was the balance that had been struck among the arts, academic subjects, and sports in the curriculum. I still feel that way after almost fifty years, and suspect that my classmates and I were indeed lucky to have had Ms. Richey and Mrs.

Strauss, building and maintaining P.S. No. 56 and its excellent teaching staff, for over forty continuous years, before we arrived.

Our seventh grade prom, which was the first such dance ever for the seventh graders at P.S. No. 56, was held in the school gym. We spent several days decorating the old, drab gym, until it looked very festive.

Just before Christmas of 1958, my mother accompanied me again in a violin recital at the International Institute. We played Vivaldi's *Concerto in A Minor*. From my point of view, the best part of these recitals was the reception afterwards, with its wine punch and delicious little cookies. Harry Taub always arranged good food.

In March of our eighth grade year, we elected class officers for the last time: I was President; Carol Magavero was Vice President; Chris Benzow was Secretary; and the Treasurers for each of our three classes were Lucy Peale, John Reinhardt, and Sharon Caterina. We had a class tea in the spring, inviting all of our mothers. Melodye Darnell was in charge of that, I recall, and it was a lovely party.

Other fond memories involve the softball games Mr. Schamber organized in the spring, during our history class. To our amazement, one morning when the weather was clear and cool, he asked if we would like to go out on the playground and play baseball—boys and girls together. Is the sky blue? Charlie Dingboom joined us and coached one team, while Elmer Schamber coached the other. We had several, superb mornings of coed baseball, thanks to Elmer and Charlie.

The spring of 1959 was also a spring of glory for our P.S. No. 56 boys' baseball team. The playground games of the past four years had shaped us into a pretty fair baseball team. Charlie Dingboom coached us into the quarterfinals of the Buffalo schools' championship games. I pitched and played first base. After we won our first three games, a lucky home run by a player from P.S. No. 66 doomed us in the last inning of our fourth game.

Before the prom, at graduation in June, 1959, I gave a speech as class president, which I carefully crafted with Mrs. Strauss' help, thanking the teachers and staff, who had nurtured us for so many years. Carol Magavero won the "Daughters of the American Revolution" award for outstanding leadership by a girl. I won the "Sons" award. Our string quartet—Barbara Wolfson, Marl Vail, Danny Fraustino, and I—played Beethoven's *Rondo* as the prelude. Most important was our class picture on the playground, with all ninety of my classmates, three of whom were pregnant, I heard. I wish that there had also been a picture of the school faculty and staff; once familiar faces vanish so fast from my memory.

The graduating class of P.S. School No. 56, June 1959

Our graduation prom, on the night after graduation, was held in the fellowship hall at St. John's Church on Colonial Circle, where there was much more room than in the old gymnasium. Again, we spent days decorating the hall. One of the problems we addressed was how to keep my classmates confined to the hall, so that they wouldn't be tempted to explore the rest of St. John's, looking for dark rooms. I recall that I danced with almost every girl in my class, as well as with my mother, at the prom. I think that everyone had a wonderful, last evening together.

After graduation, my elementary school friends virtually all disappeared from my life. Sixty of my classmates went to Lafayette High School, right around the corner from my home. Two—Ed McGuire and Jim McGibbon—went to Nichols High School with me. Mike Weinberg went to Bennett High School and then Amherst High School. Ron Carey went to Canisius High School. Most of the girls went to Lafayette, except for Ann Melzer and Ann Jones, who went to the Buffalo Seminary, and Joy Telech, who went to the Park School. Tina Haines stayed in touch over the years, for which I was very grateful. I saw Chris Benzow at the beach often. Bruce Bleichfeld graduated from P.S. No. 56 in 1960 and went to Park School. I lost track of most of my other wonderful classmates within a year or so, and never met most of them again, to my great sorrow.

Smells and sounds trigger my most vivid memories. Burning leaves fill my nose with autumn days on Buffalo's streets. The smell of apples, or the taste of cider, floods my taste buds with the autumnal equinox at Lewiston, where picking and sorting fruit and squeezing out apple cider were favorite activities. The shouts of kids, playing football, transport my ears to the yellowing, grass, football fields on Bidwell Parkway and Colonial Circle, with their elm goal posts. The plaintive, autumn meowing of a catbird, getting ready to migrate south from my Virginia back yard, brings to my eyes the sun setting on the Hobbie cabin porch and emptying dunes of Holloway Bay. Childhood autumns suffused me both with nostalgia for the passion and spent life of another summer and with the anxiety and excitement of the start of school in each of the ten rich years that I attended P.S. No. 56.

Chapter Five—
First Two High School
Years: 1959–61

Lake Schrader and Lake Peters, with Mt. Chamberlin, Alaska, 1961

When I was five years old, Grandpa Hobbie had a talk with me about religion. I had run into his arms in the living room of the house at Lewiston to report excitedly that the door to the attic, located at the top of the stairs, had just mysteriously creaked open and then closed, as I was walking down the hall on the second floor. He asked me who was there. I stammered that no one was there. Then why was I upset, he asked, if there was no one there? Of course, I was sure that a ghost had been responsible. My concern led to a discussion of ghosts and then religion. At some point, my grandfather greatly upset me by suggesting that I should marry a Presbyterian. Well, I didn't know any Presbyterian girls. Joann Cipolla was Roman Catholic, and she was the kindergarten classmate I wanted to marry. The other alternative might be GiGi Gucker, who was my babysitter at the Kennels, but she was not Presbyterian either. My grandfather remained firm in his suggestion that I should look for a Presbyterian.

I remembered this almost a decade later, when my brother announced in early 1959 that he was engaged to a Mormon girl from California. A Mormon! I didn't even know what a Mormon was, but I doubted it was the same as a Presbyterian. For several months, my grandparents and our family's older friends talked quietly about this development, until my mother flew out to California in March to meet Olivann Rumph and her mother Irene. Mom returned to report that she was very happy with John's fiancee and her family, and that all was well, quieting the gossip.

On August 18th, my parents, Ceci, Aunt Kate, and I climbed into our still relatively new, 1957 green Chevrolet and headed west for the wedding in Long Beach, California—the first and only time I ever crossed the United States by car. We filled up with gas at the station on the corner of Elmwood and Auburn: 13.2 gallons of gas cost $4.09 (about $.31/gallon). Ceci started out driving and went through a red light at the intersection of Porter and Niagara Streets in the first five minutes of the trip. For the next nine days, we visited friends and fantastic places, such as Pike's Peak, a ranch in Colorado belonging to Kathleen Rand (a cousin of Dorothy Doenitz, my mother's close friend from childhood), Petrified Forest, Painted Desert, Meteor Crater, Grand Canyon, and Joshua Tree National Monument. Our somewhat winding route took us through Dayton, Ohio; Montrose, Illinois; Merriam, Kansas; Colby, Kansas; Trinidad, Colorado; Grants, New Mexico; Flagstaff, Arizona; and Kingman, Arizona. Maps were very important to our family, and every step of the trip was carefully tracked. With Dad and Aunt Kate in the car, every tree, bush, flower, animal, and bird en route was identified, every passing car's license plate was scrutinized, and every geographic or historical site was discussed. Once we got into the rhythm of traveling, the time went by very fast. I was most impressed by the cog railway up Pike's Peak and by the Meteor Crater in Arizona. We arrived in Long Beach, California, in mid afternoon on Wednesday, August 26th.

After meeting Olivann, Olivann's mother Irene, her grandfather and grandmother Kleinman from Utah (Grandpa Kleinman was a delight and wore a cowboy hat and a holstered revolver everywhere he went), and her brothers, Frances and Larry, I recall swimming a lot in Frances' pool with his wife Pat and son. There was a magnificent Luau with mouth-watering pork at a Polynesian restaurant on the evening before the wedding, and a lovely wedding on Saturday, in an Episcopal church (it turned out that Olivann and her mother were not practicing Mormons, in contrast to the rest of her family). Olivann was a lovely blond, friendly, and a very talented piano player—I liked her and her family immensely from the beginning.

Olivann and John on their wedding day, Long Beach, California, August 29, 1960

We left for Buffalo on Sunday, August 30, returning through Zion National Park; Las Vegas, Nevada; Richfield, Utah; Rock Springs, Wyoming; Grand Island, Nebraska; Mendota, Illinois; and Mentor, Ohio. The return trip took six days. We arrived home on Friday, September 4th, having seen a grand wedding, 409 horses, and the license plates of forty-seven states, according to my trip log.

On the Saturday night after our return, I was at the beach. I lay in the bunk bed on the cabin's porch, remembering the trip, and thought about the approaching first day at Nichols High School. I remember that night not only because it was my first night at the beach after the great trip, but also because it was one of the few nights, in my many years at the beach, when the sounds of wolves' yelping and howling in some distant woods were faintly, but clearly, audible. I liked the sound. Canadian, late summer nights were full of woods noises: crickets and other insects, an occasional whip-poor-will, the cries of foxes, and the hoots of the great horned owls that frequented Dr. Marcy's woods. The presence of wolves was rarely confirmed by a sighting, but their paw prints in muddy streambeds and nighttime chorus were proof to all of us at the Kennels that they were our neighbors some summers.

The roar of a lion was the first distinctive sound I heard through the open windows of Nichols High School on September 8, 1959. High school began on the day after Labor Day. These roars would be often repeated throughout my four years of high school. On some days, I thought they were expressions of lion love; on others they seemed more like challenges, crashing through the elms in Delaware Park between the school and the Buffalo Zoo and bursting in the air around Nichols, like English cannon balls at Fort McHenry. On other days the roars seemed sad and hopeless, as though a lonely lion was crying for a freer life. They reflected my moods.

At Nichols my world changed drastically. In P.S. No. 56 I had walked the halls and playground with a certain confidence, especially as an eighth grader. In my new role as an entering "Third Form" or freshman student at Nichols, I was at the bottom of the social order. Even worse, whereas the majority of my class of about forty boys had been at the Nichols "Lower School" for years—some since fifth grade—approximately fifteen of us were new to Nichols. The "newcomers" were from both private and public elementary schools. Eight of us were public schoolers. Apart from the economic, class distinction between the public school graduates and those who had arrived either from Nichols' Lower School or from other private schools (whose parents had been able to afford the hefty tuition for Nichols and private schools), the public schoolers had never studied a language, were behind in almost every subject, and had not played on organized sports teams very much. I soon learned that the skills in which I had excelled to some degree previously, such as playing the violin and swimming, were not important at all at Nichols.

On the other hand, I was very fortunate that my brother had attended Nichols ten years before, had been captain of several varsity teams, and had been the president of his class. He was known and respected at Nichols, and through him I had some familiarity with the school and with several faculty members, who went out of their way to make me feel welcome. Pliny Hayes, who was my father's cousin, was the Headmaster or Principal of the Lower School, Assistant Headmaster of the Upper School or high school, and a long-time member of the Lower School faculty. Don Waterman, who was the head of the Athletic Department, was married to my mother's classmate (Jo Waterman) from the Buffalo Seminary and was a family friend of many years. Both of these kind men helped me a lot, although they called me "John" for several years.

I found that the rest of the teachers at Nichols were all, without exception, anxious to help me in any possible way. And most were skillful, friendly teachers, who encouraged new students to come to them for assistance with problems. I had entered an environment where I would work incredibly hard in classes and on the athletic fields—a place of extremely intense academic and athletic training, that I would later recognize as virtually unparalleled anywhere else in my experiences.

Tuition at Nichols in 1959 was about $850.00 per year. I had been awarded a one-half scholarship, so that first year my parents paid $425 for tuition plus another $250 or so for lunches and various other fees. For them this was a sizable amount, especially since my father had lost his job as a pharmacist, when the P. Harold Hayes Company closed in December 1959, after my grandfather's retirement. By my senior year, tuition had increased to $1,050, and my scholarship was two-thirds of this amount.

We wore sports coats and ties at Nichols. School days started at 8:30 AM each day with "chapel" and ended around 5:30 PM. The last, roughly two and one half hours of each day were spent at team practices. I left home in the morning at 7:45, caught the West Delavan bus at the corner of Richmond and West Delavan Avenues, transferred at Delaware Avenue to the Colvin Avenue bus, going north on Delaware through Delaware Park to Amherst Street and then going east up Amherst past Nichols, and got off at the bus stop in front of the Nichols H.S. main entrance. The entire trip took about forty minutes and cost about twenty-five cents. I could have walked to school in about the same time, through the exceptionally lovely system of parks and parkways, designed and implemented by Frederick Law Olmsted in the 1880s. Bidwell Parkway, one block from my house, leads to Gates Circle and Lincoln Parkway, which in turn lead to Delaware Park. Nichols was on the north side of Delaware Park. The only problem with the park route was that Delaware Park Lake lay squarely across the most direct way.

The trip home by bus seemed to be a bit faster, but I was usually so exhausted on the return trip that I slept. Obliging Buffalo bus drivers woke me, when the bus arrived at my transfer site at the corner of West Delavan and Delaware Avenues and at my destination on the corner of West Delavan and Richmond Avenues.

The Headmaster or Principal of Nichols was Phillip Boocock. As a man in control of who was admitted to Nichols, and thereafter of who gained admission to the best colleges and universities, Mr. Boocock was a force to be reckoned with. He was a legend, although he appeared ordinary enough, with his slight build, short-cut hair, and glasses. Phil Boocock was very personable, and I liked him immediately. In the first week of my Nichols career, and again in the last week of my years at Nichols, I was summoned to Mr. Boocock's office for a disciplinary meeting. I regard those meetings as ironic bookends to the countless, positive volumes of experiences and knowledge that my four years at Nichols represented for me.

In the first meeting I was quite scared that I was about to be kicked out of Nichols. For the life of me, I couldn't think of what I might have done in my first week of high school to merit Mr. Boocock's attention. He told me to be seated, and in a rather stern voice said that a recent incident on a bus had come to his attention, and that he wanted me to know that standards of conduct at Nichols were different than what I might have experienced in public schools. He said that a parent of a Lower School student had reported that a freshman, by the name of Chuck, had punched the student, while riding to school on the Colvin bus on the third day of school. What did I have to say about that, I was asked.

There were three "Chucks" in my class at Nichols, although I didn't know that at the time. One of the other Chucks had been a Nichols student in the Lower School. The other was related to our family's long-time friend, Dorothy Doenitz. It took me a few minutes to remember the events of the past week, but I finally remembered that, on the day in question, a member of the faculty—George Stevens, who would become a beloved teacher and football coach—had stopped to pick me up on the corner of West Delavan and Delaware Avenues in his green, Volkswagen beetle. He could vouch for my whereabouts that morning, I responded to Mr. Boocock, whose demeanor immediately softened. Mr. Boocock then said that there was no need for him to go any further and apologized for having accused me. I later heard that classmate Chuck Moeschler had been the guilty party.

Almost four years later, in the last week of May 1963, I had to take a make-up test, for a history test that I had missed due to illness. I made arrangements to take it in the Nichols library, during lunch one day, under the watchful eye of the librarian, Mrs. Stewart, who was a favorite member of the Nichols staff. I was reported at lunchtime by someone as absent without leave and suspected of going to the zoo for lunch with other delinquent members of the graduating class. When Mr. Boocock expressed his disappointment that I, of all people, would leave school without permission, again happily, I had an alibi. Mrs. Stewart confirmed that I had been with her and that I had left a message at the front office with Mrs. Coleman, regarding my whereabouts during lunch. Mrs. Coleman—always extremely kind and caring to me—quickly verified what I had told "Boo" and winked at me. This time, Mr. Boocock didn't apologize, but he looked more sheepish than I had ever seen him look before.

Those two meetings were in Mr. Boocock's office, located just to the right and behind the front office as you entered Mitchell Hall—one of the five buildings that comprised the Nichols campus in 1959. Mitchell Hall looked like an imposing, nineteenth century residence. It was the building I preferred. As you entered the Nichols High School campus from Amherst Street, it faced the quadrangle of grass and trees from the left or west side, opposite the old gymnasium. At the head of the quadrangle, with an impressive white clock tower, was Albright Hall. The chapel, Upper School science department, and Lower School were located in Albright. On the east side of the quadrangle was the old gymnasium building with its miniscule pool and central hall, whose walls were covered with pictures of varsity teams of the past. The new gymnasium building was behind it, and connected to it. To the northwest of Mitchell Hall and bounded by the soccer field, baseball diamond, and parking lot was the hockey rink, which was the first indoor rink in Buffalo.

The buildings were all covered with ivy and surrounded by manicured lawns. Graceful elms had guarded the campus, when my brother attended Nichols from 1949 until 1953. As I entered in 1959, the Dutch Elm disease had done its work, and only a few, large trees were left. Nevertheless, Nichols was a beautiful school.

The Upper School was mostly located in Mitchell. To the left of the main entrance, and across the entrance hall from the Headmaster's Office, was the Rand Dining Hall, which ran the width of the building on the south end. It had a huge fireplace in the center of the south wall, facing the entrance, and we dined under a twenty-foot high ceiling, from which hung old chandeliers. We ate lunch in the dining hall on rectangular tables with white tablecloths, eight students to a table, each of which was supervised by a faculty member. Students served as waiters at each table on a rotating basis. The food was hot, but ordinary, with lots of bread and rolls, pasta, and salads. Our school dances were held in the dining hall, which was magically transformed into a lovely ballroom for the fall sports dance, spring prom, and other dances, during the school year.

In my first trimester of school, our biology teacher, Paul Seamans, was the teacher at our dining table. I liked him, and I think he tried to give me extra attention, because John, who had been one of his students, was studying biology in graduate school. Not many Nichols' students became biologists. One day early in my Nichols' life, Mr. Seamans complimented me on my table manners. (I had been taught an awful lot of rules for eating meals at home, such as no elbows on the table, don't talk while chewing, and cut your bread before you butter it.) His compliment, of course, doomed me to ridicule by the others at the table for several months, at a time when I was struggling to establish myself. Thereafter, I was careful to conform my manners to the Nichols' norm, a decision at which my mother would have wept, had she known.

At the other end of the main hallway, on the first floor of Mitchell, was the study hall, which was the same size as the dining hall and filled with enough desks for the entire Upper School. At the front of the study hall was the supervising teacher's desk, sitting on a low platform, so as to provide a view of the entire room. Each teacher had to supervise the study hall for several hours each week. Students had at least two hours in the study hall per day, which was the time to get most of your homework done. If your study hall was during the first period of the day, you could expect that, depending on the identity of the supervising teacher, their desk would come crashing off the platform with a tremendous noise. It was an almost weekly prank to position the first period, supervising teacher's desk on the low platform, so that one or more legs were on the edge of the platform. When the teacher sat down and applied any pressure to the desk, the desk fell off, to the accompaniment of guarded laughter throughout the room.

There were some teachers whom you did not dare to subject to this trick. Others, I noticed, always checked the desk's legs, before stepping onto the platform. Some of the older faculty were most susceptible to sitting down, completely oblivious to the impending crash, having forgotten that the same trick had been played on them the previous week. Once, just before Christmas in my first year, when I was looking forward to getting home early one day, the desk had been rigged, during the first period, by several Sixth Form, or senior, students, who eagerly anticipated that Austin Fox—the venerable chair of the English Department (and, as I have mentioned, a fellow customer of Charlie's Barber Shop)—would soon be ambushed, as his name was on the list as that morning's study hall proctor. Instead, Headmaster Boocock strode in to make an announcement he had forgotten to make at Chapel. He was *not* one of the faculty members on whom you wanted to play this trick. Of course, the desk fell off with a loud crash. We all ended up staying an extra hour after school, and the responsible seniors had their senior privileges suspended (driving to school and access to the senior lounge).

Our classrooms were on the second floor. My first year I had Advanced Algebra with Mr. Gillespie—one of the older faculty members; English with Mr. Stevens—later my favorite teacher, who taught me how to write; World History with Mr. Pedersen—another favorite teacher; Biology with Mr. Seamans—who made a tough subject interesting and enjoyable; and French I with Mr. Sutter—probably the best teacher I ever had.

Mr. Sutter was Nichols' premier language teacher, known as "El Supremo," and taught Spanish. His students always had the best Spanish achievement scores in New York State, and it was not unusual for several to get perfect scores on the college boards. They not only read and wrote Spanish flawlessly, they also spoke Spanish fluently after a couple of years with him. He annually won the award as the best Spanish teacher in the state. Despite my brother's advice to take Spanish, I opted to study French as a freshman, although I was aware of Mr. Sutter's reputation for excellence, for his legendary status was a bit intimidating.

When I reported to my French class, during my first day at Nichols, El Supremo was before us. Mr. Sutter only taught French I for one year in his long career as a language teacher. I was fortunate enough to have him that one year. He spoke only French in class. He piled on the homework. We had hundreds of rules to memorize. He was a strict teacher, and tolerated no inattention or laziness in class, but he also had a nice way of laughing with us at our mistakes to ease tension in the class. When he broke into English to say "Hobbie old boy," you knew you were in trouble. I struggled with French and was close to failing the course at the end of the first trimester. Language was something I had never thought about much prior to Nichols. Learning the rules of French was very hard for me. Mr. Sutter encouraged me as much as possible in class, and taught us memory tricks to facilitate learning. I went to him for help after school. He always had the time to explain how I could better remember the order of words or the pronunciation of difficult sounds.

After the first trimester examination, Mr. Sutter excitedly called me at home to tell me that I had passed with flying colors. He was even happier than I was. I only had him as a teacher for that one year. I took French for three more years at Nichols and three years at Dartmouth, studied in France at the University of Montpellier in 1965, and graduated from college with a minor in French, but I learned more French with Mr. Sutter in one year than in the rest of the years combined. And the discipline in language learning, that he taught me, helped me enormously, as I studied Korean in later years.

In Mr. Gillespie's Algebra class I sat next to a tall, lanky boy named Bob Ramage. We became very close friends. Bob was kind, intelligent, athletic, and had been in the lower school at Nichols. He was respected by all, as our class president, star kicker and tackle on the football team, and discus and shot-put thrower on the track team. Above all, he was a nice person. Bob lived in Snyder, New York, a suburb of Buffalo. He had five sisters and a brother—all younger than he was. His mother was an attractive, youthful-looking, blond woman, who persisted in trying to persuade me to take out one of Bob's sisters. His father was kind, but gruff, and was usually watching television and drinking scotch or smoking a cigar, whenever I visited the Ramages. Many years after high school I found out—on the occasion of his burial at Arlington National Cemetery with high honors—that Mr. Ramage had been awarded the Navy Cross for his heroism as a Navy bomber pilot over

Japan in World War II. He never said anything about the war, when I knew him. I was very fortunate to have had Bob as a close friend.

Next to Mr. Gillespie's classroom was that of Norman A. Pedersen, whose World History classes I looked forward to every week. I found history perhaps the most interesting of all my classes. Mr. Pedersen was a wonderful teacher. He was later the assistant varsity football coach, and varsity track coach, and went on to become a famous, beloved Headmaster of the Brunswick School in Greenwich, Connecticut.

At the end of the hall was a flight of steps, climbing to the McNutt Library, located above the dining hall. Nichols' sweetheart of a librarian, Mrs. Stewart, made this her domain. The first time that I wandered into the library she greeted me and told me that my brother had been one her favorite students. She showed me the seal of Dartmouth College in the stained glass door of the library (which had been donated by a Dartmouth alumnus), and said how happy she was that John had gone to Dartmouth. I loved the peacefulness of the library, with its shelves of books and comfortable chairs. It was my favorite room at Nichols and where I opted to take any make-up or take-home tests, during my high school years. Mrs. Stewart provided a sympathetic ear to any problems, and seemed to know when a student was upset about something.

After classes were over each day in the autumn of 1959, I reported to the gymnasium, changed into my football gear, and reported for freshmen football practice. I tried out for running back, but the competition was fierce. Another public schooler, a big guy named Mike, was faster, stronger, and shiftier than any of us. Mike Quinlan, who everyone said was built like a hydrant, became our fullback, and went on in later years to lead Nichols to its best records in football and to set the school rushing record. He was awesome!

Nichols' football team ran the single wing formation, which once had been the most popular formation on collegiate and high school teams, but in the fifties had been replaced elsewhere by variations of the T formation. In the single wing, the fullback took the direct snap from the center, in a position several yards behind the line, then either passed, handed-off to another back, or ran. Because the varsity football team ran the single wing system, the freshman team used it also. You needed a big, fast back, who could run and throw, like two-time Heisman Trophy winner Dick Kazmaier of Princeton. The Nichols varsity coach, George Stevens, who graduated from Nichols in 1948, knew all about that, as he had been the Princeton quarterback in the Kazmaier years. Mike was perfect for that role. He was impossible to stop.

In almost every play, the left guard pulled out from the line to block for the passing back, to lead the blocking through the middle of the line or around the end, or to serve as a decoy. Which player on the other team you were supposed to block was determined by how the opposing team lined up. Audible signals from several key players on the line told the rest of the linemen whom to block. I guess because I was pretty big and fast, I became the pulling guard on offense and enjoyed the action a lot. I soon learned that Mike was so fast and bullish, running the ball, that I had to get through the line ahead of him quickly and find my target—usually a linebacker—before Mike piled into me from behind!

On defense I settled into the position of left linebacker at first, and later, left defensive end. I recall that football practices were brutal in September's heat. Under the freshmen coach, Dave Allen, we ran countless wind sprints, up and down the field, blocked on blocking sleds, and did hundreds of pushups, leg lifts, jumping jacks, and every other kind of exercise you can imagine. I had never been so tired in my life! The next day I was fine, but on the second day I could hardly walk. We also started to learn the playbook—a complicated set of about forty plays, which we had to memorize. Four of us who played on the line—Bob Ramage, another classmate, Tom Goldstein, whom I liked a lot, Jim McGibbon (from P.S. No. 56), and I—cemented our friendships on the freshmen football field, as our team won 3 and lost 2.

In November, I attended my first Nichols dance—the Fall Sports Dance. Sandy Maisel, another classmate, asked me if I would double date and share a rented car. The "car" was a "stretch" limousine, big enough for ten people. My date, Marny Wilson (a pretty freshman at the Buffalo Seminary), and I joined Sandy and his date for dinner at the Swiss Chalet restaurant on Main Street in downtown Buffalo, with the limo and driver waiting outside, before driving to Nichols for the dance in the Rand Dining Hall. This was the first of many dances in high school that I enjoyed. I never again engaged a limo. It was too expensive. Getting around on dates was a problem at the age of fourteen, so transportation was an issue, unless you had older siblings who were willing to drive you around. Mine were both in college or graduate school, away from home. But my mother and father were very obliging chauffeurs, and whenever possible I double-dated with a classmate who had older siblings, willing to pick up and drop off our dates.

After the Falls Sports Dance at Nichols, there were several holiday season, debutante balls at various country clubs, for which I was obliged to buy a tuxedo. Several girls, whom I knew through their families (their siblings had been classmates of Ceci or John or their mothers had been classmates at the Seminary of my mother), asked me to escort them. At first, I enjoyed going to these dances. They provided an opportunity to meet girls from the Seminary, to drink at open bars (I was never asked if I was eighteen, which was the legal drinking age), and to get to know my classmates better in social settings. And I enjoyed dancing. I probably attended a dozen such affairs, before I decided that I missed the girls I knew at P.S. No. 56. There were some wonderful freshmen girls at the Seminary, but I felt uncomfortable with them—probably because I was socially immature and thinking too much about their superior economic status. They also seemed to be more interested in sophomore boys than in a lowly freshman. So I started to turn down invitations, and put away my tuxedo.

Nichols had the trimester system, with final exams each term in November, March, and June, respectively. After really struggling academically during the first trimester, in the new year—1960—I began to do better and to catch up with those classmates who had been better prepared. I found, however, that my homework and school sports consumed all my time and energy. I lost track of former public school friends. I no longer had time to attend concerts, or to visit the Albright-Knox Art Gallery, which was one of my favorite places in Buffalo. Nichols took over my life!

During the winter term of 1960, the frenzied, academic work continued, especially in French, my difficulty with which kept me off the honor roll until the spring term. I loved to watch the Nichols' hockey games in the old rink, which thundered with cheering and shook with the excitement of those games, but at the same time, I deeply regretted that I was such a bad skater that I could never even think of playing hockey. For the past four years, during the winter, I had been in training for competitive swimming at P.S. No. 56. At Nichols, without swimming in the winter, I felt lost.

With the spring term and the melting snows on the Nichols' campus, I turned to an old love—baseball. I was a pretty good outfielder, but I had trouble hitting. I got contact lenses when I was fifteen, and these helped some, when I played Junior Varsity baseball for the next two years. I recall a lot of strikeouts, one good bunt, and only one sterling play in those two years. We were playing the Park School. In centerfield, I managed to make a one-handed catch of a deep, fly ball to center-left field, after a long sprint, and to throw to Ed Marlette at shortstop, who doubled-off a runner to end the inning.

My former P.S. No. 56 and dance school classmate, Ann Jones, invited me to the Buffalo Seminary Prom in the spring of 1960. I had known Ann since kindergarten. She was a good friend. I dusted off my tuxedo, and my father drove. When we arrived at the Buffalo Seminary, I accidentally closed the car door on Ann's hand, as she was getting out of the car. My father took one look at Ann's bloody hand and said that we needed to get her immediately to a doctor. Ann suggested, instead, that we go to her house and let her parents—both physicians—bandage her hand, which we did. Then we returned to the prom and danced a few dances, with Ann's bandaged hand held gingerly in mine, before she was elected as the freshman "queen" and took her place as a part of the "court" on the stage. The evening was a success, and I was tremendously relieved that my mistake had not irrevocably spoiled the prom for her.

Later the same month, my parents and I drove to South Hadley, Massachusetts, for Ceci's graduation from Mt. Holyoke College. The campus, with its many copper beeches and spacious lawns, was beautiful in June. Ceci and her friends were radiant. It was a lovely graduation. Ceci then prepared to head for Middlebury College in Vermont, where she would work and study for the summer.

Although I struggled with French in my first year at Nichols, otherwise I found that, by the end of the year, I was doing just fine. P.S. No. 56 had prepared me well. I ended up on the honor roll for the year. Mr. Boocock had a very nice custom of writing notes to my parents with each trimester's final report card. These chronicled the ups and downs of all my academic efforts at Nichols for my four years there. His notes assured me that, even when I had a relatively low grade in a subject, I would improve.

During the summer of 1960, I had my first summer job. I applied for a camp counselor position at the Point Abino Day Camp in Canada, where I had attended as a camper, eight years before. The camp director now was my former counselor, Bob Kreuger. I got the job. Bronwin Baird, who was the sister of Nichols classmate Bruce Baird, and Ginny Irwin, a junior at the Buffalo Seminary, were two of the other counselors. I had to be at the camp entrance on Point Abino Road at 8:00 AM each day. Some days, my mother or father dropped me off from Buffalo; on other days, after staying the night at our cabin, I walked east along the beach from the Kennels, about one and one half miles, until I came to the Baird estate, and then through the estate, about half a mile, to the camp entrance.

I was in charge of getting the lunches to the lunch area, and of teaching swimming, as well as being the counselor for about twelve boys. One of the boys was Jimmy Bergantz, who several years later entered the Nichols Lower School and reminded me, when I was a senior, that I had been his camp counselor, years before. My squad of boys and I roamed the sand dunes and woods of Point Abino, played Capture the Flag, softball, touch football, badminton, tennis, and other games with the other three groups, swam in the pool and on the beach, rode the horses in the Baird's stables, paddled around the large pond on paddleboats, and otherwise had a tremendously fun time!

Camp was over at 3:00. To get home, I walked back to our cabin, around the curve of Holloway Bay's beach, hitchhiked to Buffalo, or caught a ride with one of the camper's parents. I really liked both Ginny and Bronwin, who were older girls, and very attractive in different ways—Ginny, an athletic blond with short hair, and Bronwin, a very pretty, longhaired brunette with freckles—and kind. When the summer ended, I was as brown as a berry, had nothing but fine memories of my one summer as a camp counselor—especially of a kiss from Bronwin—and had finished the fifteen books that were required summer reading for all Nichols students.

Pre-season football practice began in mid August of 1960, just before my second year at Nichols. It was really brutally hot and exhausting. Chuck Kreiner, who was the other defensive end, passed out from the heat. We practiced three hours in the morning, broke for two hours at lunch, and then resumed practice for another three hours. Exercises, wind sprints, blocking sleds, tackling drills, cross-blocking drills, countless laps around the field, and scrimmages all merge in my memories into one huge, sweaty, grueling, hot, smelly, thirsty, exhausted, dirty, and satisfying image.

Towards the end of the pre-season practices, Coach Stevens announced that we would be scrimmaging against Riverside High School, whose coach was my former gym teacher at P.S. No. 56—Charlie Dingboom. That year, he would coach Riverside H.S. to the city public high school championships in both football and swimming—the first of many. Riverside had a big senior fullback, who was strong and fast, like our Mike Quinlan. Charlie Dingboom came over to me, before the practice game began, and asked how I was enjoying Nichols, expressing regret that I had not accepted his invitation to come with him to Riverside. I appreciated his kind words and have often thought about him with fondness.

During the scrimmage, I was playing left linebacker in the last quarter. On a blitz, I went tearing into the Riverside backfield and met the fullback head on. There was a tremendous collision. I was knocked groggy, and the fullback was helped off the field. I think I was barely conscious, when my teammate, Jack Walsh, helped me up and congratulated me. That was the first of several occasions, playing football, that I had my "bell rung." Afterwards, Charlie Dingboom shook my hand and then his head, and asked, jokingly, if I was trying to single-handedly destroy his football team. That was the last time I ever saw Charlie, who went on to coach successfully for over fifty years.

In my second year at Nichols, we studied poetry in George Steven's English class, and my world changed. Mr. Stevens was an excellent teacher, and he was particularly skillful at conveying his own love of literature and poetry to his students. It certainly helped that he had been the quarterback—and outstanding blocking back—of an undefeated, championship team at Princeton in 1951, thereby earning the instant respect and attention of his students. He never talked about that, but was eloquent in discussing such American poets as Frost, Dickinson, Jeffers, or Whitman. I got hooked on poetry in his class, and it has been a source of peace and great pleasure, throughout my life.

At Nichols, we used a writing manual called the *Harper's Handbook*.

Essentially, it was a book of dozens of writing rules, each numbered, with subcategories and with examples of correct and incorrect prose. When Mr. Stevens corrected an essay, he would mark a mistake in grammar, punctuation, or style by circling the error and noting in the margin the number of the applicable rule. We then had to look up the rule, write it fifteen times, correct the mistake, and write the corrected version of the sentence or paragraph ten times. In this way we had grammar, spelling, and style drummed into our heads. For example, rule 52f was "Do not carelessly misspell words." I probably wrote this rule several thousand times during my four years at Nichols. But I learned how to write, and to check spelling, thanks to George Stevens!

I also learned how to drive my second year at Nichols—except for how to express myself, it was perhaps the most important thing I ever learned. During the second trimester of my sophomore year, with most of the rest of my classmates, I took Driver's Education. Our teacher, Mr. O'Connell, was a saint, and totally unflappable. Our class was before school in the morning, often while it was still dark outside. Several huge snowstorms during the term assured that we all learned to drive in the worst of conditions. Mr. O'Connell sat in the right front seat, and while each of us took turns driving, the other three boys were wedged in the back seat, praying that we would survive. There were no seat belts in those days. We drove through blinding blizzards and on glare ice. Mr. O'Connell taught us that you had to develop good driving habits from the beginning. He drummed into our heads: "Anticipate, anticipate, anticipate! Drive as though everyone else is crazy! Never tailgate, and in snowy conditions do everything with great deliberation." I thought we would all die on several occasions. Mr. O'Connell had one primary rule: no screaming in the back seat.

I recall one particularly harrowing experience, when even Mr. O'Connell got upset. It occurred while Bernie Pitterman was driving in a raging snowstorm one morning. He had started slowly down a long, steep hill, when suddenly, we all saw the snow plow at the bottom of the hill, beginning to back up the hill with its salt-spreader engaged and spewing salt—a huge fan-like, rotating blade at the rear of the truck. The truck was perhaps a quarter of a mile away. Bernie slammed on the brakes and lost control. The driver education car kept sliding on the hill's icy surface, straight down towards the backing truck with its spewing blade. It seemed as though everything was happening in slow motion and that it took an eternity for our car to finally slide to a stop against a curb, about twenty feet from the truck. Five shaken riders emerged, and four started yelling at Bernie.

In March, I decided to apply for a summer job with the Appalachian Mountain Club, in New Hampshire's White Mountains, as a "hutman." As I mentioned above, John had been a hutman for four years, working first at the AMC's headquarters at Pinkham Notch and then at Lakes of the Clouds Hut on the shoulder of Mt. Washington. Ceci had worked for two years at Pinkham, and I had visited many huts with them and with my parents on summer visits, years before. I wrote to George Hamilton, who had taken over as the Manager of the Huts System from the legendary Joe Dodge only the year before. I was very disappointed to receive a letter back almost immediately, telling me that, unfortunately, all positions had already been filled. But George told me to renew my application in the fall for next year. I was extremely sad that my summer plans had unraveled.

In the spring of 1961, the dreaded Fourth Form (sophomore) oral report in English II was prepared and delivered. This was a fifteen-minute, oral presentation on a subject in English literature that had been approved by Mr. Stevens. By this time, we were all used to writing fifteen to twenty page papers on a variety of subjects, as well as to making brief statements in class, but none of us had made this kind of a scholarly, oral presentation before. Its prospect made all of us extremely nervous. The presentations were spread out over a one-week period in May. You could not read a prepared paper in giving your report. Only note cards were permitted.

My presentation was entitled "The Poets of the South" and featured such poets as Sidney Lanier, Edgar Allan Poe, and Henry Timrod. I rehearsed it several times at home with my parents and godmother, Ruth Culliton, who taught English at Kensington High School. It was twenty-five minutes long. The morning of this frightening event was extremely warm. The windows of Mr. Steven's corner classroom, on the second floor alcove, were wide open to catch the breezes. Pigeons had nested on the ledges outside of the windows, and their twitterings and cooings accompanied a strong, sulfuric smell of rotten, pigeon eggs that drifted through the classroom. My presentation was third. Mike Keiser's oral report went well in the lead off position. Harry Meyer was next and was looking sort of green as he stood up. My stomach, already churning with anxiety, was not helped when Harry went over to the window and leaned out, sick to his stomach. We both got through our oral reports. The smell of sulfur invariably recalls for me that stifling, May morning of rotten, pigeon eggs.

Several weeks later, a telegram arrived. My brother had become a limnologist, specializing in the ecology of arctic lakes. Under a research grant, he and his new wife, Olivann, had spent the winter at an isolated, research facility in northeastern Alaska on Lake Peters, in the heart of what is now the Arctic National Wildlife Refuge. Lake Peters lies in a remote, rugged part of the Franklin Mountains in the northeastern Brooks Range, at approximately 69 degrees N latitude and 145 degrees W longitude. Mount Chamberlin's glaciers feed the lake from its southeastern shore. John's telegram invited me to join them at Lake Peters for the summer, as a research assistant replacement for a graduate student, who had become ill at the last minute. Mr. Seaman's biology classes were suddenly relevant. My despair, at not being able to work for the AMC in the White Mountains, evaporated.

With my parents' approval and Phil Boocock's blessing, I prepared to leave Buffalo for Alaska on June 1st, skipping the last two weeks of school and final exams. But first, my parents, Ceci, and I drove to New York City on May 29th to pick up my mother's cousin, Vera Holden, who was arriving on the *Queen Mary* from England to visit us for the summer—the first visit of an English cousin from my mother's side of the family. We had never met Vera, although she and my mother had corresponded for years. She lived in Erdington, which is a suburb of Birmingham, England, and was about my mother's age—mid fifties. Ceci and I went out on the New York pier—in the shadow of the magnificent *HMS Queen Mary*, which was the first ocean liner I had ever seen—to look for her with a sign: "Welcome Vera Holden." We spotted her immediately. She looked totally befuddled. As our family joyously welcomed Vera, I don't think I had ever seen my mother so happy.

It was an eight-hour drive from New York City back to Buffalo on the New York State Thruway. I remember how shocked Vera was to learn that we were driving about 100 kilometers/hour (60 miles/hour) and that it would still take eight hours to get home. She was amazed at the open countryside, forests, Hudson Valley, Finger Lakes, and wide expanses of farmland we drove through, and repeatedly commented on how beautiful New York State was—she had thought that it was all developed and heavily populated. I looked at my home state with fresh eyes and greater appreciation. Vera stayed with us for three months, and returned many times in future years.

As soon as we returned to Buffalo, my sister prepared to leave for France, where she would be studying and working during the summer. I packed for Alaska, traveling as lightly as I thought prudent.

On June 1, 1961, I took my first plane ride, flying from Buffalo to Chicago, and changing to a flight to Seattle, en route to Lake Peters, Alaska. After about ten hours of flying, I spent the night at the Blue Haven Motel in Seattle, before another long flight to Fairbanks, Alaska, on June 2nd. Most of these planes were old DC-3s, with two propeller engines. I was met in Fairbanks by staff of the Arctic Research Laboratory (ARL) and spent the night in a dormitory at the University of Alaska. I remember that I went to a movie theater after dinner and was amazed, when I emerged from the movie at about 11:00 PM into bright sunshine. Early the following morning, I boarded an Alaska Airlines plane for a three-hour flight over cloud-covered mountains, arriving at a bleak, desolate Point Barrow at about noon. Below me on the flight across Alaska, I occasionally glimpsed magnificent, jagged peaks, when they poked through the clouds.

Point Barrow is the northernmost tip of Alaska. It was the headquarters for the ARL. In June it was still surrounded by pack ice in the Arctic Ocean. There was a constant, cold wind off the ocean. After lunch with the ARL Director, Max Brewer, and other staff, I was taken to the supply depot, where I was issued clothes and equipment for the summer, including a heavy parka, gloves, boots, both cold weather and warm weather shirts and pants, a camera, binoculars, woolen socks, and other paraphernalia—most of it army surplus. Then, I was shown to my dormitory, which was a Quonset hut, amidst a sea of mud and planks. Before I could settle in, my name came over a loudspeaker to report to Max Brewer's office. There, Max told me to pack my gear. My flight to Lake Peters was leaving in half an hour. Forty minutes later, I was winging towards northeastern Alaska in a small, single engine, Cessna 195 with the pilot (Loyd Zimmerman or "Zim"), a new cook for the Lake Peters camp (Russ Gilsdorf), and a carpenter (Frank Talbert), who was to oversee the construction of several, small buildings there.

We flew for hours over the snow-splotched tundra, lying between the Brooks Range across northern Alaska and the Arctic Ocean, known as the "North Slope," as the terrain dropped from the mountains on our right to the sea coast on our left. I could not believe how beautiful the land beneath our plane was, alternating in color from the light blue of the pools, forming from melting snow, to the various shades of white and gray, marking ice and snow of differing depths and texture. The sky was overcast. Heavy fog lay on the coast. At our relatively low altitude, it seemed as though the land beneath us was totally devoid of life. Zim laughed when I mentioned this, and promised that in a few weeks this area would be the prettiest sight I had ever seen, filled with flowers, birds, and animals. This was hard to believe. In several hours the only movement we saw below were several huge white owls—Snowy Owls—that were startled into flight by the sound of our plane. White, gray, and blue on all sides. It was surrealistic. Zim was reading a *Playboy* magazine, as he flew on automatic pilot at an altitude of about two hundred feet.

After almost three, long hours, we turned south into the foothills of the Brooks Range. Zim told us to watch out through the fog for the mountains ahead. In a minute he shouted to us to look down. Several herds of caribou scattered below us on the snow—the first caribou he had seen this year and my first ever. I marveled that this was June, and it still seemed to be winter. In a minute, we climbed over a range of mountains and into a bank of fog. Zim said that we were circling above Lake Peters. I could see nothing around the plane but whiteness. We circled for twenty minutes, before Zim said that we weren't going to get down there today through this fog. So we turned north towards the Arctic coast.

Zim nonchalantly told us that we were low on fuel and that he was looking for a place to set down. I had a moment of panic. Set down? As far as I could see, there was nothing but snow and ice. Twenty minutes later, we spotted the Distant Early Warning (DEW) Line Station at Barter Island, which was a military, radar facility on the Arctic coast. Zim radioed Barter Island that we needed to land. The response was negative, but Zim brought us down on the runway, anyway. We were immediately surrounded by angry, military police, who were upset at Zim for landing there. He knew some of them already. We refueled, had a hearty dinner with the two dozen men at the base, and radioed Point Barrow for instructions. Zim was told to keep trying to get through to Lake Peters all night, if necessary, so we took off and headed south towards the mountains, again in the quiet light.

This time, we found a hole in the three thousand-foot ceiling of low clouds and dropped into the Lake Peters valley. I saw mountain peaks all around us through the fog, but could not see anything below, until suddenly the frozen lake was visible, and our plane's skis touched down on the lake's ice. It was about 9:00 PM. We had been en route for six and one half hours. Zim seemed relieved. He then explained that, the day before, a C-123J (two propeller cargo plane with retractable skis for use on compacted snow runways) had touched down on the Lake Peters ice and almost gone through the ice, before gunning its engines and flying out without stopping. We taxied over across the ice to a point of land that stuck out into Lake Peters on its east shore—a kind of gravel bank with several, small structures on it. The temperature on that June 3rd was 45 degrees, and a biting wind blew across the ice, as we hopped out of the Cessna. Thanks to John, in the past three days I had flown about six thousand miles on five different planes—my first airplane flights—across unforgettable landscapes. I entered an amazing Aladdin's cave of life that evening.

John and Olivann welcomed me. With them at the Lake Peters camp were the camp manager, Frank Riddell; a limnologist from Indiana University, Dr. David Frey; and an ornithologist from Syracuse University, Dr. Tom Cade. Frank was an older man, who was famous throughout the north country, I later learned, for having helped track and kill in 1932 a murdering trapper, known as the "Mad Trapper of Rat River," in the Yukon Territory, in Canada's most famous and most violent manhunt. They all told me that I had set a record in getting to Lake Peters in less than ten hours from the time of my arrival at Point Barrow.

The next day the weather cleared. The breathtaking silence of the Lake Peters valley was broken, early in the morning, when several, huge, Air Force cargo planes wheeled into the valley and dropped twenty-seven barrels of fuel on the ice, without breaking one. Each plane descended to within fifteen feet of the ice, and then the barrels rolled out, bouncing on the ice. The second morning, the planes were back, this time dropping construction supplies by parachute. Three parachutes failed to open, so some lumber, paint, and furniture were total losses. The sight of those gigantic planes, straining to turn in the narrow valley, and then swinging around to make repeated drops across the frozen lake, gave me goose bumps!

John, the other men, and I spent most of our time, for the next several days, collecting barrels, lumber, and construction supplies on the ice, and bringing them to camp with the help of a bombadier, which was a small, tractor-like vehicle, moving on chain link treads. The camp consisted of a tiny, two-room laboratory building (20'x16'), the main building (20'x16'), where the kitchen and dining room were located, two Jamesway (Quonset) huts, a generator shack, an outhouse, and a large tent. All of us slept in one of the Jamesway huts on cots, except John and Olivann, who stayed in the laboratory. Within two weeks, the carpenters had built another small building (16'x24') for our dormitory, as well as a new outhouse and generator shack. We became a tiny village almost overnight. As each week brought a couple of new scientists to our group, the added accommodations were just in time.

Lake Peters Research Station in the foreground on the shore with Mt. Chamberlin and its glacier in the upper right, 1961

Surrounding the lake on the south, east, and west sides were mountains, rising approximately five thousand feet above us. Our camp rested on the tip of an alluvial fan, which had been created by deposits from a stream, emptying into Lake Peters on the east shore. There were four such large, alluvial fans on Lake Peters, and several smaller ones. From the air, they looked like small, fan-shaped peninsulas, with the narrow part of the fan anchored to the stream heads, emerging from the bottom of the mountains that rose from the east shoreline. Ours was the second from the south end of the lake. The lake valley itself had been scoured from the mountains by glaciers. Although not visible from camp, these glaciers had retreated to the sides of nine thousand-foot high Mt. Chamberlin, a couple of miles to the southeast of camp. They fed the streams that dropped into the lake, depositing glacial silt, which formed the alluvial fans and turned the waters of Lake Peters cloudy. At the tip of the wide end of our alluvial fan was a large, gravel bank, inhabited by about sixty ground squirrels and seven humans. The bank was ten feet above the water of the lake. The squirrels, which are similar in appearance to prairie dogs, constructed their homes under the gravel; we built on top. Both men and squirrels were avoiding the pools of water, forming from the melting snows and glacial runoff and surrounding the hummocks of vegetation on the lake's shores and lower slopes of the mountains.

From our gravel bank, facing north, you looked across the several miles of rapidly melting ice, towards the north end of Lake Peters, where there was a small outlet, linking Lake Peters to another lake—Lake Schrader—surrounded by rolling hills, just north of the Brooks Range. About sixty miles further north, and not visible, lay the Arctic coast. To the west, directly across the lake, rose a long ridge of peaks, the sides of which swooped gracefully down to Lake Peters, as though formed by an ice cream scoop. More high mountains lay to the south. Their razor-sharp ridges, like those all around the lake, dropped silvery cascades of water to a narrow stream valley that emptied into Lake Peters' southernmost waters.

In early June, the snow was gone from the valley and lower slopes of the surrounding mountains, but topped the adjacent mountains. As we were hundreds of miles north of the tree line, and about three hundred miles north of the Arctic Circle, the only trees anywhere were low willows, growing in the shelter of stream valleys. Otherwise, the lowlands looked like brown fields, stretching as far as you could see, and broken only by rolling hills, streams, and pools of melt water.

One evening, shortly after arriving, I went with John and Tom Cade to Tom's bird blind, about half a mile from camp, next to some willows in a stream bed. Tom had built the blind to observe the nest of a northern shrike and the baby shrike in the nest. The blind had blown away, but the nest and babies were there. Not far away were several "meat trees," on the twigs of which the shrike had impaled their kills for safekeeping: bumblebees, mice, and small birds. Tom had a tame northern shrike, named "Greenie," which he hunted like a falcon. The bird sat in a cage until Tom gave it a signal. Then, it flew out, looked for game, struck, and returned with its kill to the cage. We spent many, fascinating hours with that tame shrike. When it unexpectedly drowned at the end of the summer, Tom stuffed it and gave it to me.

For someone who has always loved to watch birds, it was wonderful to have both my brother and an ornithologist in camp with whom to go bird watching. John could answer every question I had about the ecology of the Lake Peters valley, as he had been studying it for years, and Tom could answer virtually every question I had about the birds of the area. Tom and I went hunting on the tundra for nests, finding literally hundreds. We took a long chain, tied some rags along it, and carried it between us, as we walked about ten feet apart across the tundra, crisscrossing the terrain in ten-foot wide swaths. As the chain and rags passed over a nest, the camouflaged bird on the nest was startled to flight, showing us where to search for the nest. Sometimes, it took quite a while to find the nest, amidst the grasses and other tundra vegetation, for they were very well hidden. Within my first week at Lake Peters I had seen over thirty new species of birds and had found the nests and eggs of many of these. I was in heaven!

Several days after my arrival, Olivann left on a return plane for Point Barrow and then California. She was expecting a baby in late August, and ARL did not want to risk any problems at such an isolated site. I took over her job as camp meteorologist, in addition to working as John's assistant, and soon learned how to record temperatures, wind speeds, precipitation, types and heights of clouds, and other weather measurements. John and I made regular rounds of his various instruments throughout the valley, retrieving information on temperatures, humidity, and precipitation. We also took samples of water from various locations on the lake, measured the temperature and turbidity of the water, and took ice samples from cores. As the ice still covered Lake Peters, to get to the water we had to fashion holes through the ice with a drill, being very careful, whenever we were on the ice, to drag our small boat with us, just in case. We carried the samples back to the laboratory for storage and analysis at a later date.

The largest and most magnificent birds in the valley were golden eagles. A pair was nesting on a ledge, under an overhang on a cliff about one mile from camp. The nest was huge and barely visible from below. We climbed up several hundred feet to a point above the overhang on the steep slope, and then, with a climber's rope fastened around both of us, and after making sure that the adults were not in the vicinity, took turns bracing each other's descent to a point where you could see into the nest. No eggs or eaglets were there, only feathers and bones. But it was still a thrill to see a golden eagle's nest so relatively close up.

On the way down the mountain in a light rain, we spotted below us a golden marmot, sitting on a rock. Marmots are like woodchucks, but larger and with thick, golden-brown coats, which are highly prized by the Native Americans. It is very difficult to see them, for they are usually quite high up on the sides of mountains and spot you before you are within a quarter of a mile.

We were lucky to get within eighty feet or so by approaching the animal from above. As soon as we were spotted, the marmot gave its long, warning whistle and disappeared. I learned to rely on that whistle, and on the alert ground squirrels at lower elevations, to warn me of the approach of any animal, or even of a plane, long before I could see or hear it.

On these trips we usually carried a rifle. I was very aware of the dangerous grizzly bears in the area; we often spotted holes, where bears had dug out a ground squirrel burrow, or found bear scat. In fact, you could say that I was obsessed with watching out for bears, as I stopped whatever I was doing, about every two minutes or so, and took a long look around me with my binoculars. If I saw squirrels happily going about their business without concern, I was reassured. If I heard a marmot's whistle, or a ground squirrel's warning chirp, I scanned the land and skies to make sure that it was an eagle, and not a bear, which had prompted the warning.

In mid June we had a lot of rain and fog. One day it poured all day, and I measured over an inch of precipitation. Considering that the average, annual rainfall in the valley was only about ten inches, so much rain was very unusual. Happily, we were able to move into the new dormitory, built by Frank "father" Talbert and Harry Brower in about one week, just before the rains came. We had spent days piecing together the beds and chairs, broken in the airdrops. Now we had bunk beds with mattresses and real chairs to sit on, instead of crates. Wonderful luxury!

On rainy days we usually stayed indoors, working in the laboratory. Even on overcast, foggy days, we had twenty-four hours of continuous daylight in varying intensity. Window shades in the dormitory permitted a dark room for sleeping. From about 9:00 PM until 3:00 AM, the sun was very low on the horizon, casting long shadows from the peaks into the valley. The light of the midnight sun was lovely—a soft, golden light that gave everything it touched a diffuse, unearthly aspect.

The camp's generator provided enough electricity so that we could run the scientific equipment needed to analyze samples, have plenty of indoor light, and also play music on John's stereo system. If there were any disagreements among the camp staff, working in the laboratory, it was usually over which records to play. John's collection was all classical music. Fine for me. There was one popular music record: the 1956 original cast recording of "My Fair Lady" with Rex Harrison, Stanley Holloway, and Julie Andrews. We played "My Fair Lady" so many times that both Tom Cade and I knew all the lyrics by heart by the end of the summer. It is still my favorite musical. Tom had a great voice and did a fantastic imitation of Stanley Holloway.

We had big appetites. The Navy fed us well. A typical dinner was roast chicken, stuffing, mashed potatoes, beets, tossed salad, bread and butter, rolls, tomato juice, coffee and pudding. Breakfast and lunch were equally hearty. I started to put on weight, gaining about a half pound each week, despite all the exercise I was getting. I got a kick out of reading the cereal boxes at breakfast. A lot of our food was military surplus and a bit outdated. The cereal boxes had "offers" on them that had expired ten years earlier.

After breakfast, and after dinner, we cranked up the radio and reported the weather to Point Barrow, to the Barter Island DEW Line station, and to the ice island stations, T 3 and Arlis II, which were hundreds of miles to the north, floating in the Arctic Ocean. The radio and the biweekly planes were our fragile links to civilization. One of the first things I was taught was how to operate that radio.

Each day in June, the ice got thinner. For several weeks no planes came, because they could not land on the lake anymore. All of us awaited the day the lake would be free of ice and once again provide a safe landing for our lifeline Cessnas. I predicted that the ice would be gone from Lake Peters on June 24th. We had an "ice pool" to which we each contributed one dollar. The person who correctly guessed the date that the ice disappeared would win. There were fifteen men at the camp by mid June, so the pool was fifteen dollars. By the 24th, the ice had transformed itself into millions of "candles"—ice structures that looked like row upon row of upright candles, jammed together. When the wind blew, the candles bobbed up and down in waves and clinked together like wooden wind chimes. The candled ice would support no significant weight, so planes could not land or take off, and boats could not be used on the lake, either. We did a lot of hiking for a couple of weeks to make the rounds of John's instrument stations, located throughout the valley and on the shores of Lake Schrader to the north.

In mid June, I started making ground squirrel observations for Dick Swade, a mammalogist from Princeton, who paid me two dollars per hour. I got up every morning at 4:00 and recorded for two hours the various times and places that squirrels appeared in the ground squirrel colony around our camp. Every half hour, I also took a light intensity reading. The theory being explored was that there was a correlation between light intensity and activity on the part of the squirrels. I enjoyed getting up early and watching the colony come alive each morning, together with our camp and the birds and animals of the valley.

After a week of noting the times that squirrels emerged from their burrows, I became familiar with which squirrels belonged to which burrows and what time each squirrel usually came up into the morning light. One day, in the second week of my observations, I got up as usual at 4:00 AM, dressed warmly, and went outside. I immediately noticed that several baby squirrels and adults were already outside, unusually early. Then, one old mother began whistling excitedly, which got my attention quickly. I scanned the area with my binoculars to see what was causing her alarm, and spotted movement behind the row of empty oil barrels at the back of camp. After retreating to the safety of the camp perimeter, I finally spotted an ermine, just as the mother squirrel spotted it. To my surprise, and to the evident surprise of the ermine, she charged her archenemy, running straight at it. For two minutes she chased the ermine around the camp, with me in hot pursuit, taking notes, before several male squirrels emerged, and a posse of squirrels chased the ermine far up the alluvial fan, towards the mountain.

Later, I found that, during the night, the ermine had wiped out a litter of four baby squirrels. It seemed to have killed without a real interest in eating its prey, since all of the bodies were intact. After I told Harry Brower, our Eskimo carpenter, about the ermine, he set a live trap and caught it the next night. My ground squirrel observations continued for several weeks. The squirrels and I became good friends. Harry called me the "Squirrel Man." Forty-five years later, I was tickled to discover the scientific article that had been based in part on my observations and credited me in a footnote as "*Dr. Charles Hobbie*": "Circadian Locomotor Rhythms of Rodents in the Arctic" by Richard H. Swade and Colin S. Pittendrigh, *American Naturalist*, Vol. 101, No. 922 (Nov. - Dec., 1967), pp. 431-466. I was the first sixteen-year-old "doctor" to be cited in the *Naturalist*.

Me, at our camp headquarters, Alaska 1961

When we were not working, our camp's staff fished, hiked, or boated—in our small boat, with a two and a half horsepower motor—to our hearts' content. Lake Peters had abundant lake trout, arctic char, and grayling. From the shore we easily caught huge trout in minutes, some measuring over thirty inches and weighing over twenty pounds. The grayling were smaller, but tastier, with delicious, reddish flesh.

Towards the end of June, on a clear, sunny day, John and I hiked down to the south end of Lake Peters to measure the flow of water in the Chamberlin and Carnivore Creeks, which carried water from the Mt. Chamberlin glaciers into the valley. After successfully crossing Chamberlin Creek in our high, waterproof boots, and taking our measurements, we could not get across the deeper, swifter Carnivore Creek and had to turn back. The scenery at that end of the lake was the most beautiful I had ever seen, as I could see the entire length of Lake Peters, looking northwards, as well as down the connecting valley to the south for about nine miles, with huge mountains, towering above us on all sides. I thought, as I looked out over the valley, how extraordinary it was that there were no human beings in any direction I looked for close to sixty or seventy miles, except at our small camp.

On the last Sunday in June, I climbed the 4,600-foot mountain directly behind our camp—the steepest climb I have ever made. There was no trail. I climbed right up the side and made it to the top in two and a quarter hours and down in one hour twenty minutes, nervously keeping a watchful eye for bears. I recall that the weather that day was the clearest since my arrival at Lake Peters. From the summit, I could see fifteen miles of snow-covered mountains in every direction. Below me lay the incomparably lovely Lake Peters valley. Beyond it, in the foothills to the north, lay Lake Schrader. And in the distance, beyond Lake Schrader, was the Arctic Ocean. To the south was the Chamberlin Glacier, and above it rose the nine thousand-foot peak of Mt. Chamberlin. Words are inadequate to describe the view and my elation. At the same time, I had a prickly feeling on my scalp, as I realized that I was several miles from camp, only steps from the tops of hundred-foot high cliffs, on the far side of the peak from Lake Peters, and totally alone, without a weapon.

Then, my breath was taken away. Several hundred feet below me, on a small meadow with greening grass, amidst the rocks and snow, were six, white, Dall sheep—two rams, two ewes, and two lambs, grazing peacefully, and unaware of my presence above them. While I was watching them through my binoculars and marveling at how close I was to them—with their telescopic vision they usually see movement miles away and flee before you can get close at all—a shadow crossed my line of sight. A golden eagle was soaring above the sheep and about fifty feet below me. Incredible! All thoughts of danger left me. I exulted in the moment.

Later the same week, we awoke on June 30th to discover that the thin sheet of rotten, lake ice had disappeared. Both Lake Peters and Lake Schrader were free of ice. John won the ice pool of fifteen dollars. As the ice left, the caribou arrived—a herd of about ten thousand animals had appeared on the northern horizon. That evening, three of us piled into the boat to get a closer look at the caribou. As we approached the north end of Lake Peters, I began counting. Caribou were everywhere, as far as we could see on all sides of the valley. I stopped counting at about five thousand animals, with well more than half to go. I remember thinking that my awe was akin to what the Plains Indians must have felt a century before at the sight of thousands of buffalo. When I mentioned this to Harry Brower, he laughed and promised that caribou meat was better than buffalo meat.

Harry was a good friend for the short time I knew him, and the first Eskimo I ever knew. He talked a lot about his family—he had dozens of siblings, uncles, aunts, nieces, and nephews and was proud of them all. He introduced me to his *seven-year-old* uncle, who visited him one day during the summer. Harry asked me a lot of questions about life in the lower forty-eight states. I told him what I knew about life in Buffalo, and he taught me some carpentry, how to shoot a rifle, and about Eskimo culture and language. I especially recall being amazed that there are about a hundred Eskimo words for snow and ice. For Harry, the caribou were nothing very special. For me this herd was a once-in-a-lifetime experience.

Harry quickly shot two caribou. As a Native American, he was the only one of us who could legally kill them. He shot an old bull first, with a tremendous rack of antlers. Then, he killed a yearling. Harry immediately set about cleaning the dead animals, skinning off the hides, and cutting up the meat into manageable chunks. We then struggled to get the meat quickly back to the refrigerators at camp in our small boat, leaving the carcasses for the wolves, bears, and wolverines. For several weeks we feasted on the best, most tender, leanest steaks I have ever eaten. Caribou was much better than beef, I told Harry, but I couldn't compare it with buffalo meat, since I had never eaten buffalo. But you are *from* Buffalo, he said, astonished.

Harry also showed me the nest of a jaeger on the south shore of Lake Schrader. There was one, newly hatched, baby bird in the nest, and another was just pecking through the shell. The parent birds, which are the size of gulls, were wheeling, screaming, and diving at us the whole time, making a tremendous commotion. We left the nest and baby birds intact, of course. After that experience, I was not surprised, later in the summer, to watch a pair of jaegers, attacking a golden eagle, five times their size, and driving it from the valley.

(Almost fifty years after my brief friendship with Harry, I sat next to an Eskimo on a flight to Cleveland one day. He was the mayor of Point Barrow township, he told me, and was returning to Alaska from a conference of mayors. I asked him if he knew Harry Brower. He responded that Harry was his uncle and was alive and well, still in Point Barrow.)

The caribou continued to arrive for more than a week, streaming past our camp in long lines without stopping. They did not seem at all bothered by our camp's buildings, or the noise of the generator, as they walked by for hours on end. Thousands and thousands of beautiful animals were everywhere in the valley.

On the Fourth of July, we awoke to find that the temperature had dropped from the fifties into the twenties, and a storm had dropped five inches of snow on the valley—my first arctic storm. All was magnificently and brilliantly white, except the gray lakes! To celebrate the Fourth, we set off several flares, fired volleys from the camp rifles, shotguns, and pistols, and whooped and hollered appropriately. We were all out celebrating in the snow in our slippers and pajamas. It snowed all day and night, preventing any flights from reaching us.

The next morning, although it was still snowing, with a very low, cloud cover, the ARL pilot, Bob Fisher, found a hole in the clouds, followed the river to Lake Peters, and came in very low, buzzing our camp about twenty feet above us. None of us heard or saw him, until he was right above us, scaring the daylights out of everyone. Bobby landed the Cessna with its pontoons on the lake, bringing mail, supplies, and two Swedish botanists. When he left the next morning, Russ—our cook—ran out and hopped on the plane, never to be seen again. Either the snow or the gunfire had spooked him, I think.

During the subsequent week, six flights arrived. One brought Pete Duvenek, a boy my age, who was to be an assistant to the camp manager, Frank Riddell. Dr. Bill Steere, the Director of the New York Botanical Garden, and other scientists also arrived on another flight. Pete was a good guy, with a fine sense of humor. I liked him a lot, but because Frank kept him so busy, and helping John kept me occupied every minute, we seldom had time to do anything together or to get to know each other. Pete didn't know how to cook, but we soon taught him. The other new arrivals were good men and decent cooks. Without Russ, we all took turns cooking for two weeks, until a new cook arrived.

The early July snow quickly melted, but John and I almost froze to death, one day, when we went north to Lake Schrader to anchor a buoy in the lake to which we could tie up in the future, while taking water samples and turbidity readings. A sudden storm came up, the lakes got quite rough, and the rains thoroughly soaked us, before we got back. We were numb with cold. Surprisingly, there were no after-effects, no sniffles, or other cold symptoms, because in the arctic there are few of the germs that usually prompt "colds" at home.

**Looking north across Lake Peters amidst carpets of alpine flowers,
June 1961**

Dr. Steere and his team were at Lake Peters to study the magnificent wild flowers, which appeared on the tundra, as the ice was leaving the lakes. Carpets of three to six-inch high flowers of every color imaginable were everywhere. Most of them were species I had never seen before. There were acres and acres of white-tufted cotton grass, purplish Arctic Lousewort, and pinkish Siberian Phlox. All were miniature blossoms of awesome delicacy and beauty, stretching as far as you could see on all sides. Within a week of the ice's departure, the eruption of the biotic orgy that is the arctic summer was complete. Flowers and birds were everywhere, framed by the blue waters of the lakes and the white summits of the Brooks Range. The riot of color and life, however, was always tempered by the constant wind, which whispered in its bite that this scene would be short-lived. These weeks of glory were the exception in the Lake Peters valley. They would soon be replaced by the ice and snow that lurked on the peaks in summer, awaiting the longer nights and dropping temperatures in which they would steal down the slopes and envelop all in near lifeless white.

I had my second ride in a helicopter in early July. A Pan American Oil Company helicopter with two men landed at our camp one morning, and we invited them in for breakfast. In return, they took us for a ride of about six miles, circling the Lake Peters valley, landing on several of the surrounding summits, and buzzing Mt. Chamberlin and the Chamberlin Glacier. It was wonderful to see so much of the surrounding area from a vantage point just above the mountains. Absolutely unforgettable! On the other hand, only by hiking the terrain, or going out in the boat on the lakes, do you really see, hear, and feel the wildlife, vegetation, and varying moods of the lakes that make this area so very special.

My second helicopter ride, Lake Peters, Alaska 1961

The mosquitoes came in force in July—the "state bird" of Alaska. They were terrible! We wore nets, gloves, and sufficiently heavy, outer clothing to withstand their biting. In the brief, three-week-long period of the peak mosquito season, we went through three cases (seventy-two cans) of mosquito repellent. Anything that moved on land had a cloud of mosquitoes ten feet high, buzzing, swirling, and biting. My head net and outer clothing were a mass of humming, bloodthirsty insects most days. On the positive side, the mosquitoes made it easier to spot wildlife, since even small animals had a tremendous, black cloud of insects, trailing them everywhere. You could spot a fox a mile away. Only on the lake, or at slightly higher elevations, where there was some wind, could you escape the mosquitoes. I noticed that the caribou often escaped by jumping into the lakes. The carpenters, who had built the dormitory, with its screened windows and doors, suddenly were gods.

I saw my first grizzly bear from the small motorboat. John and I were going through the narrow channel, which connects Lake Peters with Lake Schrader at the north end of Lake Peters. I was reading the latest mail and not particularly paying attention to what was going on around me, when suddenly John shouted. There was a huge, brown and golden bear on the bank of the channel about fifty feet away. My whole body felt like jello, even though forty feet of water separated us from the bear, and we were perfectly safe in the boat. It was the unexpectedness of the encounter, as well as the hugeness of the bear, that shocked me. Neither John nor I had brought a camera—the only time all summer that I ever went anywhere without a camera, of course. As soon as he became aware of us, the bear reared up, wheeled, and dashed away up the shore towards the mountains, as fast as it could run. I was astonished that it could run so fast. It was close enough that I could see the muscles and rolls of fat rippling, as it moved. I only saw one other bear the entire summer, and it was over a mile away on the side of a mountain.

John and I spent many days the following week on Lake Schrader, mapping the bottom of the lake. We measured a base line on the shore, marked it with flags, and then, while John moved across the lake in the boat, taking soundings at regular intervals and notifying me by radio, I stood on shore at one end of the measured baseline with a radio, recording his position at each interval by using a transit, like a surveyor. On the day that we saw the bear, we had been heading to Lake Schrader to begin this process. After we had set up the baseline, and John had departed by boat for the middle of the lake, over a mile away, I realized that he had the rifle with him in the boat. I was then standing about one mile from where we had seen the bear, so I was more than a bit anxious. With the transit, which was like a telescope, I made periodic sweeps of the horizon on all sides to reassure myself that I was not going to have an unwelcome visitor.

After John had been gone about an hour, on one of these sweeps I spotted a dot on the horizon, coming towards me, and getting bigger and bigger every second. I frantically called John on the radio—he was closer to the dot. John reassured me that it was just a male caribou, running like crazy, and sure enough, within a few minutes the big bull stormed by without even glancing at me. Then I got to thinking. Why would a lone caribou be running for his life in the middle of nowhere on the tundra? That was not a reassuring thought. I kept a sharp lookout, assembled the flags we were not using in a kind of stockade around me (as though these would have deterred a bear or wolves), and kept working. Except for a few thousand mosquitoes, I had no further visitors.

The next day I had the ride of my life! A party of five archaeologists from Columbia University, headed by Dr. Ralph Solecki—the archaeologist who discovered the Neanderthal burials in Shanidar Cave in Iraq (to whom a tribute was made in the introduction of the novel "Clan of the Cave Bear")—was a day late in arriving at our camp, after a three-week field trip. Zim and I went up in the Cessna to look for them. After about fifteen minutes of searching, I finally spotted them, as they were starting to cross the Sadlerochit River near Lake Schrader. We circled them until they were safely across, and dropped them a note that a boat would be waiting for them at the east end of Lake Schrader.

On the way back to camp, Zim took me on a flight around the peaks surrounding camp. On our first sweep around the valley, we were very high, and I was able to get a much better idea of the rivers and mountain ranges of the Brooks Range around Lake Peters than I had been able to in my helicopter rides. On the second sweep, we were flying right down on the peaks and below them. Then, Zim took me on one of the rides that he was famous for: up valleys, around glaciers, down into canyons, and finally skimming over Mt. Chamberlin and swooping down to just above the glacier. We cleared some of the peaks by about twenty feet. Chunks of snow and ice went rolling down the mountain from the back draft of our single propeller, we were so close. Nothing in my outdoor life has ever compared to the thrill of that flight.

After picking up the archaeological team with the boat that evening, I heard the stories of their expedition, including how a bear had drifted into their camp and destroyed their tent and a lot of their equipment, before they were able to scare it away with gunfire. They had discovered several sites of early man in the area, unearthed several, ancient hammerheads and flint chips from about five thousand years ago, and were very excited about the archaeological potential of the area around Lake Peters and Lake Schrader. Bert Salwen, one of the Columbia team, gave me my first haircut of the summer.

Several days after their arrival at our camp, Bert Salwen, Ralph Solecki, and two other men wanted to survey two of the small bluffs at the eastern end of Lake Schrader, which they had noticed, when we picked them up by boat. John and I took them by boat, and hiked with them up to the tops of the hills, overlooking Lake Schrader. After a few minutes of walking around near the summit of one of these hills, Bert excitedly pointed to a circle of rocks, about fifteen feet in diameter, hidden in the tundra grass. He identified it as a tent ring; the stones had been used by early humans to hold down the outer edges of a tent-like structure. In the middle of the circle, several inches below the surface of the ground, the team found the blackened remains of ancient campfires, probably very old, they thought. Hidden among the rock debris they also found several dozen "choppers," which are crudely edged stones used by Paleo-Indians to skin their prey. Early humans had clearly camped and hunted here, on the bluff overlooking the lake. I was entranced by these discoveries. Carbon dating set the age of the campfires at about ten thousand years. The August 25, 1961 issue of *Time* magazine reported that this was the oldest campfire yet found in North America of the ice-age humans, who had crossed the land bridge between Siberia and Alaska, across the Bering Sea. We were all excited when we heard the results of the dating tests, and from then on, wherever I hiked in the Peters Valley, I thought of those early men and how difficult life must have been for them.

Coincidentally, in the same issue of *Time* was another article by a visitor to Lake Peters earlier in the summer: limnologist David Frey from Indiana University. Dr. Frey explained in the article why all fresh water lakes were slowly dying in a predictably, irrevocable process, hastened by the impact of man. I realized again how fortunate I was—as one of only a handful of people—to see these arctic lakes, in their relatively pristine condition and setting.

At least once a week throughout the summer, a storm blew through the valley. One of these hit just as John, several members of the archaeological team, and I were wrapping up an afternoon's work at the site on the eastern end of Lake Schrader. Dark clouds swarmed over the mountains into the valley. The wind cleared the air of mosquitoes with a blast of cool air. The rains came and soaked us with little warning. After waiting an hour or so for the wind to subside, we tried to start across Lake Schrader, but the little boat was soon swamped by the lake's churning waves. We managed to pull the boat out of the water and turned it over on shore. Then, it began to snow heavily. The six of us crawled under the boat for shelter. An hour or so later, the wind subsided enough so that we could slowly boat back to camp, hugging the shore all the way. It took over two hours. By the time we got back, all of us were frozen stiff.

After the good fortune of their important discoveries, which pushed back the earliest known presence of humans in North American by five thousand years, some bad luck hit the Columbia University team, shortly after our adventure in the storm on Lake Schrader. One of their members, Jerry Jacobson, developed a severe, kidney disorder, just as sunspot activity caused a blackout in our regular radio transmissions to Point Barrow. After several days of no radio contacts, with Jerry lapsing in and out of consciousness, we were finally able to contact the U.S.N. icebreaker *Burton Island,* which relayed our emergency message to Point Barrow. A day later, just when Jerry looked as though he might not make it, a Navy plane arrived unexpectedly with a physician on board, who was able to treat Jerry. When he was finally able to travel several days later, Jerry was evacuated by air to a hospital in Fairbanks and survived. This incident shook me. I realized how tenuous our contact with the outside world was. As long as there was no accident, illness, or other emergency, we were pretty self-sufficient. When the unexpected occurred—a surprise storm on the lake, an accident or illness, a bear destroying equipment, or human error—suddenly we were very vulnerable.

Around mid July on a gloomy, foggy morning, I spotted what I thought were two bears on the western shore of Lake Schrader. We boated down for a closer look and discovered two very large moose on the shore. It was unusual to see them so far north. Later the same day, we saw several golden plovers near the southern end of Lake Peters. I had never seen either moose or golden plovers before.

In late July, we had the warmest weather we had experienced to date during the summer: sixty-eight degrees in beautiful sunshine. After the steady drizzles and fog, week after week in mid July, the clearer weather was welcome. The sun was setting each evening now about 11:00 PM. One evening we saw a gorgeous sunset to the north—one of dozens in late July and throughout August—while a storm was gathering at the south end of Lake Peters, producing a magnificent rainbow.

I was most in awe of the grand, ever-changing beauty of the Lake Peters valley and Lake Schrader at any given moment. While the sunsets and rainbows were spectacular, equally beautiful, in a subtler way, were the hues of brown, green, blue, gray, and white that shifted literally every day and every hour. Clouds and fog drifted overhead and on the lakes in a ceaseless variety of shapes and tints. The vegetation on the mountain slopes and lakes' shores went from brown to green, to mottled splashes of bright floral colors, to rust, in a period of six weeks. The lakes' waters could be brilliantly blue in the sunshine, bright blue or green with white-capped waves, when the wind blew, slate gray under stormy skies, or white under a blanket of fog. Sometimes, the lakes' surfaces were roiled with five-foot waves; sometimes, they were so placid that they perfectly reflected the sky and mountains.

Lake Peters valley with Mt. Chamberlin behind, August 1961

Among the three dozen or so scientists, who visited the Lake Peters camp during the summer, were botanists and zoologists from Sweden, an ichthyologist from Finland—who amazed me by swimming across Lake Peters and back every morning (the water temperature was in the forties), officials from the Office of Naval Research, and oil company geologists. I liked all of them, and had an opportunity to get to know them well, as I ferried them around the lakes. On these trips we often passed a derelict camp, created ten years earlier by oil company staff on the northwest shore of Lake Schrader. It was a horrible eyesore, and damaging to the surrounding environment with its leaking barrels of fuel, piles of refuse, discarded cans everywhere, and caterpillar tracks, crisscrossing the tundra in all directions around it. The sight offended all of my passengers. In the Arctic, scars do not heal quickly. At this oil company camp there were ten-year-old food cans, scattered around in profusion, which still had paper labels intact and looked brand new. Vehicle tracks made a decade before looked freshly made. Once despoiled, it was obvious, that area would never be the same.

Earlier in the summer we had heard that this part of Alaska had recently been designated as the Arctic Wildlife Refuge—a nine million acre preserve that would be off limits to the kind of wanton, environmental destruction that the abandoned oil company camp symbolized. Camps, such as Lake Schrader's eyesore, would be closed and cleaned up. The Refuge would be off limits to all except scientists. Hopeful as we were at this news, most of our camp's visitors were very skeptical that the Lake Peters valley and North Slope Eden would survive much longer in the face of predictably relentless pressure from Big Oil to tap the oil reserves supposedly in the area.

As August started, I began to train for pre-season football. After my squirrel observations ended each morning at 6:00, I exercised, and ran several miles around the alluvial fan, causing great consternation among my squirrel friends. When I arrived at Lake Peters in early June, I weighed about one hundred fifty-five pounds. Now I was almost at one hundred seventy pounds, and climbing. I was determined to turn my blubber into muscle, before I started football practices in the September heat of the "lower forty-eight." Biff Reed, one of the geologists in camp, sometimes kept me company, and threw an old football around with me. I ached all over most of the time, but in a month I got into great shape, despite weighing about one hundred seventy-seven pounds by early September. I have never run in a more spectacular setting or on spongier terrain.

One depressing day, we received word that mail destined for Lake Peters had been air dropped by mistake to the Navy's floating ice island, Arlis II, over one hundred miles to the north. The Navy had established several weather and science stations on drifting masses of ice in the Arctic Ocean, which over the past twenty years had been occupied and abandoned several times. We kept in touch with these stations daily by radio. One was called T 3; another was Arlis II. Arlis II advised us that books, letters, and packages for me, and some mail for John, were now with them, probably until the icebreaker *Staten Island* reached Arlis II in October.

There were seven of us in camp in August, as the fog settled in for days at a time. The fog was a sure sign of the end of the six-week-long summer. No more scientists would be coming to Lake Peters. No one would be staying for the winter, as John and Olivann had the previous year. I missed having the opportunity to talk with different scientists in so many fascinating fields. We were so busy, wrapping up John's research and otherwise slowly closing up the camp, however, that visitors were no longer welcome.

We celebrated the completion of one of Frank Riddell's projects in early August. Besides being the camp's manager, Frank was the camp engineer and mechanic. During the summer, he had been restoring a vehicle, known as the weasel, which had been damaged the previous winter. The weasel had sunk through the ice on the lake, been pulled out, and towed to shore. In attempting to clean it up and dry it out, John had covered it with blankets and lit fires near by. The blankets caught fire, and the weasel was badly burned. During the summer, Frank had replaced parts, repainted the weasel, and restored it to working condition. One of the camp staff christened the refurbished weasel and painted its name on the side: "John I." While the rest of us thought this was hilarious, my brother did not seem to be amused.

At the end of the first week in August, one cold and foggy evening we heard a plane's engine on Lake Peters about 8:30. British Petroleum, an oil company camped on Lake Schrader, had sent a man in their plane to taxi up the lake to our camp for help. One of their men had a seriously injured arm, which had swollen up to twice its normal size. Blood poisoning had evidently set in, as he had a high fever and was unconscious. They could not fly him out, because of the fog, so they asked us to try to get instructions from a doctor over our more powerful radio. At this time of night, the ARL radio in Point Barrow was not operating, but after an hour of attempts, we were able to contact the Flaxman Island Dew Line Station. All of the DEW Line stations were equipped with microwave telephones, so the operator at Flaxman called the ARL at Barrow and told them to turn on their radio. When we finally got through, the reception was too poor for the kind of lengthy and detailed communication needed. Luckily, the Navy's other floating ice island station, T 3, broke in and offered to relay our message to ARL. By this means we were able to get our message out to ARL. But to contact the doctor, we asked Flaxman Island again to assist. With a telephone "patch," the doctor advised us that it was essential to give the man all available penicillin and to get him to either Barrow or to Barter Island, where there were medical facilities, as soon as possible. Biff Reed and I set out through the fog and darkness in the boat at midnight with penicillin, and finally reached the oil company camp. With penicillin, the man recovered consciousness quickly, and his overall condition improved considerably. Two days later, the fog lifted enough to evacuate him by plane, and he made it safely out.

By mid August, there were only five of us left at the Lake Peters camp. No other scientists were scheduled to visit, as the season of life in the Lake Peters valley was almost over, and colder weather was settling in. With the first signs of autumn, the Dall sheep began to move down, from the high ridges around the valley, to the lower slopes, still lush with vegetation. We counted thirty-two sheep one morning, including several rams with curling horns. On August 14th we watched as two rams battled each other in a high meadow across the lake. What a sight!

With the flowers gone, the mountain slopes changed from green to their fall colors of red, orange, yellow, and brown. Berries appeared everywhere, adding their bright colors to the autumn palette. Wherever a stream ran down a slope, there was a bright green swath of vegetation. The pattern of green ribbons against the background of autumn hues was exquisitely lovely.

The sun, which had never set during most of June and early July, was now setting around 10 PM and rising about 2:30 AM, giving us welcome hours of complete darkness. As the temperatures dipped into the twenties at night, and heavy winds and snow buffeted the valley on several days, John finished up his research and gathered last minute information. We spent most of one morning calculating the surface areas of Lake Peters (2.57 sq. miles) and Lake Schrader (5.11 sq. miles), as well as the areas of the basins, which they drain. Peters drains 66.27 sq. miles and Schrader drains 54.19 sq. miles. The rest of the men moved food and equipment from the Quonset huts and tents into the wooden frame buildings in preparation for winter.

One flight in mid August brought another high school age boy, Ted Humphrey, to help close up the camp. It also brought our missing mail and packages of books, which ARL had retrieved from the ice island, as well as a single rock and roll record. I was forbidden to play the record, after once putting it on the camp's loudspeaker system for an hour. Ted caught a forty-inch long, thirty-five pound lake trout one evening, breaking the camp record. The next day "Diamond Jim McGoffin" and his wife landed in his plane, bringing their big, black, friendly Labrador retriever. The dog caused great concern among the ground squirrels, as it raced back and forth on the tundra, and almost caused Pete Duvenek to have a stroke. Pete had not heard that we had visitors with a dog, and upon encountering the dog about half a mile from camp on the tundra, thought it was a wolf. We could hear his yelling from camp. He took a lot of teasing after that for mistaking a Labrador for a wolf.

On August 22nd, we heard by radio that John's wife had delivered a baby boy—Lawrence John—on the 20th. We celebrated appropriately with much scotch and retelling of the summer's adventures.

August was snowy, cold, and foggy until the day we left. That day, August 27th, there was not a cloud in the sky, when the sun came up at 2:30 AM. I made the rounds of the ground squirrels, saying farewell. They had gotten fat during the summer, with so many people hand-feeding them scraps. Even an ermine was in the area of the squirrel colony to say goodbye. The squirrels seemed unconcerned with his presence, now that the young squirrels were fully grown. John and I said our farewells to Frank and to the several men who would remain in camp for four more days, boarded the plane after breakfast, and regretfully watched the valley and its spectacular mountains flash by, as the plane took off across the calm surface of Lake Peters. I thought, sadly, that I would never see that paradise or my summer friends again.

Point Barrow was enveloped in fog and rain when we arrived. Our plane skipped across the rollers, which were thumping in from the Arctic Ocean and pounding the shore, as we landed, after a beautiful, three-hour flight west across the North Slope. I remember that we watched *The Honeymoon Machine* at the Barrow movie theater that evening, and I took my first shower in three months! I also weighed in at one hundred seventy-seven pounds. John weighed one hundred sixty-eight pounds. For the first time in my life, I was both taller and heavier than my brother.

On September 1st, we arrived in Seattle, Washington, met my father, who had flown out from Buffalo, picked up John's new Volkswagen bus, and together drove south down the west coast to Long Beach, California. It was a fun trip, through spectacularly beautiful scenery, along the coast. I spent the whole time telling my father about the summer's experiences. We didn't have a license plate on the van, because the paperwork had not been ready in Seattle. A state trooper stopped us in Oregon for not having a license plate on the car. Dad explained the situation, and the trooper didn't ticket us. Instead, he wrote a note, excusing our violation, for us to present to any law enforcement officers we might meet.

We made it safely to Long Beach, where Olivann and the new baby, Lawrence, awaited us. John had been very anxious, during the entire trip south, to meet his new son. Dad was very pleased to see his first grandson, and we were all happy to have enjoyed such a pleasant trip together down the coast—the last trip the three of us would ever take together. Dad and I flew home to Buffalo, two days later, where the shimmering, blue waters of Lake Erie welcomed us. My great Alaskan adventure was over. I went swimming at the Kennels the next day, enjoying Lake Erie's bath-like temperature, smiling at the weak attempts of Canadian mosquitoes to bother me, and thinking of the thin sheets of ice, forming on Lake Peters.

Chapter Six—
Last Two High School
Years: 1961–63

Mom, Grandma Hobbie, and Dad with me at graduation from Nichols High
School, June 1963 (John Mooney and his parents in the right background)

After graduating from Mt. Holyoke College in 1960, and spending the summer at Middlebury College in Vermont, Ceci entered Cornell University in September 1960, to pursue a Masters degree in Romance Languages. My father and my grandfather were both very happy and proud that Ceci had decided to attend their alma mater. Ceci had a job in the Cornell library and was a teaching assistant to help pay her expenses. In the fall of 1960, we all drove to Ithaca, New York, to help her get settled there. Dad was as pleased as punch to be back at Cornell, with his daughter as a Cornellian.

In June 1961, while John and I were at Lake Peters, Alaska, Ceci introduced a Cornell undergraduate student to Mom and Dad. She had met John W. Pehle in May. He was a psychology major from the Washington, D.C. area. He visited Buffalo, just after the arrival of my mother's English cousin, Vera Holden. My sister departed for her summer job in France soon afterwards. From her letters during the summer, I could tell that Ceci was not particularly happy in France, and I suspected that she did not want to be there without Mr. Pehle. Ceci wrote to me a lot during my childhood. I appreciated her letters throughout my life, especially because she was pretty frank about her feelings and wrote to me as someone who was not seven years younger than she was. From Mom and Dad's letters, I sensed that, even though he was Catholic, John Pehle was someone they liked, in contrast to most of my sister's previous boyfriends.

After my month of conditioning in Alaska, I was in excellent shape, when I showed up for football practice at Nichols in the fall of 1961. I had missed pre-season football practices, but my additional fifteen pounds pleasantly surprised the coaches. I was now starting at defensive left end and sharing offensive responsibilities at left guard on offense with a tough classmate, Timmy Wright, who was much smaller than me, but very gutsy. I liked Timmy a lot. He dubbed me "Wood Duck" upon my return from Alaska. The other defensive end, Chuck Kreiner, was nicknamed "Woodchuck."

Nichols was in the Interstate Preparatory School Athletic Conference. Although Nichols was much smaller than the other schools in the league, our teams usually put up a good fight, before losing. Our big rival was the University School in Shaker Heights, Ohio. In football, we also played Cranbrook School in Bloomfield Hills, Michigan; Shadyside Academy in suburban Pittsburgh, Pennsylvania; Western Reserve Academy in Hudson, Ohio; Kiski Academy in Saltsburg, Pennsylvania; University of Toronto School in Toronto, Ontario; and Olean High School in Olean, New York. For many of our away games, we took a bus there the day before, stayed the night, and returned after the game on Saturday or Sunday.

I tremendously enjoyed those bus trips and visiting other schools. I especially remember being awed by the football field at Cranbrook, which was a carpet of springy, carefully maintained grass, without a weed. It seemed a sin to play on that field. I also recall the several dozen pieces of statuary on the carefully manicured, Cranbrook campus, which reeked of money. The other schools' campuses were almost as impressive and made Nichols, despite its lovely campus, seem like a second rate school in comparison. Nichols was inferior physically. There was no doubt that the other schools were much bigger and had more money. We liked to think that Nichols had smarter and tougher students, however.

On the bus trips we sang songs, told jokes, and generally had a great deal of fun. It was a fine opportunity to get to know the coaches and their wives, who often went along. Coach Stevens' wife, Jill, became virtually one of the football team. She seemed like an older sister to us. Mike Quinlan, Craig Butler, and Whitey Sahlen, our strong, tough running backs, impressed me with their one-arm pushup contests on these trips.

My student-faculty advisor was the Assistant Director of the Athletic Department and basketball coach, Hal Gerard. He was a kind and knowledgeable mentor. In the fall of 1961, with an eye to beefing up my resume for college admission purposes, he counseled me to become involved in more extra curricular activities. In many ways, committees of students and faculty, which together planned the curriculum and events of the year, ran Nichols. There were dozens of such groups, involved in every facet of life at Nichols. At that time, I was a member of the Assemblies Club, which planned our weekly assembly programs; of the Creative Writing Club; of the Glee Club; and of the Nicholodians, which was a small group that sang at glee club concerts. So I joined the business staff of the *Nichols News*, which involved a lot of time, billing and collecting fees from the advertisers in the Nichols newspaper, and became the assistant manager of the varsity hockey team.

My third year at Nichols, I took English III with Austin McC. Fox, French III with Bob Hershey, Trigonometry and Calculus with Bob Root, History with Millard Sessions, and Chemistry with Edgar Anderson. Each class met three times per week. I got A's in all except Chemistry. Our chemistry teacher was a man whom I admired and liked immensely. He managed to make chemistry palatable, with his stories of former students, who had blown themselves up in the laboratory, and his funny jokes. "Eddie," as we called him outside of the classroom, used to sing in a men's chorus with my father, and always told me how much he liked and respected Dad. I liked Eddie a lot, although chemistry was a bear of a course for me. My third year at Nichols it kept me off the honor roll most of the year. Phil Boocock told me not to worry about my grades in the course. Most of the rest of the students, who were also taking advanced honors chemistry, were also getting Cs, except for Bill Flor, Jim McGibbon, Sandy Maisel, Mike Keiser, and Mike Roizen, who were acing it, as they did all subjects.

At my sister's urging to try again for an AMC position in the White Mountains, in September I decided to reapply for a summer position, working for the hut system, as John and Ceci had in the 1950s. I wrote to George Hamilton again. George responded at once, and to my delight, this time George offered me a position as a hutman at the Madison Spring Huts on Mt. Madison. I would be able to skip the usual first year at the AMC Headquarters at Pinkham Notch, where both John and Ceci had worked. My friend, Bob Ramage, also applied for a position at my urging, but was not accepted. I realized that I was very lucky to have had siblings, who had been good employees of the AMC. There were more than fifty applications for each of the AMC summer positions, I later learned, because in 1961 the *National Geographic Magazine* featured an article entitled "The Friendly Huts of the White Mountains," which prompted great interest in the hut system and in summer employment there.

To celebrate my acceptance as a hutman I wrote a poem about mountains: "The Silent Teachers." In February 1962, it was selected for publication in Nichols' literary magazine, the *Gleaner*, and the magazine's editor-in-chief, senior David Milch, asked me to join the editorial staff. In the May edition, another poem and a short story of mine were published. The story reflected one of my major concerns the previous summer. It was about a man in Alaska, eaten by a bear. David went on to Yale and became a writer, television screenwriter, and producer, winning several Emmy awards (*Hill Street Blues, NYPD Blue, Deadwood*).

In October, Phil Boocock asked if I would speak in an assemblies program about my summer in Alaska. With some trepidation, I agreed, and organized the slides that John had taken over the past year at Lake Peters, as well as some of my own, into an hour-long show. I consulted with George Stevens as to what I should talk about. He advised me to just relate my experiences in chronological order, while showing the slides. The actual program, which was supposed to be limited to a maximum of one hour, including questions, went well over an hour and a half. I got carried away. The program went very well, and there were a lot of questions. Afterwards, at least two dozen of the faculty told me how much they had enjoyed it. Like it or not, I became known as the Alaska guy.

Bob Ramage took it upon himself to improve my social life in the fall of 1961. I give Bob a lot of credit for good taste. He fixed me up with three girls in the next two years. Each of them became special in her own way to me. Janet Berner, Pam Austin, and Janis Terry were students at Amherst High School in suburban Buffalo. They were all friends, and one year behind Bob and me in school. Bob was dating another girl from Amherst, who arranged dates for me at Bob's request, so that we could double date. This arrangement worked out wonderfully. Thank God for Amherst High School!

Janet was smart, tall, dark eyed, lovely, and kind. She had long, dark brown hair and was gorgeous in a white dress. Her house was just down Brantwood Road from Bob's. She was a cheerleader at Amherst. I took her to several Nichols' dances in my junior and senior years. After the dances, we would go to a restaurant with Bob and his date, and often end up at my house. Mom and Dad told me that they would rather have me doing whatever I did with girls in our living room than in the back seat of our car. I loved to dance with Janet. We played records and danced in the music room. I secretly worshiped her. But I was so nervous about kissing her that it happened rarely. She must have thought that I was crazy. Although I liked them, I felt that her parents didn't like me very much, for some reason. I was pretty harmless. Janet and I wrote to each other for several years, while she attended Cornell University, but I never saw her again, after her high school graduation in 1964.

Janet Berner, 1962

Pam was a very intelligent, funny, and cute blond, who lived at 189 Berryman Drive in Amherst. We dated for several months and were friends for years afterwards. Her parents were far too protective, even paranoid, and she rebelled against them, whenever possible. I loved her spontaneity and her giggle. She went to Wells College, visited me at Dartmouth, had several dates I arranged with my college classmates, and ended up marrying my first college roommate!

Pamela Austin, 1962

My mother had tried for years to persuade me to take out the daughter of her old friend, Kirsten Terry, who was a violinist she had accompanied on the piano many years before, when she and Kirsten had performed regularly together. Mom had often mentioned that Mrs. Terry had been a wonderful violinist, when she was young, and how much she had enjoyed playing music with Kirsten in years past. According to Mom, Kirsten had a daughter—Janis—at Amherst High School, who played the piano beautifully and was reputed to be very "pretty and talented." Of course, I stoutly resisted. My mother's idea of "pretty and talented" usually was quite the opposite of mine.

As it turned out, Janis Terry was smart, beautiful, had lovely, limpid blue eyes and strawberry blond hair, was a magnificent pianist, and stole my heart for a time. Her parents liked me, and I liked them. She lived at 188 Ruskin Road. The only problem was that Bob was dating Janis, at first. When his dates with Janis seemed to grow infrequent, I asked her out, after checking with Bob. I dated Janis fairly regularly until 1963. We spent a lot of time at the beach together, sailed in her family's catamaran at the Bay Beach Canoe Club in Canada, skied at Holiday Valley, attended concerts at Kleinhans Music Hall, and strolled hand in hand through the Oakwood Gardens at Niagara Falls, Ontario. I once took her to dinner at the top of the Seagrams Tower at Niagara Falls, where we watched the colored lights, playing on the cascading water below, as we ate dinner. (I took several girls there for dinner. It was a wonderfully romantic spot.)

Janis Terry, 1962

After high school, Janis attended Pembroke College and spent the summer of 1966 at Dartmouth, where I was taking German. She has the dubious distinction of being the only date I ever had in college with whom I got so drunk that I have no memory of attending a concert together at Dartmouth's Hopkins Center. Our presence there together was later confirmed by one of my English professors—Alan Gaylord—and his wife, who sat next to us and with whom I reportedly conversed intelligibly. Despite some spats, Janis and I remained friends for many years and went to the same law school—George Washington University—years later in Washington, D.C.

One of the most interesting and dedicated teachers I had at Nichols was Austin Fox, whom I also knew from his visits to Charlie's Barber Shop. He had been the head of the English Department for several decades and was an institution at Nichols. We affectionately called him "Augie," behind his back. I recall that he was a specialist on Washington Irving and Stephen Crane. We read several books that he had edited and written extensively about, including Irving's *The Legend of Sleepy Hollow*, and Crane's *Maggie* and *The Red Badge of Courage*. I especially liked *The Red Badge*, as I have always been interested in the civil war. Mr. Fox had an encyclopedic knowledge, particularly about Buffalo's history and architecture. I always enjoyed his classes, although I sometimes fought to stay awake, during the period right after lunch, when we usually had his class. Much more interesting than his knowledge of Irving or Crane was his expertise on local, historic buildings, and the stories that he told about Buffalo's history. In his classes we tried to steer his discourses towards historical subjects, about which he was so knowledgeable, and became so animated while speaking, that thoughts of an after lunch nap would disappear.

I often watched Mr. Fox play tennis against the younger members of the faculty, while I was waiting for my bus home. He was a skillful tennis and squash player, and usually won. George Stevens, who was an excellent athlete, used to get very exasperated, when he lost to Augie, who was almost twenty years older. Augie had four children. His son Steve was several years behind me at Nichols, but we became friends later in life, when he served in the military in Korea. One of his daughters (Sarah) became a prominent labor attorney and Member (judge) of the National Labor Relations Board in Washington, D.C. We were fortunate to have had Austin Fox as a teacher.

One thing I really missed at Nichols was any attention to the arts: music, painting, drama, or dance. In my first year at Nichols, I read about a study done at Harvard by a 1957 graduate of Nichols, Charles Halpern. It caught my eye, because I remembered Halpern from P.S. No. 56, where he was six years ahead of me, graduating in 1953. Halpern's student paper examined student values at Nichols, based on interviews with students and faculties and his own experience. He concluded, as I recall, that most Nichols high school students, not surprisingly, were interested in their grades, cars, sports, girls, and anything with immediate or practical value, but had little interest in music and the arts.

Halpern's study reflected what I experienced. I remember that some faculty tried to excite students about art. A teacher named Peter Shiras, who usually brought his beautiful golden retriever, named Robin, to classes, told us about his recent year in Greece. He taught there on a Fulbright grant, and in an assembly program, enthusiastically talked about the art and history he experienced. I was very moved by what he told us. Most of my classmates, however, were not. He was ardent about the value of the Fulbright and other like exchange programs in promoting understanding among nations. It was the first time that I had ever thought about that issue.

Another teacher, or perhaps he was a coach, by the name of Gurnsey, told us about his visit to Russia, describing the Heritage Museum in Leningrad as one of the most fabulous repositories of art works in the world. He piqued my interest. I told myself that some day I would visit Russia and other countries to see foreign art and experience new cultures.

I once remarked to my father's cousin, Pliny Hayes, that I missed art and music at Nichols. As I mentioned earlier, Pliny was the Assistant Headmaster. He agreed that this was a weakness at Nichols. Pliny was an extremely nice person and, by all accounts, an excellent teacher and administrator in the Lower School. I think that he taught Latin, before he became Assistant Headmaster. Although I seldom saw him, since he was working in the Lower School, I appreciated his frequent, kind greetings and offers of help throughout my Nichols' years, as well as his interest in bringing more culture to Nichols' curriculum.

In the meantime, for exposure to music or fine arts, at Nichols we had the glee club, one term of music, and one term of Art History, which George Stevens taught. Art History was a tremendous course! Mr. Stevens showed us slides of great art works of all kinds, explaining the context and significance of each. I loved that course.

The music course was pretty basic, and I didn't learn anything new. The glee club, while somewhat enjoyable, disappointed me. We prepared for, and sang, several concerts each year. However, in comparison to the choir at St. John's Church, our efforts were not impressive. There were probably forty boys in the glee club. It was a popular activity, because there were several joint concerts with the Buffalo Seminary's girls, and associated dances. Almost no one was really interested in music or in singing in particular. Ray Glover, the glee club director, struggled to get us prepared for each concert. He was a fine musician. I recall that he presented an excellent, piano recital, during one of the assembly programs. Despite his hard work, very few of the boys could carry a tune, it seemed. I was pretty frustrated with the glee club's quality, but I sang in the club for three years.

My classmates never failed to amaze me with their athletic or intellectual prowess. Most seemed to have a special gift. The three "Mikes" in our class, for example, were either great athletes or had great minds. I have already mentioned Mike Quinlan, who was a ferocious athlete. Mike Keiser was a fine tennis player and soccer player, as well as being a skilled writer. Mike Roizen, one of my youngest classmates, was one of the ten smartest guys in our class. ("Dr. Mike" later became one of the best selling authors in America with his books about health and prolonging a healthy life.)

Another classmate, Clay Hamlin, was one of the best tennis players in the East and was ranked first in his age bracket in the state. I don't think he ever lost a match in his four years at Nichols. Warren Gelman and Jack Walsh were outstanding hockey and baseball players, as well as being class officers. Warren, especially, who was among the smallest boys in our class, astounded me with his athletic skills and determination, captaining the hockey and baseball teams. He and Jack later formed the nucleus of Yale's best hockey team. Bill Loweth was an incredible soccer player.

One of the several geniuses in our class was Bill Flor, who was so smart he made my head spin. I still recall that his science project involved the migration of leucocytes. Sandy Maisel was also extremely intelligent. We sometimes did projects together. Jim McGibbon was the best arguer I ever met. I was sure that he would be a great lawyer some day. His

English and history papers were models of carefully crafted argument in support of whatever thesis he was advocating. Harry Meyer was an excellent pitcher and extremely smart. John Mooney was a gifted athlete in soccer, hockey, and tennis, as well as being an Honors student consistently. Tommy Goldstein was a gifted writer, extremely smart, a fine athlete, and one of the most decent guys in our class. Paul Sullivan was a fast runner, good hockey player, and probably the "playboy" of our class, along with several others. "Sully" was always friendly, even from the first week of school at Nichols, when others were not. I always appreciated that quality in him. Chuck Kreiner was smart and a fine athlete. "Woodchuck" anchored the other defensive end position on the football team, ran track with me, and was a good friend.

There were other boys, whom I also liked and admired immensely, such as Bob Jacobs, Cal Brainard, Pat Hennin, Gary Conover, Bill Mathias, Bill Rashman, Hank Sturdevant, Bob Rosenthal, Scott Ryerson, Jeff Jacobs, Bruce Baird (Bronwin's brother), Bill Cooley, Bernie Pitterman, and Steve Vogel, to name just a few. Bob Ramage was a step above all of us, as I have mentioned. I think our class was quite unique in the high quality of the young men who graduated in 1963. Most importantly, they were all friendly and considerate of each other, most of the time.

Because Nichols was on the trimester system, we had first trimester final exams just before Thanksgiving. Over the two weeks of our long holiday break in December, we were required to write several, long papers for English and History. I spent many, snowy, vacation days at the Buffalo Grosvenor Library on Franklin Street, researching and writing those papers, between Christmas and New Year's Day. The second trimester exams were in March, just before our spring vacation. The last trimester ended in June, with exams just before graduation. We wrote final exams in little blue books with lined pages. All exams were administered in the study hall at the north end of Mitchell Hall. I tended to become very nervous as exams approached, and although I spent long hours preparing, I was almost physically sick to my stomach at the start of each test.

In 1961, Grandpa Schultz was hospitalized after a heart attack in early November. As soon as he was released and returned home in January 1962, my mother went into the hospital to have her appendix removed. I remember how weak both my mother and my grandfather looked that winter. Grandpa Hobbie had suffered a stroke several years earlier and was still struggling to recover from it. It was a tough time for our family.

In the spring of 1962, I went out for the track team. I tried several distances: mile, 880 yards or half mile, and quarter mile. Pat Hennin, another classmate, was an excellent miler and already well established on the team. I finally settled on the half mile. I remember my first race in a meet against Park School. I was totally inexperienced, and had not yet learned to pace myself correctly, so I erred on the side of caution, sticking with my two classmates, Paul Sullivan and Tom Goldstein, for the first quarter mile, while Park School's star runner pulled way out in front. At the halfway point, I suddenly realized that I wasn't particularly tired and would never catch up to the lead runner—at least one hundred yards ahead—unless I started to really run. So I sprinted the last lap, as fast as I could—unfortunately, too late. I lost by about six inches. At least I scared the hell out of that runner.

After that first race, I earned two varsity letters in track, running the 880 and the last leg (440 yards) of the 4 x 4 mile relay. I liked running, and I liked the track coach, Norman Pedersen. In two years, however, I only won two of twelve races, usually placing second or third. In the half mile my best time was 2:06. I never really learned the strategy or psychology of running. I ran either too fast at the beginning of a race, or too slowly. On several occasions, I got "boxed in" by three members of opposing teams, preventing me from passing them, so that I could not run the race I wanted to. The half mile, sometimes, seemed to be a metaphor for my life. It was, at least, great preparation for running the trails on Mt. Madison, during the coming summer.

Shortly after the start of the track season, my sister announced that John Pehle had proposed to her. Three months later, the engagement was officially announced in June. Our entire family was very pleased and started planning for the wedding. I remember that my parents began to plant roses and other flowers in our backyard, and to otherwise paint and fix up our house and backyard, as if their lives depended on it, so that the garden and house would be ready for the reception. Ceci decided to wear my mother's wedding gown and to be married at St. John's Church—twenty-nine years after my parents' wedding. Same gown, same church, different minister. The wedding was planned for August 25, 1962, during the coming summer.

There were some worried discussions by Catholic friends about attending a "mixed" wedding of a Catholic and an Episcopalian in an Episcopal church. My godmother, Ruth Culliton, who wanted very much to attend, felt that she could not, based on advice from her priest. On the other hand, our long-time family friend, Father Carlton Sage (whose family lived next door to my grandparents' house at Lewiston, New York), was a Catholic priest and said that he was coming. Carlton was a professor of Theology at St. Mary's Seminary in Baltimore and a member of the Roman Catholic Maryknoll Order. He advised Ruth that her priest was old-fashioned and out of touch with current theological practices. Nevertheless, Ruth felt that she could not attend. This issue was the subject of much concern with my mother, who wanted Ruth to come. In the end, Ruth bowed to her priest. I think she was the only one of our many, close Catholic friends who did not attend.

Early in the spring, most of our class took the National Merit Scholarship Qualifying Test. We learned in April that four out of the forty in our class— Bill Flor, Sandy Maisel, Jim McGibbon, and Harry Meyer—had qualified as National Merit Semi-Finalists by obtaining a score of 149 or better. Another fifteen of us, including me, received so-called "Letters of Commendation" for scoring pretty high on the test. My score was 145. We were in the top one percent or ninety-ninth percentile of the students who took the exam. Overall, our class had done better on the test than any class in Nichols' history, since nineteen, or almost half the class, achieved finalist status or letters of commendation.

"Mac" MacClure retired from the Nichols staff in the spring of 1962. He was the school engineer and jack-of-all-trades, at the age of about eighty. There are people like him in every institution, who have been around for decades and become the fixtures that hold the operations together. Ed MacClure had worked for Nichols since the year I was born, he told me. He remembered my brother well and always had words of encouragement for me. Mac had the keys to every building. He helped me, on several occasions, retrieve some homework from the locked gym, late at night. After that we were friends. He told me amazing stories about Nichols' past and about the faculty. Among his many jobs, including running the boiler room and doling out towels in the locker room after practices, was that of informal counselor, with advice on everything from girls to where I should go to college. "Stay away from Yale," he advised. "Too many Nichols boys go there and end up unhappy." Despite Mac's influence, I noticed that six members of the Nichols class ahead of me, the class of 1962, went to Yale, including David Milch. Nichols wasn't the same after Mac retired.

With some weekend tutoring from Eddie Anderson, I managed to bring my chemistry grade up to an acceptable level by the end of my third year at Nichols. For the third (and last) time, as a result, I made the honor roll for the year. I was ecstatic and relieved. In the back of my mind, I thought continuously about getting in to a good college, so doing well my junior year would help. As soon as the school year was over, I prepared to go to New Hampshire to start my summer job.

Ceci advised me to pack very little, reminding me that I would have to carry whatever I took to New Hampshire up to the hut on my back. I got new hiking boots in May, and broke them in thoroughly. In early June, I left Buffalo by bus for Albany, where Ceci and Aunt Kate picked me up at the bus station in the early evening. We stayed at the Vermonter Motel on

Route 9, about four miles west of Bennington, Vermont, and drove up to Pinkham Notch, New Hampshire, the next day. After one night at the AMC Headquarters at Pinkham, where I met George Hamilton and his Assistant Manager, Bruce Sloat, another hutman— Dave Hall—and I were driven to Randolph, at the base of Mt. Madison, and dropped off at the pack house near the beginning of the trail that would take us to the hut.

Mt. Madison, New Hampshire

Mount Madison is the northern most of the so-called Northern Peaks of the Mt. Washington or Presidential Range. The four main peaks extend north from Mt. Washington, and then northeast in the following order: Mt. Clay (5,532 feet), Mt. Jefferson (5,715 feet), Mt. Adams (5,798 feet), and Mt. Madison (5,363 feet). Together they form a great ridge, five miles long, that averages over five thousand feet in height. Each peak rises hundreds of feet above the spine of the ridge. Two prominent, minor summits of Mt. Adams form a part of the main ridge: Mt. Sam Adams (5,585 feet) and Mt. John Quincy Adams (5,470 feet).

On the shoulder of the ridge between Mt. John Quincy Adams and Mt. Madison, known as the Adams-Madison column, just below Mt. Madison's summit on the northwest side of the mountain, in 1888 the AMC built a stone hut next to the Madison Spring. This hut was the first of the eight huts that exist today in the AMC's Hut System. The original structure burned in 1940 and was replaced by the huts that I knew. Although the Madison Spring Huts have always been among the most popular huts for hikers to visit, "Mad" is one of the most difficult of the huts to access—located at an elevation of 4,825 feet. Ceci and John both had assured me that Madison was one of the best huts to work at, mainly because of its incredibly lovely location and relative isolation at the north end of the Presidential Range.

Madison Spring Huts, July 1962

In 1962 there were two stone huts at Madison. One was the main hut, with a large dining room, or main room, which doubled as a rest area for hikers, when meals were not being served; two bunkrooms, accommodating about sixty-six people; a large kitchen; a small room that served as the crew's quarters; an upstairs, storage area over the middle third of the hut; and a basement under the kitchen. In the main room, which we called the "goofer" room, there was a barrel stove. On cold nights we burned in the stove the cardboard boxes and wooden containers in which the food supplies were carried up to the hut. There was no wood in the immediate vicinity of the huts, as they were located just above tree line. "Goofer" was our affectionate name for visiting hikers.

Located behind and south of the big hut was a second, stone building. The second hut, which we called "Number Two," was used for storage and as a kind of emergency, winter shelter for hikers. It had two rooms with a small stove and two small windows. Several old mattresses and blankets were kept in the second room, in case there was an overflow of guests in the main hut. "Number Two" is now gone, and the name of the AMC facility has been changed from Madison Spring Huts to Madison Spring Hut, reflecting its demise.

Just to the north of both huts was a small, stone structure that housed the gasoline generator, which we ran each evening until 9:30 to provide light in the bathrooms and main room. Just above the huts, on the side of Mt. Madison, was a water tower, to which water was pumped several hundred yards from Star Lake. The lake was a small, shallow lake, about forty feet across and one foot deep, fed from a spring in the notch above the huts, between Mt. Madison and Mt. John Quincy Adams. We pumped using the generator's power.

At the pack house at the foot of the Presidential Range, Dave and I immediately attached our packs of summer clothes and personal things to the pack boards that had been given us at Pinkham, covered the packs with ponchos, and started up the mountain. It was drizzling, cold, and windy that first trip up Mt. Madison. The pack house was a small shed, about ten feet square, located several hundred yards south of Route 2, just west of a lodge called the Ravine House in Randolph, at the base of Mt. Madison. A dirt road led to the pack house, allowing AMC trucks to deliver weekly supplies to be stored in the pack house, until the hutmen came down the mountain to get them. Supplies included canisters of propane gas for cooking at the hut; five gallon cans of gasoline; cans of food; bottles of cooking oil and other cooking ingredients; boxes of eggs, candy, postcards, paper goods (napkins, toilet paper, paper towels), spices, bread, crackers, and other foodstuffs; and wooden containers of fresh meats, fruits, and vegetables. The key to the pack house was hidden on top of one of the supporting posts, underneath the floor. A large scale, with a hook, hung from a supporting beam that stuck out from one side of the house. After you had tied your pack together onto the pack board, you weighed the entire pack, board and all, and recorded the weight.

The pack boards—ingenious contraptions of wood and canvas, approximately 14 x 42 inches in size—weighed about twelve pounds. The canvas side had shoulder straps and rested on your back. You lashed what you were carrying with stout rope to the hooks on the sides, top, and bottom of the board. In effect, it was a vertical platform, with similarities to a corset, to which you tied your load. A typical pack, carried up to Madison Spring Huts, weighed between seventy and one hundred pounds, when fully loaded. Packs carried up to other huts were typically heavier, because the climb to those huts was much shorter and easier. Packing into Lakes of the Clouds Hut was downhill from the summit of Mt. Washington, and on a trail of only about one and a half miles, so packs could be tremendous. For example, during the rebuilding of Lakes in 1969, Sid Havely reportedly hauled 331 pounds of plumbing equipment to Lakes from the summit of Mount Washington! As I soon learned, the pack trail to Madison Spring Huts climbed four thousand feet and was four miles long—the hardest pack trail by far of any of the eight huts!

Madison's records were illuminating on the subject of pack loads. In 1940, to my horror, the aptly named Bud Hefti hefted 224 pounds to Madison Spring Huts up the Valley Way. And in 1922, a gang of twenty French-Canadians hauled up several loads of construction materials, each weighing 150 to 175 pounds, to Madison, every day all summer—receiving three cents a pound for their efforts.

On that first hike, we both packed only our personal effects. Our packs each weighed about fifty pounds. There were several, possible trails up to Madison Spring Huts. The pack trail, which was chosen for packing because of its relatively sheltered and direct route, is called the Valley Way. Dave and I decided to take the regular pack trail, figuring that there would be plenty of opportunities in the future to explore other trails—and to possibly get lost—when it wasn't raining.

Dave and I trudged up the Valley Way for three and a quarter hours to the huts. After leaving the pack house, we crossed the Moose River on a small footbridge, crossed some railroad tracks, and walked through meadows, filled with wild flowers, for about one mile on a slight upgrade. Part of the Valley Way is also joined at lower elevations with another trail called Beechwood Way. Together these lead through a forest of beech trees for a short distance, before the Valley Way veers to the right and starts to climb Durand Ridge, which is one of the main ridges of Mt. John Adams on the north side. At this point the dirt trail becomes rocky and steeper, and in the rain that day the trail had turned into a small stream, which we sloshed through most of the rest of the way. It was the first of the many trips when I walked up the Valley Way on rainy days, ankle deep in water at some points.

The trail climbs the ridge on its west side, angling up the mountain just above a lovely creek, called Snyder Brook, which begins at the Madison Spring, next to the hut. Most of the way up, you could either see or hear the gurgling and rushing of the water, off to the left and below the trail. On the way up, as I gasped and wheezed, Dave told me some of the rules of the hut system. The most important rule of backpacking is never to abandon your load, except in an extreme emergency. Leaving your load, or part of it, on the trail means that someone else has to come and get it for you, or worse, that the contents will be lost. Either option is unthinkable. So it is very important to gauge correctly, when you are tying on your pack, what weight, and what combination of things to be packed, are appropriate for the weather, your physical condition, the condition, steepness, and length of the trail, the time of day, and the speed with which you need to cover the distance. For example, if you are packing late in the day and darkness is approaching, or if a bad storm were coming, you would pack a lighter load, so that you can move fast. If you have a broken leg, your pack load should be lighter than usual. If you would like the bread or other foodstuffs to smell and taste like gasoline, you should combine these with a gas can into one pack.

Rule number two: never, never let another hiker pass you on the trail. To do so would forever destroy the reputation of the hutman, as being the super being of the mountains. Rule number three: walk deliberately, anticipating loose rocks, overhanging branches, slippery surfaces, and other problems. Rule number four: always let someone you trust know your hiking plans, so that if you don't show up as scheduled, someone will go looking for you. Rule number five: never bushwhack with a heavy pack. The trails have been around for over a century. If there were a shorter, easier route between two points, someone besides you would have thought of it long ago and made a trail. Rule number six: don't poop on or near the trail. There were several other rules that decorum suggests I not relate here.

Dave also warned me about "thousand yards." This is a stretch of the Valley Way, about three and a half miles up and half a mile from the hut, which goes straight up for about one thousand steps in a series of switchbacks, as the Valley Way climbs off the side of the Durand Ridge onto the higher elevations. After "thousand yards," if you were still able to walk, the going is much easier—almost delightful—as the trail meanders through Krummholz, or scrub trees and brush, on a slight incline, up to the head of the Snyder Brook valley and the brook itself. A few hundred feet further up lie the Madison Spring Huts, about five hundred feet in altitude below, and .4 mile from, the summit.

The magnificent views of nearby, rounded summits from the upper parts of the Valley Way, and the brook accompanying most of the trail, happily cascading through well-worn valleys, reminded me on that first trip up that these mountains are among the oldest in the world, in contrast to the very young mountains of the Brooks Range that I had climbed the previous summer. In Alaska, the mountains are jagged and twice as high as the White Mountains. The Presidential Range around me in the summer of 1962 was massive in size, but for the most part without sharp peaks. Over millions of years, erosion had worn down what must have been huge mountains to the rounded, lower giants around me.

In Alaska, I had been above tree line the entire summer. Here, in contrast, the trail starts out in an old, hardwood forest of tall trees, with an occasional clearing of wildflowers, climbs through a forest that becomes increasingly pine or other softwoods as you go higher, and then, as the trees become smaller and smaller as you climb, emerges into scrub trees and brush, before ending on the rock strewn summit of Mt. Madison. At the top, as in Alaska, there are only miniature alpine flowers and grasses, except in very sheltered depressions, where scrub pine trees have eked out an existence, undisturbed for centuries. Both the Brooks Range and the Presidential Range are incredibly beautiful in different ways.

When I arrived at the hut with Dave, I met several members of the opening crew and one of the summer crew—Willy Ashbrook—a muscular, high school sophomore from Terra Haute, Indiana. I knew Terra Haute; its rock and roll radio station—WOWO—had filled my Buffalo ears on many a night, under the covers. The opening crew—Bill Barrett, John Adams, Dick Low, and Joel Mumford—had been hard at work for two weeks, packing load after load up the trail, and getting the hut ready for the summer crowds that would soon arrive. Most of the opening crew had been there since June 1st. They would stay another week and leave only when they were replaced by the permanent crew, who would be together for about ten weeks. Willy had arrived two days ago. I was the second of the permanent crew to arrive.

For the next week, I packed every day. I left the hut each morning, just after breakfast, with the other packers. We ran down the Valley Way with empty pack boards on our backs, arriving at the pack house around 8:45. The trip down took about three quarters of an hour. I learned to keep my feet moving in a kind of running and jumping rhythm. On my first trip down, the trail was wet and slippery, and I fell at least three times. At the pack house, I was taught how to lash boxes onto the pack board, so as to balance the total load on my back at shoulder height and above. I started out at sixty pounds. We helped each other get the completed packs on the scales and then get the packs on our backs. Although the trail was muddy, the rain had stopped the night before. I was cautioned to be careful to avoid "throwing the load," that is, losing my balance and having the load fall over my head, which is a common occurrence on slippery trails, especially when the center of gravity is so relatively high. I started off confidently. After the first mile, I started resting, or "crumping," about every fifty yards. To do this, I had to find a "crump" rock, on which I could balance the load and take the weight off of my shoulders. Crump rocks were flat-topped rocks, at least three feet high, that you could back up to and rest the bottom "feet" of the pack board on. After two weeks of packing, I knew and loved every crump rock on the Valley Way intimately.

Each time I crumped, the black flies came streaming out of the woods to attack, much like Alaskan mosquitoes. They bit ferociously, but had the positive effect of spurring you off the crump rocks, most of which were so comfortable that you could have spent all day there. Half way up, I stopped to eat my lunch of peanut butter and jelly sandwich, raisins, orange, and a Hershey bar. These made up our trail lunch invariably on packing days.

Four and one half hours after beginning, I was at the bottom of "thousand yards," looking up and wondering if I was going to die at that moment or perhaps on the steep switchbacks. The other three packers had gone ahead, after coaxing me up the Valley Way to this point. They had been encouraging me the entire trip, reassuring me that everyone experienced the same pain on their first, several pack trips. My legs, knees, and shoulders ached as they had never ached before in my entire life. During the first roughly five-sixths of the trail, I had fallen half a dozen times and had re-lashed the load twice. Several times, I contemplated either abandoning the pack (to hell with the shame of committing this mortal sin for a hutman) or purposely breaking a leg, so that I would have a legitimate excuse for failure. One hour later, I struggled over the lip of the Snyder Brook valley and into the hut. It took me an hour to go the last one half mile. I was half dead. It was about 2:30 PM. After an outdoors, cold water shower, under Madison Huts' single showerhead, by the back cellar door, I went to my bunk and collapsed for three hours, until dinnertime.

That afternoon the weather cleared. The large windows of the goofer room in the main hut faced west, providing spectacular views of distant mountains, lakes, and sunsets. I could hardly walk. I tended my six blisters and went to bed early. The next day I was up at 6:00 AM again. Clouds had rolled in the night before, just after the magnificent sunset, and we were now totally enveloped in fog and mist. Again, four of us left at 7:45, after breakfast, running down the Valley Way in the fog for the first half mile. After scrambling down "thousand yards," we were out of the fog; another mile, and sunshine poked through the pine boughs above us. I was tremendously exhilarated on those runs down the Valley Way.

At the pack house, we lashed on our loads and turned around. This time I packed up seventy pounds, and the trip was just a little bit easier, taking just four hours. At least the bites of the black flies didn't bother me. Pain is relative. For the next ten days, I packed every day. After my tenth trip, I was up to seventy-five pounds and beginning to get into a rhythm. Several of the opening crew, who had been packing for weeks, were carrying over one hundred pounds. I decided that eighty pounds was my limit. That weight became my usual load.

At the end of the first week, our crew was up to eight boys. Anthony MacMillan ("Tony"), the Hutmaster; Pete Trafton, the Assistant Hutmaster; Harry Brown, another member of the summer crew; Willy Ashbrook; and I were permanent crew. The rest were opening crew or construction crew, who had been temporarily assigned to Madison to help with initial packing. We were joined late in June by the last member of the permanent crew, David Ingalls, from Dobbs Ferry, New York, in the Hudson Valley. Tony and Pete were in college. The rest of us were either juniors or seniors in high school.

1962 Madison Spring Huts Crew: me, Harry Brown,Tony MacMillan, Pete Trafton, Willy Ashbrook, and Dave Ingalls

The unsung heroes were the ten donkeys, and their muleskinner, the "AMC mule train," which made daily trips up the Valley Way, laden with fifty-pound gas cans—two to a donkey—and propane gas cylinders. The gas ran our generator—electricity for the hut's lights and to pump water to our water tower from Star Lake; the propane was our cooking fuel and heated the water heater. We carried the empty cans and cylinders down on our backs, when we ran down each morning, nimbly avoiding the donkeys' periodic contributions to the fertilization of the trail.

After ten days of packing, I took a day off to rest, cleaning the bathrooms, sweeping bunkrooms, making bunks, cleaning windows, washing dishes, digging a garbage pit about one hundred yards from the hut, and otherwise doing repairs and chores around the hut. During this period, a few goofers stayed at the hut. The first two were a couple of reporters from the *Providence Journal.* I remember long hours of conversation with them, as they asked about my first impressions of Madison Spring Huts and the life of a hutman. They were shocked at our low pay and long hours. First year hutmen received fourteen dollars per week, or about twenty-four cents per hour, based on a sixty-hour week. Of course, we also received room and board, and divided up tips from the goofers. We worked eleven days and then got three days off. On our days off, we hiked to other huts, where we could eat and stay for free, sometimes covering almost fifty miles in our three-day-long breaks. Often, we linked up with other hutmen, or with the girls working at Pinkham Notch, for company on our treks.

That first week there were also other visitors: a man and two children appeared one afternoon, wearing Cranbrook School sweatshirts. Cranbrook was one of the schools in the athletic league to which Nichols belonged. Of course, I started talking with them immediately. The father was a teacher and the hockey coach at Cranbrook, and a close friend and former college classmate of the former Nichols' hockey coach and teacher, Dick Ohler, who had retired in 1961. Dick used to work in the hut system, I learned. Until his retirement, Dick and the Cranbrook coach had had a friendly, hockey rivalry for decades, he told me, admitting that Nichols had won most of the games over the years.

On the first weekend, a troop of thirty-eight girl scouts stayed at Madison. It was chaos, since Tony had not yet arrived and the crew was in total disarray. Pete Trafton, the Assistant Hutmaster, had a tendency to yell at everyone, when things seemed to be going slowly. He was excitable. We managed to get the scouts fed, nevertheless. Harry spent hours, lying in the storeroom attic that evening, peering through peepholes into the women's bathroom. After Tony's arrival on Sunday, we began to function, under his calm and capable direction, as a well-coordinated crew. Tony set up a schedule for the rest of the summer. Every other day, each of us packed in a rotation that had three boys packing each day. Two boys stayed at the hut. The last crew member was on "days off." On the days when I was staying at the hut, I would either cook or clean, which we did on alternate days at the hut. So each week, I had roughly three days of packing and three days at the hut on average, cooking two days one week and one day the next week. I have already described packing, which was not my favorite activity. I tremendously enjoyed learning how to cook, under Tony's skillful tutoring.

Tony MacMillan was a remarkable person. He was a senior at Brown University and had worked in the huts since 1960. Funny, kind, and liked by everyone, Tony was a gourmet chef—by far the best cook in the hut system. He had packed up his ten volumes of cookbooks and his huge collection of copies of *Gourmet* magazine. At least once a week, he put on a show of culinary magic at breakfast and dinner. When one of the rest of us was cooking, he hovered in the background with suggestions, clucks of approval, or snorts of contempt. He had a great sense of humor, and turned many of our cooking disasters into either delicious meals or funny stories. Tony was one of the nicest, best-organized people I have ever met. He had tremendous warmth, enthusiasm, and creativity.

In the third week of the summer at Madison, the AMC "clinic" participants arrived for two days. These groups, of about fifty, young people with hiking experience, were in training for positions as guides throughout the mountains. That Friday night, with the clinic and other goofers, we had a total of seventy-eight guests. Since the hut officially accommodated only about sixty-six, we had people sleeping everywhere, even on tables in the goofer room. Three girls shared our crew's quarters.

That Sunday was my day to cook. I cooked breakfast for about eighty people, including the crew and visiting girls. Then, on Sunday afternoon, two hours after the clinic participants had left, and just when I had begun to think that I would have an easy time preparing dinner, a Boy Scout troop *and* a Girl Scout troop walked in without reservations. I cooked Sunday night dinner for sixty-two, making nut bread, beans, potatoes, a twenty-five-pound pot roast, and gingerbread.

As the crew began to know and like each other better, our work went smoother. By early July, I was satisfied that I liked all the other crewmembers and would have a glorious summer, despite the pain of packing. My blisters healed. My soreness began to dissipate. The newest crewmember, Dave Ingalls, had even more difficulty than I did adjusting, at first, to the rigors of packing. On two occasions, I volunteered to run down the trail and pick up loads that he had abandoned. After a while, however, he became a stronger packer than I was, averaging about eighty-five pounds or more a trip.

After Dave Ingalls' arrival, all hutmen were called to headquarters, at Pinkham Notch, for a mandatory meeting "for the instruction and benefit of the newer boys in the system." Leaving Tony and Pete—the two experienced hands—at the hut, the rest of us ran down the Madison Gulf Trail and the Old Jackson Road Trail to Pinkham. It took us about two hours to go 6.1 steep miles. In a three-hour period, with about thirty other boys, we were taught the basics of cooking, packing, first aid, and positive social interaction with "guests." The word "goofers" was forbidden. I had already learned most of what we were taught. We turned around the same day and headed back to Madison. The return trip took just over four hours, up a very tough trail that climbed the headwall of the Madison Gulf on Mt. Madison's southeast side.

A typical day at Madison Spring Huts began for the cook at 5:30 AM. The cook had to be up to start cooking the oatmeal or other hot cereal on the huge stove in the kitchen, start the coffee urn, prepare any breakfast breads or muffins and start them baking, and start the bacon or sausage cooking. The rest of the crew was up at 6:00 to shave, dress, eat, and help the cook. Breakfast was at 7:00 sharp. Tables had been set the night before. All the crew helped to serve. A typical breakfast was fruit or orange juice, hot or cold cereal, scrambled eggs, bacon or sausage, muffins or banana or nut bread, and coffee, tea, or cocoa. Sometimes, we served French toast or pancakes, instead of eggs and bread.

By 7:45, breakfast dishes were cleared, tables wiped, and the kitchen cleanup began. The packers departed to run down the mountain. One of the crewmembers, who would stay at the hut that day, washed at the kitchen sink. The cook rinsed, and dried, with the help of goofers. Dishes were put away. Pans were scrubbed, dried, and put away. Goofers were checked out, and payments collected. Advice as to the best trails, weather conditions, and things to watch for was doled out. Trail lunches were assembled and given out to those who wished to buy them.

A typical trail lunch consisted of a peanut butter and jelly sandwich, orange, small box of raisins, and a Hershey bar. It wasn't much, but it was very welcome and tasted wonderful, if you were on the trail in the middle of nowhere and hungry. After the goofers had departed, all crew remaining at the hut—except the cook—started to clean the hut. We started with the main room, which had to be swept out, the floor mopped, and tables wiped clean. Sometimes, windows had to be cleaned, inside and outside. Next were the bathrooms. Toilets and sinks were cleaned, floors mopped, and paper towels and toilet paper replenished. Finally, the bunkrooms had to be swept, bunks smoothed, blankets folded in the "AMC style," and pillows plumped and arranged on each bunk. There were about sixty-six bunks divided between two bunkrooms: male and female. The hut cleanup typically took about three hours or more.

The cook prepared soup and sandwiches for lunch, with coffee, tea, or cocoa. Usually, there were very few people at the hut for lunch. Most goofers left the hut after breakfast and headed for the next hut. Newly arriving goofers arrived after 2:00 PM, since it took at least four hours to climb the Valley Way—the shortest route to Madison—and most people did not start up until after mid morning. Hikers, coming across the range from Lakes of the Clouds Hut or from Mt. Washington, took at least six hours to make the trip.

After lunch, there was time for an hour's nap. Then, the cook would start preparing for dinner, and the remaining crew at the hut would dig in the garbage pit. We buried garbage in those days in pits, hacked with pick axes out of the rocky ground, several hundred feet from the huts. Digging was backbreaking work, but I enjoyed the quietness of the pit, and the opportunity to watch the birds and hares in the vicinity of the huts. The latter were a larger variety of the arctic hare I was familiar with in Alaska.

By 2:30, the packers would return. About 5:00, all of the crew would set the tables and otherwise help prepare for dinner. Goofers were supposed to make reservations for staying at the hut. As they arrived, they were checked in and a count was made for dinner purposes. There were always unannounced visitors, either goofers without reservations, New Hampshire "valley" girls, who visited us for fun and earned their keep for a week or so by helping with hut chores, other AMC personnel on "days off," or the "ridge runners," who were U.S. Forest Service men, whose job was to police trails in the White Mountain National Forest—especially on the Range at high elevations—to assist hikers in trouble. We had plenty of help from everyone, so even if we were short on crewmembers, we could easily do everything we needed to do.

Dinner was often a true feast. The crew ate first, around 5:30. At 6:00 sharp, we rang the dinner gong, which you could hear for miles. We served a bread and salad course, a meat and vegetable course, with potatoes or rice, a dessert, and a hot beverage. Sometimes, we had Italian dinners with a pasta dish. On other occasions, Tony cooked a delicious roast lamb. We had roast beef, turkey, pork loin, pork chops, dozens of chicken dishes, and Asian concoctions, depending on what the cook decided to do and the pre-planned schedule of main courses put out by headquarters. (Each hut's main course was coordinated with neighboring huts' planned meals, so as to avoid subjecting a goofer to the same dinner, night after night, at successive huts.) The desserts and breads were my specialties. With a full house, we cooked for around seventy people on many occasions.

On one of their visits to the hut, several girls, who were frequent visitors—and became friendly with Harry and Willy especially—brought us a present: a cute kitten we named "Postmistress" or "PM" for short. She was fed milk at first, and then became fat on table scraps and mice from the garbage pit. It was good to have a mascot, and Tony adored her.

In early July, I went on my first of several "raiding" trips. Three of our crew ran the seven and a half miles across the Gulfside and Westside trails to Lakes of the Clouds Hut, one night in the clouds. We literally ran across the top of the world, as most of the trip was well above five thousand feet on the ridge, formed by the Presidential Range, between Mt. Madison and Mt. Washington. We chose a cloudy night, because our objective was to steal the so-called "Moccasin Telegraph," which was a kind of mailbox maintained at Lakes, and we needed the cover of a stormy night. The trip over took about four hours. We carried bolt cutters, and arrived at Lakes around 2:00 AM, finding the hut totally asleep with doors unlocked. It wasn't hard to grab the mailbox, although it was chained to a wall. The trip back took less than three hours. We thought we were being pursued, but it turned out that the theft was not detected until the next morning.

At Madison, we bolted the Moccasin Telegraph to a table with inch-thick bolts. For the rest of the summer, we would be on tight guard against an attempt by the Lakes' crew to return the favor. The Lakes' crew members were all good guys: Allen Koop (whose father would become the Surgeon General), Frank Dean, Stan Cutter, Paul Buffum, Richard Meserve (a future neighbor of mine in Falls Church, Virginia), David Raub, and Peter Ward. When they did strike back, it made Tony really angry—the only time I ever saw him mad at anyone. The Lakes crew stole PM.

We had missed PM for several days without concern, for she often disappeared in good weather on her hunting trips for several days at a time. When she didn't return after two days, we became worried, until a goofer told us about the new cat at Lakes of the Clouds Hut. Within a week, PM was back at Madison. Tony had prevailed in arguing that the life of a cat should not be involved in the traditional raids among huts, particularly where there was real danger in traversing the Range, which often had snow storms and extremely high winds in the summer. I think Tony made threats of unimaginable retaliation, too, if PM was not promptly returned. The worst of these was the "blue bottle," which was the last resort of retaliatory weapons. A group of goofers, who had ingested the contents of the "blue bottle" in their food or water, would have uncontrollable diarrhea, with the result that bunkrooms would be filthy and toilets overflowing for days.

In mid summer, Dave Ingalls's family, from Dobbs Ferry, visited the hut for a few days. His parents were older than most parents of kids our age, as were mine. I liked them a lot. His younger sister, Sandi, was with them. She was extremely beautiful, in a quiet, demure kind of way, with blue eyes and sandy blond hair. I think that she was fifteen. I was cooking that day. After dinner had been served and cleanup completed, I asked the Ingalls if they would like to go up to the top of Mt. Madison for the sunset. Dave and his parents declined, but Sandi said she would like to.

We climbed up to the summit, just in time for a gorgeous sunset. Because Mt. Madison is the most northern, and last, of the high peaks in the range, its summit provides a magnificent view. You can see for sixty miles in three directions. We sat and watched the sky and world below transformed into slowly changing colors; the horizon was a blaze of reds, oranges, and yellows, and the darkening mountains were shifting shadows of blues, greens, and purples, as the light retreated and disappeared. The only thing lacking was a full moon, and, as if on cue, it soon rose slowly and silently behind us in the east. Sandi and I sat and sat, watching the moon, talking, and snuggling together for warmth in the stiff wind, as the sky filled with stars. In the moonlight and starlight, we stumbled down the half-mile trail through boulders back to the huts.

By this time, both of the huts were dark. The goofers and crew were all tucked snug in their bunks, while visions of trail lunches danced in their heads. The main hut was locked. The key had been removed from its outside hiding place. Sandi and I were alone, locked outside in the rapidly cooling night. The "croo" had struck a blow.

We debated whether to try to wake someone up to unlock the door to the hut, or to stay in Number Two, which was always open. I was thinking that I had to pack the next day and needed my sleep. When I asked her, Sandi said that she didn't mind staying with me in Number Two. So we made our beds on the mattresses inside the small, stone house, closing the door against the cold outside. We talked most of the night, gradually moving closer together for warmth under the blankets. I recall that I shivered all night, although we were soon warm and comfortable. I couldn't stop shivering.

Perhaps "vibrating" would be a better word than "shivering." I had never before in my seventeen years felt so alive, vibrant, and in tune with a girl. Sandi seemed to know just what to say and do and how. She told me about herself, her home in Dobbs Ferry, her family, her feelings, and her aspirations. I told her my dreams. It was as though we had been friends for years already. As we lay in each other's arms, I thought about the mystery for me of the emotion in my favorite music and poetry, such as in the soaring, heart-trembling passages of the Tchaikovsky *Violin Concerto* or of the Dvorak *Cello Concerto*, or in Shakespeare's sonnets. I had marveled at these creations, but never before fully understood how passion produced such works or why they had been written. I felt that I knew now. Perhaps "trembling" is the correct word. Sandi was my first love.

Sandi Ingalls

I never returned to the summit of Mt. Madison again, despite climbing up to the hut dozens of times during this summer and many subsequent ones. From that week on, it was a special place. I preferred to remember the summit as it was with Sandi. I could experience the wonder of that time with her in my memory better than by ever revisiting the place, where the murmured yearnings of those special days and nights began.

Sandi stayed for several more days. I was a physical wreck, and barely managed to struggle down the Valley Way and back up the next day. But, emotionally, I felt exhilarated to have met such an extraordinary girl. Sandi turned out to be a wonderful writer, and I looked forward tremendously to each letter from her. We corresponded and remained friends for years later. For the rest of 1962, I thought about little else than sandy, blond hair and a creamy neck.

While Mt. Madison was a special mountain for me, the neighboring mountain to the southwest of Mt. Madison *is* a holy mountain, I found out. Mt. John Adams is very special to the Etherians. In August, the Etherian Society members visited the hut for a week. They explained their beliefs and mission to us, over the next several days, and persuaded most of the crewmembers to join them on the summit of Mt. Adams. The Etherians have a complicated theology, but in short, I recall, they believe that aliens from another place in space have visited earth and stored a kind of positive, beneficent energy in several of the highest mountains around the world, including Mt. Adams. This energy may be released by true believers, who may only do so from the mountain's summit by sitting and extending their arms, with fingers outstretched and pointed outward. By means of a ritual ceremony, including some incantations, the energy stored in the mountain is then released, through the fingertips, to accomplish good in the world. We joined them in their work. It was easy, and the view was superb. Our crew adopted these gentle people, who were very friendly, kind, and helpful during their stay with us at Madison. They also tipped well. Tony later wrote an article about their annual visits in the *AMC Journal*, featuring a picture of us with the Etherians on top of Mt. Adams.

Most of the time, Tony, Dave Ingalls, and I packed together. On one occasion, however, when I was cooking and Dave was staying at the hut, Harry, Willy, and Tony decided for fun to pack naked. They set off earlier than usual, so that the goofers would not be up to watch their bare departure. I was busy cooking, while Dave cleaned the hut. He took a long time, as he was a very careful cleaner. About 2:00, a troop of girl scouts arrived from the Madison Gulf Trail, having climbed up on the other side of the mountain from the pack trail. There were perhaps forty, young girls. I expected Tony and the rest of the packers to arrive about 3:00. After some consultation with the older, scout leaders, I went back to the kitchen. From the window I watched the girls position themselves and hide in the Krummholz, near the top of the Valley Way. When Harry, Willy, and Tony arrived about fifteen minutes later, barely presentable after the long hike up the Valley Way, they had a royal, scout welcome. Some of the girls gave the three-finger salute.

After dinner, the first order of business was cleanup. There were often eight or ten goofers in the kitchen with the crew and other visitors, such as the ridge runners or valley girls, helping with drying and putting away dishes and utensils. We sang Christmas carols or popular songs; there were also several off-color songs that were popular and belted out with feeling, such as "I'm Your Mailman," sung to the tune of "Bye-Bye Blackbird."

Whenever we had a big group of young hikers staying at the hut, we broke out the bingo cards. Tony had the idea of starting bingo games in early July, when the scout groups and camp groups began to hike through. Almost every girls' camp and boys' camp in New England visited Madison at some time during the summer. After dinner, until the lights went out at 9:30, the kids were restless. Sometimes the crew performed funny skits, with themes relating to trail safety and ecological sensitivity. Bingo games kept everyone occupied and happy for at least an hour, and helped to fill the crew's tip jar. A bingo card cost ten cents. We often sold one hundred cards for each game. The prize was a Hershey bar. The difference between the cost of the candy and the cost of the card went into the tip jar. It was a nice arrangement for all. By the end of the summer, we had accumulated a total of about eleven hundred dollars in tips, mostly due to Tony's fantastic cooking and the bingo games.

The huts were among the clouds about twenty percent of the time. I loved to see the clouds begin to roll in, sweeping down from either the summit of Mt. Madison, behind the hut, or insinuating over the top of Mt. John Quincy Adams and creeping down the slope, from the summit, to Star Lake and the huts. Some days, we were totally enveloped in the clouds. The fog outside was so thick you could see only about thirty feet. Massive, rock cairns marked the trail's upward progression, toward the summits and onto the major ridge of the Presidential Range. Even in the clouds, you could always find your way by following the cairns. In a heavy rain or snow, however, the fog was impenetrable. On bad weather days, when we knew that a group of goofers was heading north to us from Mt. Washington, across the ridge, in dangerous conditions, one of us would often climb up about half a mile to the top of the ridge on the Gulfside Trail and wait to guide the group down to the huts through the clouds. On those occasions, I loved to sit quietly among the huge boulders that covered the ridge, watching the swirling fog and straining to hear the sounds of the hikers above the wind. The looks of pure joy and relief, when the goofers spotted me, and their expressions of gratitude, when they recognized me as a hutman, more than made up for any discomfort I might have experienced in the snow or rain.

On my days off, my favorite hike was across the range on the Gulfside Trail to Lakes of the Clouds Hut on Mt. Washington, or to the summit of Mt. Washington. It is all above five thousand feet and thus above tree line, so the views are unobstructed in all directions. Providing the weather is clear, it is one of the most spectacular hikes in the world! At the same time, it is one of the most dangerous hikes anywhere, because extremely high winds and very low temperatures are likely to occur, with little warning, at any time of the year. Sometimes, the temperature may drop fifty degrees in fifteen minutes. Summer thunderstorms come out of nowhere, forcing you off the exposed ridge, down steep trails into the ravines that are gauged into every side of the range. I always checked the weather carefully before going up on the ridge.

From Madison Spring, next to the huts, the Gulfside Trail starts out at about five thousand feet of elevation and climbs up six and a half, beautiful miles to an altitude of about six thousand, three hundred feet at the summit of Mt. Washington. I usually bypassed Mt. Washington's summit, skirting to the west of the "cone" of Mt. Washington, on the Westside Trail to the southern flank, where Lakes of the Clouds Hut was located. The trip from Madison to Lakes was about seven and a half miles, as I have mentioned. For most hikers, it took between four and five hours. Hutmen could make it in less than two hours in ideal conditions.

J. Rayner Edmands first named the trail in 1892. He located and made most of the trail, and one of the so-called "columns" or "cols," which the trail traverses along the ridge, is named for him. The Appalachian Trail follows the Gulfside Trail through this part of New Hampshire. From the Madison Huts, the trail first heads up a steep, open slope of rocks and scrub brush to the shoulder of Mt. John Quincy Adams. This was where I would wait in stormy weather for incoming goofers. From this point, Mr. Edmands laid a path of flat rocks for about half a mile. You could ride a bicycle along the trail on those rocks, which created a natural sidewalk. I always ran this part of the Gulfside, while marveling at how much work it must have taken in the late nineteenth century to lay those rocks. At the end of the "sidewalk" there was a huge cairn, memorializing two teenagers, who died in a thunderstorm there, many years ago. We called it "Thunderstorm Junction." This was the first of perhaps a dozen or more memorials, along the Gulfside Trail, to people who had died on the Presidential Range.

For me, this trail was divided roughly into thirds. The first third ends at Edmands Col, about two and a quarter miles from the huts, after hiking across rocky terrain that occasionally skirts close to the edge of magnificent cliffs, which drop off into the Madison Gulf on the east side of the ridge, or into Kings Ravine on the west. In this first third, the trail passes the summits of Mt. John Adams and Mt. Sam Adams. There used to be a metal, Quonset hut kind of shelter on Edmands Col, which the Forest Service erected to provide shelter in emergencies. Near it is the memorial tablet for Mr. Edmands.

The second third of the Gulfside is from Edmands Col, around Mt. Jefferson, to the point midway between the Jefferson-Clay Col and the Clay-Washington Col. I liked this part of the trail, especially in mid summer, because it crosses the Monticello Lawn, which is a grassy, flat, smooth plateau at about five thousand three hundred feet, filled to the brim with alpine wildflowers in July. The flowers at Monticello Lawn rivaled those on Mt. Madison, surrounding Star Lake, just south and upslope from the huts about three hundred yards.

From the Clay-Jefferson Col (the ridge between Mt. Jefferson and Mt.

Clay) to the summit of Mt. Washington, or to Lakes, the third part of the Gulfside Trail crossed the ridge between Mt. Clay and Mt Washington, after skirting Mt. Clay's summit to the west. To go to the Washington summit, the trail continued straight up the cone. Or to go to Lakes, you took the Westside Trail, curving around the cone, crossing the tracks of the Mt. Washington Cog Railway, and scooting around to the southern side of Mt. Washington, where Lakes of the Clouds Hut nestled near two small, ice-cold lakes. It was always a breathtaking hike.

Sometimes, upon returning to Madison Spring Huts from a hiking trip elsewhere in the White Mountains on my days off, I would reverse the traverse of the range. I got to the top of Mt. Washington up the Crawford Path from the south, or up the Cog Railway (hutmen rode free), or up the so-called "stage coach" that climbed the Mt. Washington Auto Road. Then, I would race back to Madison—mostly downhill—along the Gulfside, exhilarated by the alpine flowers, incredible views, and admiring glances (I thought) of the goofers I tore past along the trail.

Coming back from one set of days off, with the intention of going to Mt. Washington's summit on the auto road and then crossing to Madison on the Gulfside Trail, I found that the Mt. Washington Road Race was about to begin, from the start of the road near the Glen House. I tried to get a ride up the road on the press truck, and ended up driving the truck. It was an experience. The truck was an old Ford, just like the old Ford truck on the Morgan's farm, which I had driven in my younger days. I was required to stay just in front of the lead runner, to drive as smoothly as I could, without jerking or sudden stops, and to make sure that the cameramen, in the back of the truck, were able to film the race. We started off in sunshine and seventy-eight degree heat. As we climbed the road, the weather got colder and colder. About half way up, it started to snow. By the time we finished the seven and a half mile racecourse, we had gained 4,650 feet in altitude, and the temperature had dropped to twenty-eight degrees. I was amazed at how well the lead runner handled the cold, high wind, driving snow, and the average twelve percent grade. While I called on all my Buffalo, winter-driving skills, the last quarter mile he chugged up a thirty percent grade, through two feet of snow. He was a former coalminer, I recall, and his record time that afternoon of 1:04:57 stood for the next forty years. After parking the truck at the summit in the snow, and waiting several hours for the snowstorm to subside, I slipped and slid in the snow across the Gulfside Trail back to Madison.

On July 2nd, I got word from a ridge runner, bringing news from Pinkham, that Grandpa Hobbie had died the day before. I ran down the Valley Way to Route 2, and hitchhiked to a public telephone in Randolph. Dad advised me not to come home for the memorial service, because I would be coming home for Ceci's wedding in late August, in less than two months, and missing work time then. I was upset to miss Grandpa's service. He had never recovered enough from the stroke he suffered, several years earlier, to be able to walk by himself again, and he had been frustrated that he was largely confined to a hospital bed, in what used to be his library, on the first floor of the old house. He was eighty-eight years old, when he died. He had been a physician for sixty years, commuting almost daily to Buffalo from Lewiston, until his stroke several years before his death. He was active in civic affairs, president of many clubs, president of the Niagara Frontier Planning Association, a church elder at the Presbyterian churches in both Lewiston and Tonawanda, and a kind, gentle man. I still miss his soft, under-the-breath whistling and his stories, as we shared bowls of peach ice cream on hot afternoons on the porch at Lewiston.

In August, we decided, at Tony's instigation, to celebrate "Christmas in August" at Madison Spring Huts on August 25th. Tony prepared food for weeks. Presents of nuts and candy were put together for all the goofers and visitors. We packed up a Christmas tree, lights, and decorations. The theme was Christmas food from all over the world. Invitations went out to the other huts and leadership of the hut system. I was in Buffalo for my sister's wedding on the actual date, but I enjoyed all the preparations, helped prepare most of the food, and feasted on all the leftover food and goodies, when I returned. Tony's brother, Andy, got dressed up in a Santa Claus costume and appeared with a huge bag of Christmas cookies, candy bars, and other treats, racing down from the summit of Mt. John Quincy Adams, just as dinner was about to be served. This was the first of many such Christmases at Madison.

While the Christmas preparations were under way, we also decided to found a ski patrol at Madison. In New England, virtually everyone skis from December until April. Every ski resort or ski area has a ski patrol, consisting of expert skiers, who patrol the slopes, assisting people who need help and otherwise keeping order. In the winter, being a ski patrol member is a kind of status symbol, for the position identifies you as a very good skier. As an added benefit, if you are a certified member of a ski patrol anywhere in New England, you could ski without paying tow fees. Sometimes, resorts even provided free food and drinks for ski patrol members, with the understanding that a member would wear an identifying emblem or patch, and help with maintaining the safety and order of the ski areas. So there were certain advantages to being a member of a ski patrol.

None of the members of the Madison crew were very good skiers. At that time, before I learned to ski at Dartmouth, I was pretty mediocre. Tony could barely get up a ski lift. But it seemed like a good idea to begin our own ski patrol, even though there was no ski area in the vicinity and no skiing on Mt. Madison at all. So we did, complete with patches, headbands, membership cards, and armbands identifying us as "Mt. Madison Volunteer Ski Patrol" (MMVSP) members. Years later, even when he was dying of cancer, Tony reportedly liked to stand at the top of particularly difficult ski runs on other mountains in winter, dressed in his ski patrol outfit, giving advice and directions to passing skiers, but petrified of moving himself. By the end of the following summer, we had over two hundred members. My "membership" came in handy many times over the following years, and the patrol is now a part of the lore of the hut system.

Several years later, during Peace Corps training in Hawaii, another trainee appeared for a volleyball game wearing a MMVSP T-shirt. He had worked at Lakes of the Clouds Hut in the summer of 1967, and in 1968 had helped to close Lakes, before coming directly to Hawaii from the White Mountains. Brian Copp and I became close friends, and together we planted the MMVSP flag on top of several of South Korea's highest mountains. Forty-five years later, I still have my carefully preserved parka, T-shirt, membership card, and patches.

Ceci's wedding took place on Saturday, August 25th, as planned. Aunt Kate picked me up on the Wednesday before, at Randolph, New Hampshire, at the bottom of the Valley Way, just after dark. I recall that I was not used to being on the Valley Way after sunset and whistled loudly all the way down, partly in tribute to my grandfather, who was always softly whistling, and partly to alert any bears, that might be taking evening strolls, to get out of my way.

The night before the wedding, Dad and I went to pick up the wedding cake at a famous Polish bakery on the south side of Buffalo. As we entered the bakery, a pretty young lady, lounging outside the bakery, asked Dad if he wanted to come home with her. We were both very surprised. In the car on the way home with the cake, Dad said that, although it wasn't the first time in his life that he had been solicited, it was the first time in many, many years. He was pleased to have this story to add to his repertoire.

The wedding took place at St. John's Episcopal Church on Colonial Circle. Reverend Clare Backhurst presided. It was a fine, warm, summer day in Buffalo. John's best man was his younger brother, Dick Pehle. I got to know Dick, who is just a little older than me, pretty well. He has a fine sense of humor, and I connected with him on many levels. My brother and I were ushers, along with several of J.P.'s friends (we called Ceci's husband "J.P.," at his suggestion, to distinguish him from my father and brother, as well as from his father, who was also John). J.P.'s parents (John and Francha Pehle) from Bethesda, Maryland, were there, as was as his grandmother from

Connecticut and most of the Hobbie family. It was a great wedding, heralded by thunderous peals from the organ at St. John's. Ceci was beautiful in Mom's wedding dress. I thought that the huge bell above the front entrance, which I had rung hundreds of times over the years, had never sounded so exultant!

Ceci and John Pehle, August 25, 1962

The reception was at our house and backyard. Mom and Dad had planted hundreds of flowers that were in full bloom right on schedule. The garden had never looked so gorgeous before. The house was resplendent in new paint. We took pictures of the wedding party in front of the mock orange bushes in the backyard. Ceci and J.P. seemed made for each other. He was very laid back and a fine addition to our family.

I returned to the White Mountains two days after the wedding, catching a ride with John and Olivann and one-year-old Lawrence. John and his family had been in Bloomington, Indiana, during the past year, where he was working on his Ph.D. in limnology at the University of Indiana. We were all happy that the wedding had been a tremendous success. The only sad thought was that Grandpa Hobbie's death, six weeks earlier, had deprived him of the happiness he would have felt at Ceci's marriage.

Upon my return to Madison, I found that, in my absence, the crew had assigned membership numbers to each of the founding six members of the MMVSP. As a joke, they made me number sixty-nine.

In the remaining two weeks of the summer, the Madison crew made plans for the following summer. Tony would be back as Hutmaster, Willy wanted to come back as Assistant Hutmaster, and I wanted to come back. Harry, Pete, and Dave Ingalls indicated that they would probably not return, at least not to Madison. On Labor Day, which was September 3rd, the permanent crew started to leave, and the closing crew started to arrive. I had no more days off. I alternately cooked for three days, cleaned for three days, and packed for four days. We had big crowds of about sixty on the Labor Day weekend. On September 10th, I left for home, carefully taking with me and guarding my *A.M.C. White Mountain Guide*, the maps on which I had red-lined the one hundred seventy miles of trails, other than the Valley Way, that I had hiked during the summer, my list of the fifteen mountains over four thousand feet in elevation that I had climbed on days off, and two dozen precious letters from a girl in Dobbs Ferry.

My senior year at Nichols started in mid September. I had missed most of the pre-season football practices, but I was probably in better condition than anyone else on the team. I enjoyed football a lot. Wind sprints and exercises were nothing compared to packing up the Valley Way. We had a glorious, final football season, losing only one game. I was listed at six feet, 210 pounds (a slight exaggeration), wearing number 61. Coach Stevens said that we were the best team he had ever coached. The soccer team, staring Bill Loweth, Warren Gelman, Gary Conover, Mike Keiser, Clay Hamlin, Bill Cooley, and John Mooney, went undefeated, and was also the best team in Nichols history.

Our only defeat in football was to University School of Shaker Heights, a suburb of Cleveland. I broke my left wrist in practice the week before the game, so I missed the only game we lost. I like to think that my absence was a factor in the loss, but in reality it was a Cleveland snowstorm, a muddy field, and three bad breaks that allowed University School to clobber us. That happens in life sometimes.

For the last game, I was back, with my arm in a soft cast, playing defensive end and offensive left guard. Dr. Brown felt it was too early to play with my fractured wrist, but I insisted. I wanted my last football game at Nichols to be my best, if possible. Craig Butler, who played left linebacker, played like a demon right behind me. I took out the blockers on Kiski's end runs, and Craig tackled the runners. He and I always worked well together. We beat Kiski handily in the mud and rain. With the help of my cast, I made some sweet blocks and hard tackles in my last football game, which was the muddiest, and most fun, game I have ever played in. Kiski tried, but could not, sweep the left end of the defensive line, as University School had the previous week. I recall that we had a fantastic, celebratory party at Assistant Coach Pedersen's house afterwards. After that party, we all called Mr. Stevens "George" and Mr. Pedersen "Norm." Nichols' football was a great experience for me.

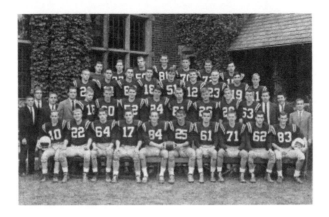

Nichols High School varsity football team, 1962

In September, I started work in earnest as the chair of the Assemblies Committee and as the Business Manager of the *Nichols News*. The former position required planning and arranging for guest speakers or other assembly programs. I remembered that for me one of the best guest speakers had been Buffalonian Fran Striker, the creator of the Lone Ranger, the Green Hornet, and dozens of other fictional characters, who had spoken at Nichols during my freshman year. I tried to arrange for him to speak again, and was informed that he had died the week before I called.

Even without Fran Striker, I was determined to arrange an outstanding schedule of assembly programs. Perhaps the best were several, great, classical music programs, including the superb Buffalo String Quartet, of which Harry Taub was the leader, and a fine brass quintet. Other programs included Marny Wilson (my first date as a high school student, four years earlier), a senior at the Buffalo Seminary, who spoke about her American Field Service experience in Uganda; Norman Pedersen, who spoke about church architecture; and an engineer by the name of James McCormack, who spoke about rocket science. Introducing guest speakers or performers, before the entire school at chapel, was something I looked forward to.

As Business Manager of the *Nichols News*, I handled a budget of several thousand dollars, but most of the work was in billing and collecting from the thirty or so companies that usually advertised in the *News'* eight editions each year. Billy Rashman was the Sales Manager, and he did a superb job of arranging such advertisers as Kleinhans, the Squire Shop, Grever's Flower Shop, Siegfried Construction Company, Tinney Cadillac, Berger's, and Dick Fischer Athletic Goods. Billy and I were a good team. I liked and respected him a lot. Fritz Zeller was my faculty mentor. He taught me a lot about bookkeeping and getting advertisers to pay the invoices I sent them.

My senior year I took English IV with Austin Fox, French IV with Jim Herlan, History with Millard Sessions, and Physics with Eddie Anderson. Again, all of my teachers were excellent. I had hoped to have an easy senior year, but in my last high school year I struggled with Physics, which kept me off the honor roll all year. I enjoyed the course, which was a new course, designed by physics teachers to facilitate learning a difficult subject. I remember learning about wave theory, for example, in the gymnasium, with four, huge, sixty-foot long "slinkies" or tightly wound coils of wire. It was much easier to visualize how waves moved, when a "slinky" coil, held at each end by a student, was stretched out to one hundred feet or so and then gently moved up and down, causing waves to move along the coil. Bill Flor, I recall, enlivened our class by accidently letting go of the end of the stretched coil he was holding, which then snapped back towards the other end, held by Jim McGibbon. Jim dove for cover, as the coil whipped back at him. He had never moved that fast on the football field, and the rest of the class, including Eddie Anderson, dissolved in laughter, as all the coils were let go.

In the late fall of 1962, Sandi visited me in Buffalo, staying for several days. She was constantly on my mind. We had a fantastic time together, and my feelings towards her were as strong as ever. She told me, however, early in her visit, that she had a boyfriend back in Dobbs Ferry. She still wanted to remain friends with me. After she left, I locked myself in my room and cried for two days, to the great consternation of my parents. I don't think that up to that week I had really cried about anything, except Grandpa Hobbie's death and Gypsy's death, since I was about ten. I have never been more miserable emotionally in my life than I was at that time. Happily, my female friends at Amherst High School, together with Bob Ramage and John Mooney, pulled me through the winter. I owe them a lot. A Mt. Holyoke friend of Ceci's, Zilpha Bentley, who stayed with us for several months in Buffalo, talked me through some of my most difficult moments, reassuring me that she had been through what I was experiencing and had survived. Zilpha counseled me that time would heal my hurt, and that finding a new love quickly would also help. The latter was more easily said than done.

Also in the fall, I was surprised to be named the editor-in-chief of Nichols' literary magazine, the *Gleaner*. Tommy Goldstein, Harry Meyer, and Sandy Maisel were the other seniors on the board—all excellent writers. I have no idea why or how I was selected. Seven other students, from other classes, rounded out the editorial board. We solicited contributions from students constantly during the school year. Sometimes, a teacher would submit for consideration a student poem, or short story, or a piece of literary criticism, produced in class. We published the *Gleaner* in February and again in May. A typical issue of twenty pages had about a dozen pieces. When the board met to select which submissions would be published, the writers' names were not identified, so at least, in theory, the works to be published were selected on the basis solely of merit. In the spring, we selected a faculty member to choose—without identifying the authors to him—one poem and one short story to be awarded the top literary prizes at Nichols, the *Gleaner* Prizes.

My brother left for Antarctica in November to spend several months there, during the Antarctic summer. At Christmas, he called to talk with all of us. Although the call came by telephone, it was relayed by radio from the South Pole, so that, in order to converse, you had to pause and to indicate with a verbal cue—such as "over"—to the other person that it was their turn to talk. My mother never caught on to this. "Why does he keep saying 'over'?" she asked in confusion. Listening to her trying to converse with my brother, without cueing him properly, and watching her frustration, had us all in stitches. John returned from Antarctica in March, safe and sound. I persuaded him to make a presentation at Nichols in April, talking about, and showing slides of, his experiences in Antarctica.

Just before Christmas, several of the *Nichols News* staff attended the 40th Conference of the Western New York Interscholastic Press Association. Tommy Goldstein, Bob Ramage, Greg Elevich, Bill Rashman, and I represented Nichols and accepted the award for the *Nichols News*, in its fiftieth year, as the best student newspaper in Western New York.

The Nichols hockey team had an amazing season that winter, winning 9, losing 5, and tying 2. Anytime that the hockey team had a winning season was big news. A lot of the competition in hockey was fierce, including Canadian high schools, which were five-year schools, so that the teams we played were the equivalent of American college freshmen teams. Warren Gelman. Paul Sullivan, Bill Cooley, and Jack Walsh were the big scorers on the team, but there were a lot of very good players. As manager, my main job was to make sure that logistics for practices, games, and trips were taken care of. I also kept game statistics, such as shots on goal, assists, penalties, and the like. In this role I got to know better Don Waterman, who was the long time Director of the Nichols athletic program.

Mr. Waterman was a large man with a big heart. He had played football, and been on the track team, at Harvard, and had taught at Nichols for years, before taking over as the Athletic Department Director. He was full of stories about Nichols' past. He once told me that, when Albert Sutter had first joined the faculty, "El Supremo" had had a problem controlling his class. It was hard to believe this, as Mr. Sutter's class was one of the most disciplined, no-nonsense classes at Nichols. Other faculty, including Don, had assisted Mr. Sutter, initially, in taking charge and figuratively whipping his class into shape. Don gave me lots of advice as to how to cope at Nichols in my first two years, for which I was grateful. Knowing the financial straits of our family, he used to give me little gifts of athletic socks and other athletic equipment that he said was either used or overstocked. He was a very kind man. Don's wife, Jo, was the head of the athletic department at the Buffalo Seminary and also extremely nice. As I have mentioned before, she was a classmate of my mother's at "Sem," and our families often got together during the summer for dinners.

January was the deadline for college applications. My father wanted me to go to Cornell, of course. I wanted to go to Dartmouth. Phil Boocock tried to be neutral, but was indirectly pushing me to apply to Harvard. Several faculty members were suggesting Yale or Princeton. We were told to apply to at least five schools, and to make one of them a sure bet. By this time, I had taken the College Board exams three times. Each time my scores inched upwards. Because of my relatively high scores on my final Scholastic Aptitude and Achievement Tests (I think they were in the high 700s), my faculty advisor, Hal Gerard, thought that I should aim high. In the end, I applied to Colgate, Cornell, Dartmouth, Harvard, Princeton, and Yale. All of these schools were expensive places, but somehow that did not seem important. I was told that if I got in to a good school, the school would offer financial aid in the form of a scholarship, or student loans, or both, on a financial-need basis. I would need that. My parents' gross annual income was about $6,500 in 1963, and Mom had been working at the American Red Cross in its blood program to help make ends meet, while I was at Nichols.

Just after I submitted my college applications, Ceci called to tell us that she was pregnant. We were all very happy about that. The baby was due in September.

In February 1963, I tripped, while racing down the stairs at Nichols, and broke a bone in my left ankle. I had to wear a cast, and then a support, for months. My major concern was whether the injury would affect track and packing. I limped around Nichols for several months, under the concerned eye of coach Pedersen, who had witnessed my tumble on the stairs, and then my ankle seemed to be all right. It was my second break within four months—third, if you count my heart.

There were about fifty submissions from students to be considered for publication in the February issue of the *Gleaner*. After several weeks of meetings, the board voted on which twenty or so would comprise the next issue. (As editor-in-chief, I only voted to break a tie, and there never was one.) Two of my poems were selected: "Summer" and "Epilogue." Both were reflections of my struggle to cope with my feelings about Sandi. Just to give you an idea, the former ended with this line: "Summer is the cruel season." I was happy to be published again.

Just before I left to visit Ceci for a week in March, Bill Flor and I were featured in the *Nichols News* as the "seniors of the month." I took a copy with me for Ceci and J.P. It was my first visit to Florida. Ceci and J.P. were living at 1615 Northwest 3rd Street in Gainesville, while J.P. studied for his Ph.D. in Psychology at the University of Florida. Ceci was working at the university library. I took a bus down and back, during spring break. One way took twenty-two hours. The smell of ripe vegetation and the humidity were overpowering, when I got off the bus. We had a great time together, visiting various tourist spots and watching birds. I added several species to my lifetime bird list. I found J.P. to be a very smart, gentle, and sensitive person, and enjoyed his company.

After I returned from Florida, Nichols was notified that, based on the results of the New York State Regents examinations, which everyone in our class had taken the previous October, sixty-five percent of us had won New York State Regents Scholarships. This was the highest percentage of winners in Nichols' history. If I attended a university in New York, I could use this scholarship.

On the track team in the spring, I found that my left ankle still was a little painful. I managed to run through the pain for the season, but didn't win a race and didn't beat my best times as a junior. A Nichols junior, Terry Williams, was running the 880 about a second faster than I could. So I was pretty disappointed. I was glad that Bob Ramage did very well in the discus and shot-put. Nichols came in fifth, as usual, in the Interstate Championships, but overall had a record of seven wins and two losses in track meets with other area schools—the best record of the past seven years.

In early April, I got the good news that I had been accepted at all the schools I applied to. Cornell gave me the best scholarship. Dartmouth gave me the next best financial aid package. Colgate, Yale, Harvard, and Princeton gave me smaller aid offers. I chose Dartmouth. I have never regretted my choice. Seven classmates chose Yale, including Bob Ramage. Jim McGibbon chose Princeton. John Mooney chose Tufts. Several classmates went to Harvard. At least one chose M.I.T. Others went to Cornell, Williams, Brown, Columbia, Hamilton, Amherst, and similar colleges. The day I sent my acceptance, I also registered for the military draft, having just turned eighteen, never expecting that military service would enter my life.

In May, we published the second and final issue of the *Gleaner*. Two of my submissions were selected for publication: a short story entitled "The Town" and a poem entitled "Night Flyers." The two-page story was about Dobbs Ferry, New York. The poem was about migrating birds. I was very pleased and surprised that each won the *Gleaner* Prize for best work in prose and poetry, respectively. It was a nice way to end my literary career at Nichols.

Just when I was beginning to worry about my prom date, Mike Quinlan, our All Western New York fullback, asked me to double-date with him in early May. He had a blind date for me, he said, whom he was sure I would like. I was extremely leery. Mike's date was Chris Benzow, my old friend from P.S. No. 56 and the Kennels. Chris didn't know the girl, she reported to me. We were going to have a picnic and drink beer at the Kennels. Mike introduced me to a girl, from Kenmore West High School, named Lindsey Jewel. I am forever indebted to Mike for his introduction.

Lindsey was smart, personable, athletic, and sensitive. She was also a long-legged, longhaired, gorgeous, blue-eyed blond, with full lips and a nice figure. Her name fit her perfectly. She was on the precision swimming team at Ken West. We hit it off immediately. Her parents were wonderful, and she had a cute dog, named Nikki. It was one of the couple of times in my life when I thought that divine intervention had occurred. We dated heavily for the rest of the spring and when I returned from the mountains. She gave me a fine, brown, mohair sweater that she had knit for me. I gave her my Nichols letter sweater. We both loved Leonard Bernstein's music in "West Side Story." I think of her whenever I hear it. Our special place was the Clarkson House restaurant in Lewiston, where we often went for dinner together.

Lindsey Jewel, 1963

On May 31, 1963, we had Class Night at Nichols. The highlight was the ivy-planting ceremony, conducted by visiting professor Montmorency Minnegerode, alias classmate Henry Sturdevant. It was a tradition for seniors to plant ivy along one of the ancient, Nichols buildings' walls, to help keep the walls standing. Being green, tenacious, and important to keeping the buildings intact, ivy was symbolic of Nichols' alumni giving program, we surmised. At Class Night, George Stevens, who was leaving Nichols with our class to become the Headmaster at the New Canaan Country Day School in Greenwich, Connecticut, presented several of us with awards for our contributions to Nichols' publications, such as the *Nichols' News*, the *Gleaner*, and the *Verdian*, our yearbook. Mr. Stevens had been associated with Nichols since his graduation in 1948 and had become an institution. He would be sorely missed. George was my favorite teacher and coach.

In early June, we had final examinations. I got a sixty-four in the final physics exam. Fortunately, more than half our class did worse than I did, and Mr. Anderson threw out the results. Despite our physics problems, at our graduation in June, the class of 1963 was lauded as having had overall the best academic and athletic records in Nichols' history. We were pretty proud. My parents were pleased that my picture was in the Buffalo *Evening News* for being awarded the Headmaster's Award, in recognition of my contributions to the school "as a scholar, athlete, poet, and musician." Harry Taub sent me a telegram of congratulations on June 7th—the only telegram I ever remember receiving in my life.

Graduation from Nichols High School, June 1963

Lindsey was my prom date. We had an awesome time. The "twist" was big that night. After the formal dance was over at the Nichols' dining room, our class retreated, around midnight, to Chuck Kreiner's lovely, summer home on Point Abino in Canada, about fifteen miles from Buffalo on the Canadian lakeshore. It was a grand party with an amazing band. At about 3 AM, four of us decided to drive several miles farther to the Kennels, where we could relax privately at the Hobbie cabin and on the beach. To tell the truth, we had all been drinking and should not have been driving. After arriving at the

Kennels, while trying to navigate the dirt road to our cabin, Jim McGibbon drove off the road into the woods and got his car stuck on a stump. John Mooney, Bob Ramage, Jim, and I spent the next hour or so, digging Jim's car out of the sandy soil, with our dates cheering us on. That sobered everyone up in time to drive back to Kreiner's house for a farewell breakfast on his porch, overlooking Lake Erie. Despite the incident with Jim's car, it was a romantic, unforgettable night.

Grandpa Schultz went into the hospital on June 14th. I visited him every night at Buffalo General Hospital. On the 20th, when I visited him by myself in the evening, he seemed fine. The next morning he died. I was the last family member to see him. I loved and admired this conscientious, hard-working, kind man, who had raised my mother so well. Right after his memorial service and funeral at Forest Lawn Cemetery's chapel, I left for my summer job, at Madison Spring Huts in the White Mountains, with the Siegner family—cousins of Aunt Betty Hobbie and friends from the Kennels—who had offered to drop me off.

My second summer at Madison was much easier physically than the first. I was now an experienced backpacker, and I enjoyed it. The crew consisted of Tony MacMillan, Hutmaster; Willy Ashbrook, Assistant Hutmaster, Dal Brodhead, John Glasser, Richard Rusk, and me. Tony, Willy, and I were the old hands. Dal, Rich, and John were new. It was an exceptionally nice crew. We continued the good times and fine cuisine of the past summer.

John Glasser was a likable, incoming freshman at Princeton. I liked Dal and Rich a lot, too. Rich was still in high school, laconic, and had a wry sense of humor. He and I started a Cribbage competition. Amazingly, I won the first eighty-six games. Then, fortune changed, and I lost over a hundred in a row. Rich's father was the Secretary of State, Dean Rusk. We never talked about the war in Vietnam or his father's foreign policy in front of Rich, although these were topics very much growing in importance in the minds of young, draft age men in the early 1960s.

Dal Brodhead was Canadian, and had an unmistakable Canadian accent. After a few weeks in the Madison crew, Dal got an urgent message from Pinkham Notch. U.S. immigration agents were waiting for him there. His work papers were allegedly not in order, and he was going to be deported, according to what we heard. The rumors flew thick and fast. Dal left Madison for Pinkham and was gone for some time. In the meantime, Rich went down the Valley Way to Randolph and made a call to Washington. A week later, Dal was back, with everything in order. Dal was never bothered again by the U.S. Immigration Service, and worked the next summer at Lakes.

**1963 Madison Spring Huts Crew: me, Willy Ashbrook,
Tony MacMillan (with PM II), John Glasser, Richard Rusk, and Dal Brodhead**

In late July, I twisted my ankle while packing and reinjured the broken bone that I suffered in my fall on the stairs at Nichols, six months earlier. I could hardly walk for a week, much less pack. I sent word to George Hamilton, the Hut System Manager, and at his suggestion went to see a foot doctor in Gorham, New Hampshire, who said that I was finished as a hutman for the summer. George offered me a position as an A.M.C. guide for the rest of the summer, but if I couldn't be a hutman, I didn't want to stay. After thanking George for his kindness, with much regret I left the hut on August 6th, after six weeks on the 1963 "Mad" crew, and hitchhiked to Buffalo, surprising my parents with my arrival the next day. I was pretty upset about my injury. It worked out all right, as Bob Ramage asked me to help him paint houses for the rest of the summer, which I did, and Lindsey was glad to see me.

Tony MacMillan called in mid August to find out how I was, and insisted that I return for Christmas at Madison. After two weeks of boring, house painting with Bob, I was ready to return to the mountains, and my ankle had improved greatly. Bob was curious about all the stories that I had told him about life at Madison. So on on August 23rd, Bob and I drove to New Hampshire, limped up to Madison, and had a wonderful, Christmas celebration with the crew and about fifty goofers on August 25th. Tony sculpted a lamb out of green jello for the occasion, in honor of my going to Dartmouth, and I cooked three, twenty-pound turkeys. Bob and I spent several more days at Madison, before returning to Buffalo.

Bob Ramage, near the packhouse at the foot of Mt. Madison, 1963

On August 31st, I drove with Lindsey and her parents to Lake Muskoka, several hundred miles north of Buffalo, in Ontario, Canada, for a week at a cabin on Crystal Lake that they rented every year. I remember that the fireweed along the Ontario highways was in full, frenzied bloom. The mosquitoes and our feelings were in like bloom. Lindsey and I had a marvelous time together. The Jewels had invited me to go with them earlier in the summer. I thought that the invitation might be withdrawn, because of an incident with Lindsey in August, shortly after I got back from Madison.

Lindsey and I had taken advantage of her parents being out one evening in mid August to watch television in her living room. The Jewels lived on the second floor of a house at 141 Washington Avenue in Kenmore. It was a very hot and muggy night. Not a breath of air was stirring. Somehow, we fell asleep in each other's arms in a state of semi undress. The next thing we knew, Lindsey's mom was shaking us and telling us to hurry up and get dressed, because Mr. Jewel was coming up the stairs. We hurriedly complied, in some embarrassment, and I kissed Lindsey goodnight. Mrs. Jewel never said a word to either Lindsey or me about this afterwards, and apparently never said anything to Mr. Jewel. Mrs. Jewel was a sweetheart.

After returning from Lake Muskoka, both Lindsey and I were busy getting ready for college. Lindsey was going to enter William Smith College, which is the sister school of Hobart College. It has a beautiful campus on Seneca Lake in central New York. We had a tearful parting, as she left for school on September 12th. Our last kiss—and it turned out to be our last—haunted me for years.

I visited Elizabeth Strauss, Elmer Schamber, Christine Kelman, and Erna Soell at P.S. No. 56 the day after Lindsey left. It was Friday, September 13, 1963. I also stopped by Nichols to bid farewell to Phil Boocock, Pliny Hayes,

Paul Seamans, Eddie Anderson, Austin Fox, Al Sutter, Don Waterman, and Norm Pedersen. The need to say goodbye to friends, teachers, and places was overwhelming. With my parents it was not a question of goodbye, but rather of wonder. I told Mom and Dad, as I packed for college, that I didn't know how they had so amazingly supported all three of us for so many years. Their income was not substantial, and I appreciated, even then, what a struggle it must have been to pay for so many, expensive, private high schools and colleges. I had taken their sacrifices for granted, most of the time.

On September 14th I boarded a midnight bus to Albany, New York, where I changed to a bus bound for White River Junction, Vermont. By noon the next day, I had arrived at Dartmouth College to begin a new life, hoping to bring Lindsey into it as soon as possible. The new life would bring many unanticipated changes, including buildings draped in black for the death of John F. Kennedy, nine weeks after I stepped onto the Hanover plain, amongst the foothills of the White Mountains, where Dartmouth resplendently sits.

I had mixed feelings as I left Buffalo. Dartmouth promised to be an adventure, and I looked forward to going to college there, in my beloved White Mountains. I knew, however, from watching my brother's and sister's experiences, I would never again really live in Buffalo, although in my heart I considered it my true home for another thirty years, until we sold 453 in 1994. Over the years, as a college student and later as an adult, I returned to Buffalo for holidays, short vacations, family and high school reunions, and then for funerals. The river, lake, parks, Forest Lawn Cemetery, beach, and old buildings didn't change much, reassuringly.

The midnight departure in 1963 was my farewell to the streets, schools, churches, and city sounds of my childhood. I also left behind that night, with the whisper of the wind off Lake Erie, the voices of so many people who had loved me, nurtured me, and helped me to fledge. Some I would hear again. Some I never heard again. Many have been stilled. In my mind I hear them all clearly yet, forty-five years later, raised in a chorus of one-winged angels. I am so very grateful.

24138 3LV00001B/101/P

Printed in the USA
CPSIA information can be obtained at www.ICGtesting.com